PRAISE FOR *INCLUSIVE FINANCE*

'A timely and insightful exploration of the role digital payments play in advancing financial inclusion. Alessandro Hatami and Meaghan Johnson capture the transformative power of technology in addressing financial exclusion and offer practical insights for driving change. A valuable contribution to the global conversation on inclusion.'
Paulette Rowe, CEO, Stax Payments

'Alessandro Hatami and Meaghan Johnson celebrate nimble fintech pioneers who are moving the needle on financial inclusion, not necessarily with global scale, but by solving the small, critical problems left by legacy systems.'
Efi Pylarinou, Global fintech and tech thought leader

'As someone deeply invested in advocating for the rights of the marginalised communities, I find *Inclusive Finance* to be a compelling and critical resource. The authors deftly connect financial inclusion with broader social and economic justice, urging stakeholders to rethink how they can make financial services work for everyone.'
Guissou Jahangiri, Secretary General, International Federation for Human Rights

'The most comprehensive analysis of every aspect of financial inclusion, brilliantly illustrated with real-world examples. A must for policy makers and innovators.'
Imran Gulamhuseinwala, former Trustee, Open Banking, and Board Member, Tandem Bank

'For many years Hatami and Johnson have been at the forefront of innovation in financial services. Their book gives a candid perspective into financial inclusion and the challenges it poses to billions of people around the world and the role that modern technology can play to address these issues. *Inclusive Finance* is one of the most insightful books I've read in a long time, full of practical recommendations and an absolute must read for anyone looking to transform financial services.'

Jeff Tijssen, Expert Partner and Global Head of Fintech, Bain & Company

'Analyses the transformative impact of fintech, showing how innovations such as digital identity systems and embedded finance are already reshaping financial inclusion. Hatami and Johnson bring the topic to life with rich case studies, making the book as practical as it is thought-provoking. This book is a must-read for those seeking a concrete, technology-driven roadmap to solving financial exclusion on a global scale.'

Huy Nguyen Trieu, Co-founder, Centre for Finance Technology and Entrepreneurship (CFTE)

'Offers invaluable insights into how fintech and innovation can transform financial inclusion across both developed and developing countries, making the powerful case that financial inclusion benefits everyone. It compellingly argues that the entire financial sector – not just governments and charities – has a crucial role to play in taking action to advance this important goal.'

Marie Walker, open banking and open finance expert, Raidiam and University of Cambridge

Inclusive Finance

How fintech and innovation can transform financial inclusion

Alessandro Hatami
Meaghan Johnson

Publisher's note

Every possible effort has been made to ensure that the information contained in this book is accurate at the time of going to press, and the publishers and authors cannot accept responsibility for any errors or omissions, however caused. No responsibility for loss or damage occasioned to any person acting, or refraining from action, as a result of the material in this publication can be accepted by the editor, the publisher or the authors.

First published in Great Britain and the United States in 2025 by Kogan Page Limited

Kogan Page
Kogan Page Ltd, 2nd Floor, 45 Gee Street, London EC1V 3RS, United Kingdom
Kogan Page Inc, 8 W 38th Street, Suite 90, New York, NY 10018, USA
www.koganpage.com

EU Representative (GPSR)
Authorised Rep Compliance Ltd, Ground Floor, 71 Baggot Street Lower, Dublin D02 P593, Ireland
www.arccompliance.com

Kogan Page books are printed on paper from sustainable forests.

ISBNs

Hardback	978 1 3986 1045 3
Paperback	978 1 3986 1043 9
Ebook	978 1 3986 1044 6

British Library Cataloguing-in-Publication Data
A CIP record for this book is available from the British Library.

Library of Congress Control Number
2025930852

Typeset by Integra Software Services, Pondicherry
Print production managed by Jellyfish
Printed and bound by CPI Group (UK) Ltd, Croydon CR0 4YY

CONTENTS

PART TWO
How do we fix finance?

FOREWORD

Financial inclusion is vital for global economic growth, yet millions of people – and not just in developing economies – remain excluded from formal financial systems. This exclusion perpetuates cycles of poverty and inequality, hindering progress for individuals, communities and nations. *Inclusive Finance* explores these challenges, offering a fresh perspective and actionable strategies for addressing financial exclusion in a rapidly changing world.

This book shines a light on the gap between the haves and the have nots and is more than a guide; it's a call to action for policymakers, financial institutions, tech innovators and development practitioners. Packed with research, real-world examples and practical advice, it provides a comprehensive roadmap to closing the financial gap. Whether you're a policymaker crafting inclusive regulations, an incumbent financial services provider aiming to serve their customers better, an entrepreneur creating disruptive solutions or a researcher exploring finance and social justice, this book delivers valuable insights and inspiration.

At its core, *Inclusive Finance* examines the multi-faceted nature of financial inclusion. It begins by analysing the global state of financial access, celebrating milestones like mobile money's growth in Africa while addressing persistent challenges such as gender disparities. Using data-driven insights, it unpacks why financial exclusion persists and what's needed to achieve universal access, aligning with the United Nations' 2030 Sustainable Development Goals.

A major theme is the transformative role of technology. Innovations like mobile money, blockchain, artificial intelligence and digital platforms are revolutionizing financial services, making them more accessible. Groundbreaking examples from Kenya, India and Brazil illustrate how technology has opened opportunities for millions previously excluded from formal systems. By integrating technology into financial inclusion strategies, the book emphasizes scalable sustainable solutions for under-served populations.

Another key focus is closing the gender gap in financial services. Women, particularly in low-income and rural settings, face significant barriers to financial access. The book highlights compelling stories and strategies to empower women financially, showing how this benefits families, communities and economies. Addressing this gender disparity is critical for achieving broader economic equality.

The book also tackles the challenges of serving rural and marginalized communities often overlooked by urban-focused financial innovations. It explores scalable models such as agent banking and community-led cooperatives that can effectively reach these populations. These examples demonstrate the importance of tailoring financial solutions to local contexts and needs.

Collaboration emerges as a recurring theme throughout the book. It stresses the importance of partnerships between governments, private companies, NGOs and development agencies to create robust financial ecosystems. Strong regulatory frameworks are vital to fostering innovation while protecting consumers, ensuring financial inclusion efforts are sustainable and equitable. The book highlights three fundamental benefits of financial inclusion: social benefits: improving the quality of life of millions of people; economic benefits, enabling the unbanked to contribute to the economic welfare of their communities; and, lastly, financial benefits, as providers get to see how technology can allow them to serve market segments that are currently out of reach, in a sustainable way.

In their book Alessandro and Meaghan offer a clear and realistic pathway for individuals and institutions to work toward a world where financial access is a fundamental right and exclusion is a thing of the past. *Inclusive Finance* is an essential read for anyone who believes in the power of finance to transform lives and communities. With its combination of visionary thinking, practical solutions and heartfelt advocacy, this book is poised to become a cornerstone in the field of inclusive finance.

Whether you're an experienced professional or just beginning to explore the subject, this book will deepen your understanding of the challenges and opportunities that lie ahead. More importantly, it will inspire you to act and join the movement to build a more inclusive and prosperous world. A legacy to be proud of.

Sir Ron Kalifa

PART ONE

What does financial inclusion mean?

1

Why does financial inclusion matter?

Introduction

Billions of people are benefiting from the services of banks, financial institutions and financial technology (fintech). Across the globe, people benefit from what these institutions are able to offer them. They enable them to send and receive money – be it a pay check, a payment for a service or even a gift. Most 'banked' people can store and protect these monies safely within the bank and when they wish to do so they can use their funds to buy something that enables them to get on with their lives or simply makes them happy. They do this through the help of organizations that provide them with services that are safe, quick, professionally run and conveniently priced.

Similarly, when they need to do something they don't have enough money for, their financial services provider (or bank) can offer them a viable solution. This can take many shapes and can be delivered with terms and conditions that are complementary to their needs, the situation and what they want to use the funds for. If they have overspent slightly their bank can offer them an affordable overdraft. If they need to buy a fridge or go on holiday, they can get a credit card or a personal loan. For bigger purchases their financial partners can help by providing them with a significant personal loan, a loan to buy a car, a mortgage or any other type of credit product with conditions and terms that they can afford to service. The ways these services are delivered are clearly defined and extensively monitored by governments and regulators.

If, on the other hand, at the end of the month they have a bit of extra liquidity at hand, their friendly banking partner will help them protect it. They will offer an array of options that suit the customer's needs which are fairly priced, easy to use and good value for money. They could be offered a savings account that rewards them with a small interest income for holding their financial surplus with their financial provider. Or they could be offered opportunities to invest the extra liquidity, whereby taking a bit of measured and clearly defined risk they can generate a greater upside than what a savings account would offer. If the customer has a more long-term perspective, the financial provider may even suggest a convenient pension product that will pay a stipend when they retire. They may also be offered an insurance policy so that, if something unexpected happened, they would be protected from a resulting financial downside.

All these services are provided by organizations that are (usually) financially sound, reliable, fair and well regulated by savvy regulators. The provider of financial services is usually a reliable organization that is easy to engage with and, most importantly, trustworthy. The financial provider is a trusted entity that benefits from making the life of their client easier. Yes, they charge fees, but these are fair, monitored and affordable.

This is how banking should feel like. And it does feel like this for many people. Customers of a financial provider mostly feel in control of their money. They are able to engage with their provider whenever they need to, gaining access to a range of products, services and engagement models that they can benefit from. So, is everything OK?

Well, not really.

Not everyone has access to this banking experience. In truth, while the average banking experience today for many customers is the best that it has ever been, too many are excluded. Billions of people across the globe (in both the developing and developed world) are not adequately benefiting from the financial services industry. Many millions of people are unable to gain full and fair benefit from their hard work and sacrifice. In today's world, if you do not have access to banking services ('unbanked') or if you do not have access to the services you need ('underbanked') you are unfairly penalized. Life for the unbanked and the underbanked is much harder than it would be if they had access to the financial services they need.

The fact is that the financially excluded and underserved are at a real disadvantage. They can only pay or be paid with cash. This exposes them to crime. Also, they are excluded from accessing places that offer them the goods and services they need remotely at more competitive prices than those they can reach in person. They are unable to get credit except from a limited range of lenders that are often not fairly priced, or worse, illegal like loan sharks. If they have a bit of surplus cash, their options are limited. The only options they have to protect any surplus is to store cash somewhere safe or to spend it fast. The latter is a really common strategy in countries with high inflation where customers cannot benefit from high savings interest rates. The University of Bristol estimates this poverty 'premium' at £490 for lower-income families in the UK.[1] Financial exclusion means that millions of people are forced to pay more for essential goods and services than the more affluent, making an already unfair situation even more painful.

The most effective means we all have to achieve economic and social welfare is our ability to earn a living. Earning a fair living is inexorably linked to our access to financial services. But access to finance is not open to all. In 2021, according to the World Bank, between 1.7 and 1.4 billion people still did not have a bank account.[2] This is a phenomenon that hits poorest countries most, but even the richest countries have a large number of unbanked and underbanked citizens. In the USA, 13 million people don't have access to bank accounts[3] while in the EU 13 per cent of its citizens are underbanked.[4] This lack of access results in poverty, social exclusion, poor health and lack of education – robbing many people of a fair and fulfilling life. Many reasons are behind this phenomenon, including outdated processes, cultural bias, technology gaps or simply legacy mindsets, and many more. All these obstacles – at least in part – can be mitigated by innovation.

As with most other aspects of our society, digital technology has and is continuing to innovate and transform financial services. Fintechs, neobanks and other challengers are reshaping the financial services, banking and payments landscapes everywhere. But they are doing this primarily for the benefit of certain segments of society, excluding certain others. Arguably, most neobanks are targeting mass affluent digital customers that are tired of the incumbent and their offering. The less affluent, digital or even educated customers are not usually a target segment.

This particular sort of financial 'discrimination' is only in small part driven by lack of access to technology. In fact the number of people with mobile phones exceeds the number of those with bank accounts. Interestingly, according to the World Economic Forum in 2022, of the 1.7 billion unbanked people, 1.1 billion had access to mobile technology.[5]

This financial exclusion can have a much more profound effect on society than many of us might realize. We could group the impact of inclusion into three categories: social, economic and financial. The social impact affects society as a whole and has implications that include fairness and morality. The economic impact focuses on wealth creation by those that receive the product and the impact this has on the economic situation of the markets they operate within. The financial impact simply states that providers of financial services to the unbanked can do so and generate returns from their services.

Social impact

Billions of people are not able to achieve what they need, hope and are capable of because they are excluded from simple financial tools that most of us consider basic. Enabling the billions of unbanked and underbanked individuals and businesses to access the financial service or product they need, and to gain access to all the financial services we take for granted, will have a profound impact on society. An inclusive society is fairer and more balanced. This vision of social harmony and equity is not just a feel-good opportunity: inclusivity leads to a more affluent, meritocratic, fair and stable society – that is everyone's gain.

In summary, financial exclusion leads people to:

- **Poverty:** When individuals are unable to access basic financial services such as bank accounts, credit and insurance their ability to generate, spend and protect their income is impaired, making them poorer than those who are not financially excluded.
- **Inequality:** Financial exclusion can contribute to the widening of the gap between the rich and the poor, creating social inequality. Poverty passes inequality to the next generation. The inability of an underbanked household to get the most out of their finances often results in family members leaving education, the inability to develop specialized skills that generate higher pay and of course the inability to borrow at fair rates and conditions in order to start a business or to buy a home.
- **Social exclusion:** People who are financially excluded may find it difficult to participate fully in society and access services that require financial transactions. In many instances we see that financial exclusion follows gender, racial and social stereotypes. People of colour, ethnic minorities, women, members of the LGBTQ+ communities are often denied access to finance – resulting in devastating unfairness in their ability to earn a living commensurate with their skills and ambitions.

Economic impact

Economies are not closed systems and the notion that the wealthy need the poor to stay poor in order to remain wealthy has proven to be false throughout history. Today the most affluent and successful countries in the world are by and large the more financially inclusive ones. But even the wealthiest and most financially inclusive countries still leave a sizable number of their citizens underbanked. According to the Federal Deposit Insurance Corporation (FDIC), in 2021 the US had 5.9 million unbanked households. Adding millions of individuals that are able to use their access to financial services to improve their economic situation will create more productivity, more buyers of services, builders of infrastructure, manufacturers of goods and ultimately more wealth. Inclusion is not a zero-sum game, the slice of the 'pie' of the rich will not become smaller – the global economic pie will become bigger for everyone.

The economic impacts of financial exclusion are:

- **Low economic growth:** Financial exclusion limits the potential for economic growth of countries and their economies. In the worldwide high inflation environment resulting from the Covid crisis and the Ukraine war, the unbanked are unable to earn a return from any capital in excess to their needs in the same way the banked can. In fact, they are doubly hit. The unbanked see the buying power of their cash income diminish due to inflation. However, they cannot hope to offset some of this loss in buying power with the revenues from an interest-bearing savings account or investment product.
- **Limited entrepreneurship:** Financial exclusion limits entrepreneurship and the creation of new businesses. The inability to access growth capital prevents creative, innovative individuals from building the business they would be capable of, limiting their ability to earn more but also preventing them from employing others, buying goods and services from others or being able to share the fruits of their success with loved ones.
- **Increased reliance on informal finance:** Financial exclusion forces individuals into a murky world of financial products offered by unregulated speculators. These offer the underbanked money transfers, credit and even investment and savings products that are expensive, unmonitored and ultimately dangerous financially – and sometimes even physically.

Financial impact

Greater inclusion also presents a commercial opportunity for financial institutions. Many providers of financial services believe that they cannot be more financially inclusive because the individuals they are excluding cannot be served profitably. Innovative businesses such as Nubank in Brazil and many more across the globe have proven that this is untrue. By providing a service that – amongst other things – enables millions of unbanked individuals to access a simple banking product, Nubank has created a business that not only affects society and the economy positively, but also makes money for the bank. Providers tend to assess the suitability of an underbanked person using approaches and criteria that are driven by decisions based on often anachronistic legacy processes that are largely made obsolete by recent innovation.

Today technology can make requirements such as identification, authentication, underwriting, risk assessment, compliance and fraud detection much less complicated and costly than in the past. In view of what is possible today, the less inclusive financial institutions are therefore excluding profitable underserved new customers because their legacy business practices, policies and operating models are not adapting to what technology could enable them to do. This means that potentially profitable customers are not being served and many banks are leaving potential profits on the table. There are scores of businesses across the globe that have tackled exclusion profitably. Businesses like M-Pesa converting a mobile phone into a bank account or ZestMoney in India providing credit to the underbanked are great examples of these opportunities.

Banks can benefit from financial inclusion in several ways:

- **More customers:** Sound financially inclusive policies and practices allow banks to serve more people and businesses. Done right, this will inevitably lead to increased revenues and profits for the bank.
- **Greater profitability:** In developing new ways of serving the unbanked, banks and financial services need to adapt their operating models, rules and practices. These more sophisticated ways of engagement with potential customers will not only enable them to address the needs of the underserved customer segments, but it will also enable them to serve core customers better. Better KYC/AML, authentication, fraud detection and compliance will impact their business for the better across all segments and customer profiles.

- **Increased loyalty:** Providing financial services to those who were previously excluded will create a loyal customer base, as these new, previously excluded, customers are likely to remain with the bank that first provided them with access to financial services. In a world where changing to another bank is possible with a few clicks, loyalty can be a valuable commodity.
- **Improved reputation:** Banks that are actively involved in promoting financial inclusion can improve their reputation and enhance their brand image. This can lead to increased customer trust and loyalty beyond the underbanked segments. Being proactively inclusive can have a very positive impact on the providers' reputation across many of the markets and geographies they operate in.
- **Better stakeholder engagement:** Challenging financial exclusion promotes diversity and inclusion in society. Today as businesses become increasingly transparent due to how technology has transformed the transparency of business practices, not only customers but also employees and investors demand better corporate behaviour. Supporting financial inclusion will not only generate the financial benefits described above but it will also drive greater engagement with other key business stakeholders.

The fact is that digital innovation can fundamentally reduce the number of unbanked and underbanked individuals across the world. As the success of digital banking is rapidly leading to a cashless society, it is of the utmost importance to find digital solutions to the banking needs of the whole population. Addressing the urgent need to provide cashless solutions to all also allows us to create the means to tackle other aspects of financial exclusion.

To achieve this, we need to create a shared vision for all stakeholders in the industry – this will include fintechs but also the global banks, governments, regulators, tech firms, social networks and of course end-users.

The vision

To eradicate financial exclusion, we need to illustrate what a financially inclusive society actually looks like. The basis of this concept should be that no human being should be denied access to the banking product they require to live their lives. In our financially inclusive society, no person is denied access to banking due to reasons such as: income, gender, sexual orientation, religion, race or ethnic background, age, education, social status, residential status or health. Most of us have witnessed or even been on the receiving end of being denied a financial product because the provider considered one of these categories as too high risk to serve.

In principle every individual (person or legal entity) should be able to access the following financial capabilities – these are not specific financial products, they are outcomes of using financial services:

- **Current account:** Every individual should be able to access a service that allows them to digitally store cash. This should be personal, secure, free, simple to use.
- **Payments:** Every individual should be able to receive, send and store a payment in a safe, quick and inexpensive manner. Furthermore, every individual should be able to send money that they own to any other individual or organization nearby or across the globe except where these funds would be used for purposes that are illegal or harmful to others.
- **Protection:** Every individual should be able to have access to financial products and services that allow them to safely and securely gain financial benefit from any funds that are in excess of their needs. These products will range from savings accounts, to investments, to insurance, to pensions.
- **Credit:** Every individual should be allowed to connect with entities that are willing to provide them with credit with fair and affordable conditions. These will range from personal loans to secured products such as car loans and mortgages.
- **Advice:** Every individual should be able to gain access to trustworthy information and advice on how to manage their money – advice that is not motivated by greed of the provider but is aimed at increasing the welfare of the individual.

Today's technology allows simple and cost-effective ways to address all these requirements. Banks provide their customers with the ability to achieve certain goals – we call these the capabilities we described above. Capabilities such as paying or being paid, protecting any financial surplus or borrowing. These capabilities are delivered through a given set of services such as a current account, a remittances service or the appropriate credit.

In delivering these capabilities we do not suggest that players should abandon all constraints and reasons in providing financial services; we believe that every jurisdiction should provide the right framework to enable provision of the following services to the extent that their infrastructure, regulation and economic situation allow. Table 1.1 describes the customer needs that should be addressed by financial services providers.

Achieving financial inclusion requires following a dual approach. Firstly, we need to understand what is wrong with our current system and how we arrived at this situation. Secondly, we should articulate what can be and in fact is being done to address what is wrong with our current financial system.

It is important to understand why financial services today are not delivering on their social contract with some of their customers. In Chapter 2 we will look at how certain groups are unfairly treated and the impact that this is having on their lives. We will outline the

TABLE 1.1 Customer needs addressed by more inclusive financial services

Service	Customer need
Identification	The means to be digitally identified and authenticated by the individual's jurisdiction of birth or residence
Current account	A basic current account for every individual
Savings	A basic savings account that can earn interest where local customs do not prevent it
Remittances	Access to inexpensive cross-border payments when these funds are available in the sender's current account
Credit	Access to affordable credit that adequately reflects the circumstances of the borrower
Data	Ability to own one's personal financial data and the means to grant or deny access to financial institutions as they see fit

systemic bias that results in exclusion and how historical biases, outdated policies and built-in operational discrimination have shaped a financial ecosystem that is letting down so many of us. We will also look at how certain creative and resourceful individuals across the globe address these shortcomings by creating frameworks, services and businesses that are transforming the financial exclusion landscape.

Looking at the past is fundamental when trying to understand the present. We will discuss how the reasons behind financial exclusion are deeply rooted in our pasts. In order to understand why the modern banking offering is letting so many of us down, it is important to be able to look at the origins of banking.

The first banks were created to serve the economic elites of the markets they operated within. These were rich people that needed liquidity to do something or that wanted to get a better return on their financial assets. The banker's clients did not ask for a financial product. They expressed their needs, and the banker would see if they could offer them the financial support they would require to address these needs. Everything the banks offered was custom made for the client by bankers who understood the client's needs and had the know-how and authority to define conditions and pricing.

As we entered the Industrial Revolution, demand for finance expanded and the banks started creating standardized products that were sold to customers by bankers who did not have the right to customize them. Product characteristics were centrally defined and the banker interfacing with customers had little or no power to change them. In the 20th century, with the introduction of automation and mass marketing, the conditions for the sale of financial products became even tighter. The digital revolution just took this approach online.

As banking became increasingly digital, so did money. Digital technology made it easier and safe for consumers to store their liquidity online. Receiving and sending payments, asking for a bank loan or opening a savings account no longer required going to a branch. This digitalization of finance was welcomed by many. But it had one terrible outcome for certain segments of society (who are often less affluent, less educated and more rural). These segments slowly found themselves excluded and marginalized. Understanding why this happened is key to resolving financial exclusion.

As banks digitized and fintechs started challenging them, new banking products were created to fulfil customers' needs. A key offering of banks is being able to send and receive payments. Digital technology has made this much more efficient than ever before. But in delivering this it has raised the costs and uncertainty associated with cash-based payments, further excluding the unbanked from most of these benefits. Sending and receiving large amounts of cash has become much more difficult in the digital age. All banks today require that cash payments over a certain size be scrutinized more thoroughly than the digital equivalent. These are mainly justified and necessary anti-money laundering (AML) policies, but they have led to a certain characterization of cash payments.

A similar narrative has affected the credit space. In the past, a customer or small business could get a loan from a friendly banker on the back of their personal relations and reputation with the bank manager or loans officer. This knowledge was based on the bank staff's direct engagement with the community they operated within. Creditworthiness was based on personal knowledge of the banks and the customer. This was replaced by access to credit scoring tools that based their decisions on information on gathering data generated by other banks and financial institutions. Choices of legitimate affordable sources of credit for the unbanked dried up in the digital age.

All the other financial products and services were similarly affected. The unbanked found that, in a cashless society, their choices were reduced, terms became less favourable and execution of trades became harder.

The digital transformation of banking has not yet been good news for the underbanked and unbanked. But this is not down to the technologies themselves. This is largely due to the way digital transformation is being implemented by financial institutions. Legacy ways of thinking are resulting in many financial institutions making decisions that are discriminatory to certain segments of society in ways that they do not need to be. But fintech can, if implemented correctly, become the means through which everyone can get access to the financial product they need.

Conclusion

It is important that after we have understood the problem, we understand the means through which it can be addressed. We need to understand how fintech can make financial exclusion obsolete; how banks are coming around to seeing the benefits in addressing the needs of the financially excluded; how governments and regulators are seeing the cost it could have to their economies; how Big Tech is seeing inclusion as a growth opportunity; and how consumers are increasingly disturbed by how certain segments are treated by financial institutions. We will begin by looking at the specific importance of the different families of financial services products.

First and foremost is the current account, which provides the means to access most financial products. This will be followed by payments, credit, savings, investments, pensions and insurance. We will then seek to understand how the banks need to regain the role of the 'trusted advisor', a role that has been watered down by the advent of digital finance. Finally, we will look at why inclusive finance is actually feared by many. The prejudices about risk/reward, fraud, cybersecurity and even political risk must be understood and – if appropriate – debunked.

Having looked at the problem, we will look at solutions.

Fintech and challengers are (allegedly) trying to address the problem by creating solutions and propositions that make it possible for providers of financial solutions to reach the underbanked and unbanked worldwide. Fintech innovation is looking at different actors in the financial services ecosystem to see how their offering can make a difference.

Creating solutions that challenge the status quo with propositions that are safe, compliant and profitable is the key. These will attract the support of customer advocates, regulators and, of course, investors. Also, it is important to recognize the role that can be played by governments – not only by regulating the sector more intelligently, but also by supporting concepts such as digital identity (ID) and mandating a free universal basic account for all the unbanked. Lastly, we will look at players external to finance that have a huge role to play in fighting financial exclusion. Big Tech firms, telecommunications companies (telcos) and retailers are just a few of the non-financial organizations that can have a real impact on financial exclusion.

The best way to explore these changes is by looking at key innovations that are transforming the financial services industry. Change areas such as identity and authentication, open banking, banking as a service, embedded finance, distributed ledger technology and many more will inevitably impact financial inclusion. For each area, we should not only look at key strategies, leading business models and key players; we should also understand and map other key elements in each area such as conferences, publications, academic research and key experts that can be points of reference in order to understand and engage with the specific innovation areas.

Our goal in writing this book is to create a resource for professionals, academia, consultants, non-profits and the general public that will enable them to better understand the importance and potential to make the global economy larger, fairer and more inclusive.

Notes

1 Personal Finance Research Centre (nd) The poverty premium, University of Bristol. www.bristol.ac.uk/media-library/sites/geography/pfrc/pfrc1614-poverty-premium-key-findings.pdf (archived at https://perma.cc/UW2Y-4BXQ)

2 World Bank (2021) The Global Findex Database 2021, World Bank. www.worldbank.org/en/publication/globalfindex/interactive-executive-summary-visualization (archived at https://perma.cc/XD8U-NEXW)

3 Federal Deposit Insurance Corporation (2021) 2021 FDIC national survey of unbanked and underbanked households: Executive summary, FDIC. www.fdic.gov/analysis/household-survey/2021execsum.pdf (archived at https://perma.cc/4BG6-Z7WZ)

4 WSBI-ESBG (2024) Nevertheless, more than 13 million adults, or 4% of the adult population, face financial exclusion, according to an ESBG analysis of the Global Findex Database 2021, recently released by the World Bank, WSBI-ESBG. www.wsbi-esbg.org/number-of-unbanked-adult-eu-citizens-more-than-halved-in-the-last-four-years (archived at https://perma.cc/3K9Y-GBUW)

5 World Economic Forum (2022) Why decentralized finance is a leapfrog technology for the 1.1 billion people who are unbanked, WEF. www.weforum.org/agenda/2022/09/decentralized-finance-a-leapfrog-technology-for-the-unbanked (archived at https://perma.cc/CMM8-JV8J)

2

What are the drivers of financial exclusion?

Introduction

Financial exclusion in banking is there by design. Banks were created to serve certain segments of society only – they aimed to almost exclusively serve people with means. Early banking offerings were perfectly customized (hyper-personalized as we would say today). The first bankers were focused on delivering exactly what their clients wanted, creating fully bespoke financial propositions. This required a lot of dedicated time and as such the bankers' returns for providing the service had to justify the effort. The customer therefore had to be able to pay for the services they received.

From the outset, banks have been taking risks – with their own money but mostly with other people's money (most lent out money left with them by trusting depositors). To succeed, banks had to generate enough returns from their services to be able to entice depositors to leave their money with them and to be able to have enough reserves not to go bust if their borrowing customers were to default on their commitments. The outcome of this is that since their inception banks deal almost exclusively with the affluent – or those that looked like they were.

One of the world's first modern banks, the Medici bank in medieval Florence, dealt with princes and dukes and other wealthy owners of assets. Sometimes these became guarantees when borrowing, so if the loans were not paid back the assets would be taken over by the banker as compensation. So, the traditional borrowing customer had to have assets (liquid ones preferably) to receive a loan.[1]

If you were a German prince, a Flemish silk merchant or a Pope, you would have access to a number of financial products. The banker would work with you, because great profits were at hand, to offer you the means to invade a neighbouring state, open a new trade route or convert a continent. If you weren't a property or asset owner, you would not have been a target customer. The rest of the population had to rely on less sophisticated and less formal means to address their financial needs. The rest of society relied – and sometimes still does today – on informal arrangements.

In ancient times, value between people – rich and poor – was exchanged through the barter of goods. The ancient Sumerians tried to standardize this process by creating comparisons that equated a certain amount of silver to a certain amount of grain. Value was then exchanged differently by different cultures, from the cowrie shells (see Figure 2.1) in sub-Saharan Africa to the rai stones of the Yapese people in Micronesia.

FIGURE 2.1 Cowrie coins

SOURCE A Hatami

The creation of money facilitated the exchange of goods in the economy. Using money allowed buyers and sellers to pay less in transaction costs in comparison with barter trading, which required the physical transfer of one good against another. Money became a liquid asset that was chosen as an efficient way of storing value and a practical way of transferring it. The first actual coins were minted in electrum, a mixture of gold and silver, by the Lydians in modern-day Turkey, probably around 700 BC. Valuable metals were used to issue the first coins because the value of the metal was supposed to equate to the value of the coin. So, in a way, the metal coins were still a form of barter. Until the introduction of paper money in China, little changed in the world of payments – the most common legal tender was the metal coin.

The introduction of paper money in the 10th century AD by Chinese merchants authorized by the Chinese state during the Song dynasty in China was followed by the state itself issuing the notes. This was the first instance of fiat money – a government-issued currency not backed by a commodity whose value is set and guaranteed by the state.

As we said in Chapter 1, the financial needs of everyone – rich or poor – can be summarized into three groups:

- **Payments:** To be able to send, receive and store money.
- **Credit:** To be able to borrow money when we have a shortfall.
- **Protection:** To be able to protect any capital in excess to what is needed immediately. These include products such as savings, investments, insurance and pensions.

The emergence of money (fiat and not) had a profound impact on financial inclusion. It allowed everyone to send and receive value for goods and services in an efficient and relatively safe way. From 300 BC in India in Asia and from 100 BC in the Roman Empire in Europe, the affluent could even use the equivalent of what today we call cheques.

Even though cash simplified the transfer of value, the non-rich had few choices when seeking credit. Their lenders included not only friends and family but, more ominously, moneylenders and pawnbrokers. The terms offered by these lenders were often very onerous, pushing all three Abrahamic religions (Judaism, Christianity and Islam) at some point to decree that charging excessive interest for a loan (usury) was a sin.[2]

More structured choices were available to some. The lucky few that lived in Perugia in Italy could borrow from the Monte di Pietà, a charitable low-cost lender established by a monk. Other lenders existed but these did not serve the less wealthy. These were, as we said, mainly available only to the well-off.[3]

Cash also allowed for the protection of assets. Until the 19th century the only option for the less affluent to save money was to find a secure hiding place. The first modern savings bank was founded in 1816 in Germany by the philanthropist Friedrich Wilhelm Raiffeisen and its aim was to create a proposition for the less affluent to benefit from their savings. The idea was to provide a means for people of modest means to save and earn interest on their savings. For the less affluent, the ability to invest, buy insurance or a pension came much later.[4]

Historically, the less affluent in society did not gain access to the range of financial products and services that were available to the wealthy. As banking evolved, the offering of financial services became slowly more democratized. Partly as a result of the Industrial Revolution, from the middle of the 18th century banks began realizing that there was an increasing demand for what they could provide. As gross domestic product (GDP) per capita grew around the world, so did the demand for financial services. In his historical analysis of the economy, *Contours of the World Economy*, Angus Madison outlines a distinct peak in the GDP per capita of individuals and economies across the world. The new affluent created a much greater demand for financial services than ever before.[5] The banks of the time adapted well by taking in deposits, arranging for money transfers and providing loans. The first modern banks appeared in centres where industry and trade thrived. Cities like Birmingham, Kolkata, Stockholm, Hamburg, Rio de Janeiro, Cairo and New York all were home to banks established before 1800.

These modern banks, aimed at serving old money, new money and affluent entrepreneurs, started off by trying to apply the principles of banking established by their predecessors to much larger pools of customers. The banks gave great importance to their knowledge and understanding of their customers. This included a clear awareness of factors such as sources of capital, the quality of the assets held, the resilience of their source of wealth and a clear view of how any credit would be used.

The first modern banks relied on the ability of their local leadership to know, understand and assess risks and opportunities inherent to each customer. This is where the myth of the all-powerful 'branch manager' was created – customer-friendly, well informed and powerful enough to make decisions. In the first modern banks, the local senior bank staff had what today would be considered an impossibly broad mandate to define the pricing and conditions of the products and propositions that were offered to customers. In most instances, the size of the facility, the required collateral and the financial conditions of a loan or the pricing offered for savings, investments and other products could be largely defined in the branch. This was possible because the branch manager was almost always part of the community they served. However, the financially exclusive risks of this model are clear. The bank managers would know their customers personally. The traditional focus on profitability often led to privilege the engagement with wealthier customers as these were more likely to generate higher returns than less affluent customers and businesses.

As the average GDP per capita across the globe grew, the number of individuals that needed banking also grew. This resulted in a growth in the number of banks and bank managers. The banks soon realized that in order to manage their businesses they needed to harmonize and enforce the rules through which customers were onboarded, assessed and served. The power of the local staff in engaging with customers was reduced and the rules of engagement became increasingly centralized.

The arrival of communication technology such as the telegraph, telephone, telex and fax machines allowed interaction with centralized decision-making hubs and thus resulted in the branch staff being controlled centrally while still being able to deliver a certain level of speed in working with their customers in the branches.

These new ways of banking still required the banks to focus on customers with the means to justify the costs of serving them. However, as the number of potential customers grew, the banks could no longer offer the personalized services that they could do when they had fewer customers. This resulted in banks becoming more prescriptive on the characteristics of desirable customers, serving a customer base that became much larger but remained affluent. Precise rules were created on who was eligible for what products, all under very specific conditions that were set centrally by the bank headquarters and not in the branches.

Prospective customers had to be able to present a form of identification that was recognized by an authority – ideally the state. They had to prove the ability to pay for any fees that were generated by the banking services. And, most importantly, they had to prove that they were able to repay credit and pay for any other bank products they were signing up to.

These requirements were rolled out across distant geographic locations and economic realities, so the profiles of potential customers became increasingly homogenous. In addition to providing identification and proof of wealth, customers now had to provide other characteristics that were considered necessary to mitigate risk by the central decision. Suddenly factors such as gender, race, religion and the like came to be seen as actual indications of the viability of a new customer.

The branch managers of old were by no means unbiased, but if they believed that a customer of the 'wrong' gender, colour or religion was a worthwhile risk they could offer them banking. Centralization of banking made this much harder.

Sometimes these rules were even enforced by the state. An early instance of modern financial regulation was implemented by the Dutch in the 17th century. These standardization practices were meant to reduce risk to the bank; the effect was often that of discrimination and exclusion.[6]

A disturbing example of this was how discrimination against women was enshrined in law during this centralization of banking in countries where women historically were not barred from having bank accounts. In medieval Venice, women were considered legal entities practically equal to men with regards to finance, trade and property.[7] This was not the case until very recently in many economies across the world, as shown in Table 2.1.

Even modern and sophisticated organizations seem to be carrying these biases in their risk assessment. In 2019 at the launch of their Apple Credit product (supported by Mastercard and Goldman Sachs), two prominent individuals – Steve Wozniak, a co-founder of Apple,

TABLE 2.1 Year women gained the right to open bank accounts without male permission

India	*1947*	After India gained independence in 1947, the constitution provided equal rights to all its citizens regardless of gender
Japan	*1947*	The Japanese Constitution and The Civil Code guaranteed equal rights to all citizens, irrespective of gender. Prior to these revisions, the legal status of Japanese women was similar to that of minors, requiring them to obtain consent from male family members
China	*1954*	The Constitution of the People's Republic of China (1954) stated that women in China enjoy equal rights with men in all spheres of life
Germany	*1958*	A reform allowed women to open bank accounts without permission
Australia	*1960s*	Formal laws varied by state
United States	*1960s*	The Equal Credit Opportunity Act in 1974 solidified these rights
France	*1965*	Before this, women needed their husband's permission to open an account or work without his consent
Italy	*1975*	Women were allowed to open a bank account without a male guardian's permission after the reform of family law
Spain	*1975*	Laws introduced after Franco's death
United Kingdom	*1975*	The Sex Discrimination Act
Switzerland	*1985*	Before this, married women needed their husband's permission

and David Heinemeier Hansson, a Silicon Valley entrepreneur – both disclosed that they were offered far superior credit limits than their spouses, even though they shared the same assets, bank accounts and financial profile.[8] This obviously received substantial media coverage, causing embarrassment to Apple and Goldman Sachs.

Similar bias was historically applied to other groups. Even if illegal in many countries, discrimination against certain groups is still widespread. Table 2.2 lists some of the biases in place in many economies around the world.

TABLE 2.2 Typical biases impacting seekers of financial services

Group	Nature of discrimination	Impact of discrimination
Non-white neighbourhoods	• Redlining: Denial of mortgages based on neighbourhood	• Reduced homeownership, wealth accumulation and neighbourhood investment
Women	• Gender pay gap: Earning less than men for similar work	• Reduced savings, investment opportunities and retirement funds
Immigrants/new to country	• Identification bias: Lack of credit history or documentation • Language barriers: Financial institutions not providing services in other languages.	• Difficulty in obtaining loans, credit cards or mortgages
LGBTQ+ community	• Orientation bias: Discrimination in lending based on sexual orientation	• Reduced access to credit, higher interest rates
Homeless	• Unhoused: Discrimination based on lack of a fixed address	• No access to basic financial products and payments
Indigenous peoples	• Colonization: Land rights disputes affecting property as collateral	• Difficulty in obtaining loans or mortgages
Low-income Individuals	• Poverty: High fees for basic banking services • Domicile: Bias based on where one lives	• Reduced savings, reliance on predatory lending
Less able individuals	• Access discrimination: Not making services accessible to the less able	• Reduced access to financial services • Forcing dependence on others for financial products

A closer look at barriers to financial inclusion suggests that they can be roughly categorized into two groups. Supply-side barriers are put in place by the providers. Demand-side barriers are put in place by the customers themselves not asking for financial products because they do not realize how they could benefit from them.[9]

Supply-side barriers

Bias

This type of barrier is the result of behaviours and rules that are defined by two types of prejudice. Organizational bias is in place by design, resulting from the organization's past rules and behaviours. Individual bias is pushed by the personal beliefs and behaviours of individuals charged with delivering the financial service.

ORGANIZATIONAL BIAS

This is where the provider of the financial product has created a set of rules and guidelines that were often not designed to discriminate against a specific group but end up doing so. An example of this is the difficulty that a person without a fixed address has in opening a bank in the UK, US, Canada and many other countries.

Most countries say that access to a basic bank account should be offered to anyone that can verify their identity. However, the means of validating one's identity is left to the provider, so the means of providing ID can vary substantially between different banks. These different rules might not be meant to be discriminatory when implemented but in reality they result in financial exclusion.[10] The decisions to stipulate a specific means of ID by different providers has often been done with the goal of meeting regulation and avoiding issues such as money laundering and fraud.

These rules, set at the organizational level, are part of the legacy framework that makes incumbent banks less agile. Many challenger banks issue basic 'bank accounts' that are often simply digital wallets and that are easier to open than traditional bank accounts. These new institutions are redesigning policies on the basis of regulation, sound business practices and, of course, technology. There are limits to this innovative mindset, as the bias shown by the Apple Card discussed earlier highlights.

INDIVIDUAL BIAS

This bias is more common in banks that deliver their services through face-to-face human interaction. An example would be a branch employee that applies some of their own prejudices when engaging with a minority customer and denying them the product that best fits their needs. This is something that the bank should monitor and address. As we are moving to more automated delivery of financial services, hopefully unfair bias towards individuals will no longer be an issue.

Legacy

In a fast-changing environment such as we have today, processes and policies that derive from legacy and tradition can become a real impediment in delivering transformative change. Legacy can become a real barrier to improvement if not monitored and addressed. For long-standing financial institutions, a strategy that is illustrated by the phrase 'this is how we do things' is no longer fit for purpose, but this approach is still used by many.

The legacy issues faced by incumbent financial players are multiple and sometimes well hidden. These are not only about outdated technology (an area already addressed by many institutions), but also about internal organization, policies, objectives and business culture. These issues can manifest themselves in a variety of ways. The most complicated issues are with operational legacy, connected to the built-in bias issues mentioned above where regulation, risk and fraud requirements are interpreted and implemented in ways that are unnecessarily discriminating on certain segments of society. Addressing these is not easy to do and it sometimes requires a redesign of the provider that many financial institutions are unable – or unwilling – to undertake.

Regulation

Regulators usually see themselves as the champions of the unbanked underdog. Unfortunately, this is often not the case, as regulation is often not aligned with the needs of the unbanked. Regulators correctly see their role as protecting the welfare of the market they regulate – this can involve limiting the provision of finance to customers whose riskiness is less difficult to assess – these are usually the more affluent.

Regulators affect inclusion by requiring the offer of basic financial services to all members of society. However, poorly thought-out regulation can have very detrimental effects of financial inclusion and requirements aimed at protecting the public can become barriers to the less affluent. For example, Know Your Customer (KYC) requirements that necessitate identification and authentication using means that are not available to all can be a real barrier to access. According to the World Bank, 850 million people worldwide do not have an official ID.[11] They are therefore excluded by most providers of financial services, as regulation in most countries requires a physical ID.

Lack of ID is a problem often associated with developing countries, but the regulatory barriers to financial inclusion are also a problem for developed countries. The UK Parliament completed a review on consumer financial services access in 2019. It found that 1.3 million UK adults do not have a bank account. The UK Parliament recognized that 'Consumers may have difficulty proving their identity, for example, those with no permanent address or who move often, those who do not have a passport or driving licence or UK paper utility bills in their name'.[12] As we mentioned earlier, many regulators require proof of address in addition to identification. This makes it very hard for people in financial difficulty to be able to get help from a bank to improve their financial situation. This has led to a number of interesting collaborations between charities and banks. In the UK, homelessness charity Shelter and the HSBC bank are working together to issue basic bank accounts to individuals that do not have a fixed address.[13]

Costs

Some governments require that banks issue a basic bank account that is free to open and which enables the user to send and receive funds and to withdraw them as cash when required – the EU and the UK both have provision for such accounts.

The reality is that banks provide financial services to their clients because they want to earn income from it. Onboarding the unbanked and offering them a limited set of services is not profitable for banks. In addition, opening accounts for the unbanked can be costly to the bank. If the customer does not have an ID and therefore needs a special type of identification and authentication process, they will inevitably be more costly to onboard. Furthermore, if they then cannot be offered the same credit products as normal bank customers (overdrafts, personal loans and the like), or they do not have enough excess liquidity to deposit into a savings account or buy an investment product, an insurance policy or a personal pension, they will inevitably be considered a less profitable – and therefore less desirable – customer for the bank.

In 2016 the UK government designated that the nine largest providers of current accounts in the UK be required to offer basic bank accounts to eligible customers. But, as formally stated by Lloyds Banking Group:

> The basic bank account is free. It provides a basic banking provision, but the cost to us is not dissimilar from other products that provide a basic current account provision. [...] These are not commercially advantageous products for us to have.[14]

As a consequence, research conducted by Citizens Advice, a UK charity, concluded that 'Basic accounts are still not visible enough in all banks, so some people won't know that they exist. This is compounded by the fact that not all banks allow people to apply for a basic bank account when consumers think they would benefit from one.'[15]

Technology can of course help to address these costs. A mobile money account costs a fraction of the cost of a bank account to activate and manage, and it provides most of the services of a basic bank account. These can be the first step for a broader engagement between the bank and the customer, eventually leading to more traditional banking services that are remunerative for the customer and the bank.

Barriers to financial inclusion also exist from the demand side. There are several reasons why customers themselves are the cause of their financial exclusion.

Demand-side barriers

Financial literacy

One key driver of financial exclusion from the demand side is that of financial literacy. It results in potential bank customers not realizing they could benefit from access to a bank account. The impacts of financial illiteracy are many, but they can be (maybe simplistically) grouped into three categories:

- not choosing the right product
- not knowing that a product you could benefit from exists
- not trusting banks and thinking that financial products are not for you

Not choosing the right product is an issue more relevant to the underbanked and the poorly banked rather than the unbanked.

We can categorize individuals that are not benefiting from financial services into three groups:

- **The unbanked** are individuals using no financial products.
- **The underbanked** are individuals using some financial products but not benefiting from all the products that could help them.
- **The badly banked** are those who are using the wrong financial products, not benefiting from or even being damaged by their financial provider.

In all three instances, lack of financial literacy is a fundamental issue. All three of these situations are in some form the result of lack of financial education and understanding – or, more insidiously, being subject to misinformation on the risk and benefits of banking.

Limited financial literacy results in customers making wrong decisions about banking. Beyond simply not engaging in banking, choosing the wrong products can create simple issues such as not realizing that you are not receiving the right return on your savings or using an overdraft or a high-fee credit card to borrow. It is fair to say that the banks in this case should advise their underbanked or badly banked customers that better options are available to them. It is also clear that, even with the regulators' consistent focus on avoiding 'misselling' of financial products, banks and financial services, organizations are still not serving their clients as well as they could.

Not knowing that the right financial product exists affects the unbanked more. Many do not even know that a bank could give them the right solution to address their financial problems. A sure way to ensure you do not receive what you need is the fact that you do not ask for it. A number of initiatives are underway to address this kind of financial illiteracy. An interesting one is the collaboration between the European Commission and the Organisation for Economic Co-operation and Development's (OECD) International Network on Financial Education, resulting in the development of a joint financial competence framework aimed at improving financial literacy among children, youth and adults in the European Union.[16] It is also worthwhile mentioning the Aflatoun International Organization based in the Netherlands. They work with a strong network of non-governmental organizations (NGOs) and governments to deliver social and financial education to children and young people worldwide.[17]

Lack of trust is more difficult to address, as it has emotional and even cultural roots. People can become averse to banking because of a poor experience in the past, perceived complexity, fear of being taken advantage of, concerns about privacy and even religious or cultural norms. The best approach to address this is again education. Banks should play a big role in addressing these issues – following up on bad experiences, simplifying the way they present their products and talking about the social implications of their products, such as identifying products or services that are Shariah compliant.

Social norms

All of us live in some form of social system. The values, beliefs and customs of these systems affect the choices we make every day. Breaking these values by any individual can have dire consequences, such as isolation, harassment and even violence. One group that is affected in their access to financial services because of social prejudice is women. We mentioned how many countries have until recently had limitations on allowing women access to finance.

A working paper of the African Development Bank presents a worrying picture about the current state of access to finance for women. In their survey of banking in 47 African countries they not only saw a gender gap in the access to banking (only 37 per cent of women have bank accounts compared with 48 per cent of men) but also self-exclusion – when asked why they did not apply for a loan, twice as many women than men replied 'I did not think I would be approved.'[18] Similar results occur across the world.

Access

Financial exclusion is often attributed to lack of access. This is the assumption that if the customer could have access to a bank branch or equivalent financial exclusion would be resolved. Financial inclusion in recent years has gone up while the number of physical bank branches has gone down across the globe.

The main drive behind the closure of branches is cost. As the number of people preferring digital engagement with their bank increases, branches start serving an increasingly small number of customers – thus making them less worthwhile from both the bank's and the customer's perspective. The narrative that branches are useful for financial inclusion has been shown to be inaccurate – as the number of branches decreases across the globe the number of people with bank accounts increases.

The issue is that even though basic bank accounts have migrated well online, other products such as credit, investments, insurance and pensions have not done so to the same extent. The role of the bank branch was not only to deliver bank accounts, but it was also that of explaining and promoting financial solutions to customers that would improve their lives. The closure of branches has not been compensated with tools and capabilities online to give customers – especially less financially savvy ones – enough support to access the other benefits banking could provide.

Conclusion

Financial exclusion is a problem that affects society as a whole. Its effects are deep and diverse. There is much discussion on what needs to be done and banks, governments, businesses, educational institutions, entrepreneurs, NGOs and even entrepreneurs are claiming that they are addressing the problem. But we are moving too slowly and not taking full advantage of the most important resource available – digital technology.

Financial exclusion is not resolved by enabling everyone to have a current account. It is a much broader challenge, and the growth of fintech provides us with a powerful tool. Let's use it.

Notes

1 N Ferguson (2008) *The Ascent of Money: A financial history of the world*, 10th anniversary edition, Penguin, London
2 Encyclopedia.com (2024) Monti di Pietà, Encyclopedia.com. www.encyclopedia.com/religion/encyclopedias-almanacs-transcripts-and-maps/monti-di-pieta (archived at https://perma.cc/GX2F-H2AL)
3 Encyclopedia.com (2024) Monti di Pietà, Encyclopedia.com. www.encyclopedia.com/religion/encyclopedias-almanacs-transcripts-and-maps/monti-di-pieta (archived at https://perma.cc/GX2F-H2AL)
4 Raiffeisen Bank International (2024) 130 years and counting, Raiffeisen Bank International. www.rbinternational.com/en/raiffeisen/rbi-group/about-us/history.html (archived at https://perma.cc/K9EE-RWRU)

5 Angus Maddison (2007) *Contours of the World Economy, 1–2030 AD: Essays in macro-economic history*, Oxford University Press, Oxford

6 H James (2015) *Financial Innovation, Regulation and Crises in History*, Routledge, Abingdon

7 E Dermineur (2018) *Women and Credit in Pre-industrial Europe*, Brepols

8 K Schwab (2019) I applied for an Apple Card. What they offered was a sexist insult, Fast Company. www.fastcompany.com/90429224/i-applied-for-an-apple-card-what-they-offered-was-a-sexist-insult (archived at https://perma.cc/H3TL-7MYW)

9 G Kumar (nd) Financial inclusion: Barriers from supply side and demand side, *International Journal of Research in Engineering, Science and Management*, 2, 313. www.ijresm.com/Vol.2_2019/Vol2_Iss4_April19/IJRESM_V2_I4_88.pdf (archived at https://perma.cc/F5R4-XGJ8)

10 M Davie (2019) How lack of identification is blocking financial inclusion around the world, Kiva. www.kiva.org/blog/how-lack-of-identity-is-blocking-financial-inclusion-around-the-world (archived at https://perma.cc/NTK4-6GXA)

11 ID4D (nd) ID4D global dataset: Overview, World Bank. id4d.worldbank.org/global-dataset (archived at https://perma.cc/D7NG-7Q6D)

12 Parliament (2019) The Treasury Committee. Consumers' access to financial services, UK Parliament. publications.parliament.uk/pa/cm201719/cmselect/cmtreasy/1642/164205.htm (archived at https://perma.cc/L27Q-KU45)

13 Shelter England (nd) HSBC: A corporate partner of Shelter, Shelter England. england.shelter.org.uk/what_we_do/corporate_partners/hsbc (archived at https://perma.cc/N6PK-9AUV)

14 Parliament (2019) The Treasury Committee. Consumers' access to financial services, UK Parliament. publications.parliament.uk/pa/cm201719/cmselect/cmtreasy/1642/164205.htm (archived at https://perma.cc/L27Q-KU45)

15 D VandenBurg and J Lane (2017) *Getting the Basics Right: Access to basic banking in the UK*, Citizens Advice. www.citizensadvice.org.uk/Global/CitizensAdvice/Debt%20and%20Money%20Publications/Getting%20the%20basics%20right.pdf (archived at https://perma.cc/B29Y-P7GK)

16 OECD (2023). International Network on Financial Education, OECD. www.oecd.org/en/networks/infe.html (archived at https://perma.cc/VCZ9-SJ7D)

17 Aflatoun (nd) Homepage, Aflatoun. aflatoun.org (archived at https://perma.cc/2JVN-4JE3)

18 African Development Bank (2019) Working paper 317: Women self-selection out of the credit market in Africa, AFDB. www.afdb.org/en/documents/working-paper-317-women-self-selection-out-credit-market-africa (archived at https://perma.cc/U3P2-XRUB)

3

The role of banking in everyone's lives

What is offered vs what is needed

Introduction

Banks as we see them today are a relatively new invention, probably less than 700 years old. Banking, though, is ancient.

We advocate the right for everyone to have access to banking – but does everyone actually need banking? Most people do – the issue is that many of us need a broader set of products and services that banks are willing or able to offer. As we said in Chapter 1, ideally, banking should allow every person to be able to access:

- **payments:** send and receive money
- **credit:** borrow what they can afford to repay
- **protection:** make the better and protect any financial surplus

And importantly:

- **advice:** insight from trustworthy entities on the best choices to make to achieve our goals

All of these services are really means through which to achieve much more personal goals – both short term (such as buying lunch) and long term (such as saving for retirement). For all of these, we rely on an ecosystem of entities of which banks and financial institutions are simply one component.

Above all, the most important players in this ecosystem, as illustrated in Figure 3.1, are:

- **governments**, which provide the rules of how financial services are delivered
- **providers**, in other words, the different actors that actually deliver the services
- **enablers** or those who provide the technology and the services needed make the ecosystem function
- **users**, who are those that are the end customers of the services

In the following sections we will discuss the role of each player in this ecosystem in more detail.

Governments

We are using the term 'government' very broadly to include actors such as the financial regulators setting the engagement rules; the monetary authorities defining the costs of the services – from the value of the currencies, interest rates and any other relevant fees; the legislators defining the laws used by the regulators and the monetary

FIGURE 3.1 Forces shaping financial inclusion

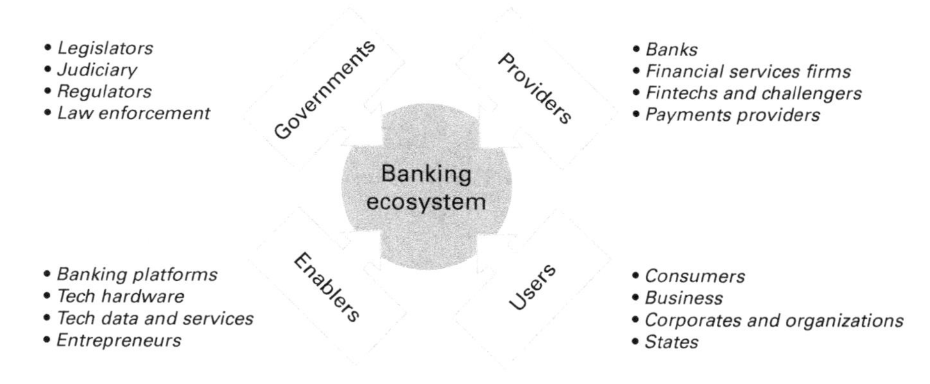

SOURCE The Pacemakers Ltd, 2024

authorities to deliver their services; and the executive and legal systems implementing and enforcing the rules set up by regulators and legislators.

A government has – first and foremost – the objective of protecting the welfare of the market they are responsible and accountable for. This means finding the right balance of laws, rules and requirements that are not too strict nor too lax; promoting reliable sustainable services while at the same time not preventing new products, services and providers from serving the market they are responsible for. The implementation of these requirements must be supported by a state that is fair and accountable.

Strict policies aimed at protecting end-users and the economy are certainly desirable. However, if these are so complex that they result in high costs, discourage innovation and, most importantly, discourage competition, they can be deeply counter-productive.

On the other hand, rules that are too relaxed can (and often do) lead to failure. We can all remember examples where a lack of adequate regulation led to failure and financial loss for the users they served. This in turn caused a real backlash for the economy of the market they operated in. As an example, take the Great Recession, as the financial crisis of 2008 is widely known, which was widely attributed to inadequate financial regulation.[1]

One other potential flaw of governmental regulation is that it is not immune from political intervention. In looking around the world, it is possible to think of markets that are innovative in some areas, but that are way behind in the development of their financial regulations because of the effectiveness of the incumbent players' lobbying activities. For example, many of us are surprised at the difference in the quality of retail financial services offered in the USA compared to Europe. Let's take a look at payments. In the EU the European Commission introduced the Single European Payments Area (SEPA) in 2008.[2] With its Instant Credit transfer scheme, banks in SEPA countries offer instant payments across member states. The only way to get an instant cross-state payment in the US is by bypassing the banks and using a peer-to-peer payment service like PayPal and Zelle. The long payment duration benefits the banks, not the end-user.

Or think about large markets where the success of specific financial institutions raises fears in the political leadership, leading to specific regulation aimed at slowing down fast-growing financial actors that the state sees as potential political challengers. For example, in Russia large tech companies like Yandex and VK Group, which have expanded into the fintech sector, face increased scrutiny and regulatory measures. The Russian government has introduced rules requiring significant financial operations to be under the purview of national security and economic sovereignty considerations, reflecting fears about the political and economic impact of these tech giants.

The regulatory situation in free market societies is far from perfect; they are not as inclusive, innovative or competitive as they could be. However, it is far better than what we have seen in controlled economies that believe that financial services should be a state-owned service. In countries with nationalized financial services, we often see a financial service offering that is not sophisticated enough to meet the country's needs.

One example was Soviet Russia. At that time, practically all banking was provided by the state bank of the USSR, known as Gosbank (Госбанк, Государственный банк). In an arrangement often referred to as a monobank, Gosbank combined the roles of a central bank and a commercial bank. It basically offered only domestic and international bank transfers, short-term working capital for enterprises and savings accounts for consumers.[3]

The range of products available to Soviet customers and enterprises was extremely limited and scrutinized by the state.[4] Even though Gosbank arguably had the intent of serving all its customers, in reality it operated as an arm of the state, scrutinizing flows of cash and rewarding favoured individual firms on grounds that were not always based on merit. Gosbank prioritized serving sectors favoured by the state rather than those needed by the country – a large part of its funding went to heavy industry and military production rather than to sectors such as consumer goods or services sorely needed at the time. This also led to the creation of a parallel financial black market, referred to as the 'second economy', which provided fund transfers and credit with little or no regulation.[5]

Even though centralized systems aim to be inclusive by design they do not seem to be able (or inclined) to deliver real inclusion in practice. But politicized banking is not just a phenomenon in tightly controlled economies, as we see many other countries interfering in their citizens' lives through financial regulation. The list here is long and diverse.

Another worrying aspect of strict financial regulation can be that it forces the providers to implement very strict rules when accepting and serving customers that end up excluding large numbers of people. On the far extreme, not supervising and enforcing rules can have similar damaging effects. A few of the risks that regulation brings to financial inclusion are:

- **Limiting the types of documentation acceptable for account opening:** Across the globe, regulators generally do not acknowledge that a sizable segment of the population does not have access to certain forms of identification, employment or addresses. The United Kingdom, unlike many other countries, does not offer a free government-issued ID. Instead, banks often ask for a passport (cost over £80) or a provisional drivers licence (£34). Many citizens cannot afford these. A cheaper alternative, the PASS Card issued by the UK Post Office, costs only £15 but most banks do not accept it. In the European Union, the EU launched a National Identity Card for all member states in 2021. The card will be available to every EU citizen and resident as a means of identification and will be accepted by all banks. Too-strict regulation has the potential to make identification a cause of financial exclusion.[6]
- **Demanding outdated modes of engagement when serving customers and onboarding the customer:** Many regulators across the globe still require the customer and the bank to meet in person. This is meant as a requirement to protect vulnerable customers. But as the cost of opening a branch is increasing everywhere, many individuals and businesses in rural areas or away from large centres are often excluded for access to finance. Regulations requiring face-to-face engagement between a bank and its customer are meant to protect the customer in reality, but they're leading to financial exclusion. In the US the

Patriot Act still requires banks to ask select individuals to present paper documents in branches to validate their identity.

- **Not implementing measures to protect from the misselling of financial products:** Banks and financial services firms are businesses with return targets. These often become sales targets that need to be met by employees. This has the potential to lead to misselling of financial products. This can have two effects on financial exclusion. Let's take an example like the misselling scandal associated with payment protection insurance (PPI) in the UK. The scandal involved UK banks misselling PPI alongside loans and credit cards. Often unnecessary or unsuitable, these policies were frequently sold without customers' knowledge or consent. By 2011, a flood of compensation claims led to banks setting aside over £50 billion, with Lloyds alone accounting for £20 billion of the compensation. A lack of adequate supervision often leads to scandals such the UK PPI example, leading to many consumers feeling that the banks are not trustworthy enough to bank with.[7] The 2021 Global Findex data from the World Bank showed that 21 per cent of adults without a formal account state lack of trust in banks as a reason for not having an account. Regulation that is unable to protect its customers leads to financial exclusion simply by making finance seem dangerous to the most vulnerable segments of society.[8]

It is clear that governments and all their manifestations play a significant role in determining the success of financial services and banking in the markets they are responsible for. All other actors in the financial ecosystem depend on the effective and fair implementation of 'the rules of the game'. Arguably the most important actor in driving financial inclusion are the governments and the rules they put in place to regulate the financial services industry.

Providers

The delivery of banking and financial services needs the help of specialists. In other words, providers such as banks, brokers, advisors, lenders, fintechs, insurers, loan sharks and the like play a key role.

Like any enterprise, these need to be profitable to survive. This means that they need to be able to earn more money from the delivery of the financial service than it takes them to supply it to their customers. These are (usually) regulated, monitored and supervised entities. Like any industry, they are subject to competition, innovation, fraud, incompetence and bad luck in operating.

From the first lenders in Mesopotamia 4,000 years ago, to the first real banks in Italy in the Middle Ages, to the first modern insurer in 17th-century Hamburg,[9] all these organizations sought to enable their customers to achieve their goals by providing a financial service that delivered a 'reasonable' profit. In order to do this, financial services providers had to be very careful with their choice of clients, catering to the more affluent segments of society. From the outset this created issues for the less affluent. Across history, they had limited choices in borrowing, saving, sending and receiving money.

This situation was stoically accepted by all until the cost of being financially underserved became increasingly large. Until the introduction of digital banking and fintech, being unbanked was a bearable situation. This shift to digital meant that cash became less frequently used, making life for the unbanked harder as digital transformation of finance made it easier and cheaper for banks to serve an increasingly large number of customers using digital channels. This was good news for many, but not all. As financial services digitized, unbanked or underbanked individuals found it increasingly difficult and expensive to access the services they needed.

But this transformation was not painless. In becoming digital most banks and financial services providers thought that they could get away with simply digitizing the processes and ways of doing things that were conceived many years ago. This did not work for long.

At the start of the digital revolution in the late 1990s many industries were profoundly transformed. The way businesses in areas such as retail, media, travel and communications are operated today would be inconceivable a few decades ago. The same happened to banks – but after many other parts of the economy.

Banks initially were largely unaffected by the digital transformation wave. At least, that was until the first fintechs started challenging them. The fintech challengers initially aimed to do what banks do at a lower cost. The digital challengers targeted the banks' most profitable customers, the digitally savvy young mass affluent – serving them a little better than the incumbents but with much lower costs. Banks of course did use digital technologies but these were large and complex centralized mainframes that ran algorithms designed for processes that were defined in the 1980s and 1990s, written in coding languages such as Fortran and Cobol.

These digital platforms were designed to operate in a legal, legislative and operational environment that often was no longer completely aligned to new market requirements. When the banks attempted to modernize their operations, they thought that they could just recode the old algorithms and processes using new code on new hardware. So old processes were transferred into new platforms, but they weren't actually re-engineered to optimize for new technology, customer needs and even regulation. This resulted in poor practices and procedures that were migrated from the past to the present – not fully benefiting from the digital revolution.

The resulting unnecessary complexity and obsolescence of these new banking platforms did not create the advantage over the digital native disruptors the incumbents were hoping for. A good example of the limits of this halfway digital transformation of incumbent banks can be seen in the fact that until recently many required the presentation and acceptance of a physical ID to a bank employee even if a customer was opening a bank account online. I had personal experience of this – when opening a bank account at an incumbent bank for a new business, I was asked to submit paper documents in the branch to complete the authentication. At the same time, I opened an account with a challenger bank who simply downloaded the documents required from the relevant entities online. The first account took a week to open, the second under 15 minutes. Paper-based authentication was obviously not a legal requirement for the incumbent bank, but an interpretation of the regulation by the bank itself. Operational legacy became a real challenge for certain segments to gain access to banking.

Along with operational complexity, another issue that incumbent banks risk transferring from their legacy platforms to new ones is bias. As banking and finance become digitized, the impact of the occasional racist or sexist bank clerk became much less of a factor for an individual being offered or denied financial products. But a direct transfer of legacy processes and policies could result in bias migrating to the new digital platforms. A direct migration of process could result in biased decision-making being transferred to the new platforms.

One blatant example is a practice common across the world known as 'redlining' in the US. This is where risk models of the banks define residents of certain areas, often with lower incomes or with high minority populations, as higher risk, therefore offering them poorer pricing, condition and selection of banking products. A well-known example of this was the settlement announced by the US Justice Department with Hudson City Savings Bank in the state of New Jersey for close to $33 million after the Justice Department found that it was avoiding doing mortgage business with African Americans and Latinos between 2009 and 2013.[10]

Another area of bias is gender discrimination. This is illegal in most countries, but it is alive and kicking in many markets. In 2022 the Inter-American Development Bank (IDB) developed an online tool to measure the impact of gender biases in credit offers. It was tested on bank personnel of both sexes to see the likelihood that these biases would affect their behaviour. It presented participants with hypothetical loan applicant cases based on real cases that bank personnel would see daily.

The IDB found that 98 per cent of participants exhibit some level of gender bias, 88 per cent of bank personnel gave worse offers to female clients (in terms of amount, interest rate or tenor). If the hypothetical cases were real, 56 per cent of the female applicants evaluated would have received an unfair offer compared to their male peers with worse credit profiles and less profitable, but otherwise similar, businesses. If biases played no role in credit decision-making, that percentage would have been zero.[11]

But this bias creeps easily into the fintech space. As has been mentioned, the Apple Card faced gender discrimination allegations in 2019 when men reportedly received higher credit limits than women with equal qualifications. Tech entrepreneur David

Heinemeier Hansson and Apple co-founder Steve Wozniak reported significant disparities. Goldman Sachs denied using gender in decisions. The incident sparked an investigation and debates about AI bias in financial services.

One additional worrying factor is the fact that many providers believe that serving underserved segments is expensive and unprofitable. This perception does not take into consideration several factors. Firstly, offering a bank product to an underserved individual will often create a long-term customer, especially if access to this product enables them to improve their financial situation and become a devoted customer. Recently the Office for National Statistics (ONS) reported that the average duration of marriage in the UK was 12 years.[12] While average customer durations can fluctuate across financial products, a study in the banking sector by the UK a few years back found that nearly 40 per cent of those surveyed had been with their banks for over 20 years, while another 20 per cent had been with their provider for over 10 years. Put simply, a loyal customer is well-worth the investment.[13]

There is also the reality that a more intelligent use of technology can make serving underbanked customers, who often belong to discriminated-against or less-affluent segments, simpler and more cost effective than with traditional branch-based onboarding and product sales practices.

Diversity and inclusion are becoming key expectations of banks by their customers, investors, employees and regulators. As employees, customers, investors and regulators demand more diversity and inclusion from banks, the banks' efforts in being more open to all segments of society will only increase in time.

Enablers

The providers of the infrastructure through which financial services are delivered today also play an important role in making sure that these services are delivered efficiently and fairly. The digital transformation of banking has had two opposite effects on financial services.

Let us look at how technology is possibly increasing financial exclusion. Arguably the digitalization of our lives has contributed to marginalizing certain segments of our societies. Before the digital revolution almost every commercial transaction could be completed in the physical world. We could all pay for the goods and services we received in cash. This had all the challenges of a physical cash economy – the complexity of dealing with a currency that occupies space, has volume and weight. Physical cash could be stolen or destroyed without leaving a trace, but it was egalitarian in the sense that to receive or make payments all you had to do was to meet your counterpart directly and exchange cash – the fact that you were banked or unbanked made little difference. As our economy digitized, the ability to buy goods and services with physical cash was severely impacted. Retailers and service providers were able to dramatically reduce their logistical costs through e-commerce and were able to pass these savings onto their digital customers. This led to two issues. Firstly, the delivery of goods and services in the physical world became increasingly uneconomical. This resulted in the closure of stores and branches and the transfer of transactions online. Secondly, people who relied on cash to transact found themselves at a disadvantage because they could not use cash online. Therefore, the digital revolution initially caused an increase in financial exclusion.

At first, digitalization was not seen as an issue for banking, as in the first decade of the digital revolution financial services were largely untouched. Banks saw digitalization simply as the transfer of services offered in branches to a desktop. This initially was seen as a new channel to be operating in parallel to the branch and telephony channels – not replacing them. Consumers that adopted these online services were almost always more technologically savvy than the average bank customer and therefore they were rarely un- or under-banked.

Things became more complex when mobile phones became smart. Suddenly the branches were no longer a place you went to (physically or on your computer) – they were in your pocket all the time inside your smartphone. This led smart-tech-aware fintech entrepreneurs to start creating financial products that were serviced not only on a PC but also from a smartphone. The main technology manufacturers realized that enabling their devices to deliver financial services would make their technology stickier with the end-user. Manufacturers had the belief that the more complex things users could do on their phone the more reluctant they would be to switch brands. Suddenly the user experience for a bank customer on their phone became superior to when they engaged on their desktop or in a branch. This move from branch to smartphone left many individuals behind, increasing the gap between the financial services the digital-savvy could get compared to what their peers that had less access to technology could access. This also had an impact on the profitability of branches. As fewer people started visiting them, banks started to increasingly close branches, making it even harder for non-tech savvy customers to bank.

In the last few years, three innovation trends started narrowing this divide.

The first is affordability. According to market research firm Persistence Market Research, the size of the global refurbished and used mobile phone market was $50.5 billion in 2022, forecasted to triple in size by 2033.[14] This is creating a source of cheaper smartphones for segments of the population that were previously not able to afford these phones.

The second trend is the ingenuity of users. M-Pesa is the most impressive example of how the ingenuity of users was able to cut through exclusion. In the early 2000s mobile phone customers working in the big cities in Kenya started transferring airtime to relatives in the hinterland. These were in turn able to sell these minutes for cash locally. This was de facto a digital money transfer using non-smart mobile phones. This approach was noticed by Safaricom, who in turn transformed it into one of the world's most successful mobile payments propositions.[15]

The third trend is entrepreneurship. The success of M-Pesa led to innovators working in or with tech firms to realize that phones – even the not-too-smart ones – could be a fantastic tool to fight digital exclusion. Across the globe, innovators started using technology to create financial products for underbanked mobile phone users. According to the World Bank, globally 1.4 billion adults were unbanked in 2021,[16] yet two-thirds of them owned a mobile phone that could help them access financial services. Services such as WeChatPay in China and PayTM in India have enabled millions of unbanked and underbanked individuals to benefit from simple financial services.

Users

The end of financial exclusion depends also on the behaviour of the end-user. We highlighted the barriers put in place by the main actors in the financial services, banking and payments ecosystems. But we also need to mention one last driver – demand.

The World Bank's research shows that the reasons why people did not open bank accounts include lack of money, financial services being too expensive, services located too far away, family members already having an account, a lack of documentation, a lack of trust and religious reasons.[17] The research points to many of the areas we discussed earlier regarding the action the different actors in banking, finance and payments could take to reduce financial exclusion. Embedded in the survey responses is a niggling concern: Are these unbanked individuals making these statements about why they are unbanked based on factual information? Let's look at each specific response:

- How much money do you really need to open a bank account or a payment account?
- Are all financial services too expensive? Aren't the alternatives used by the unbanked individual actually more expensive?
- Most of the unbanked have mobile phones – are they not able to use these to bank and not go to a branch?

- Are the users aware that different financial institutions interpret the laws setting out identification rules differently, and therefore there could be a provider that can offer them a bank account or e-wallet?
- What information is the lack of trust in banking based on?
- The religious reasons quoted are often assumed – for example, certain interpretations of Islamic law forbid traditional lending and borrowing, but payments are allowed, as are select compliant borrowing mechanisms.

From these reasons, it is clear that a lack of financial education is an important contributor to financial exclusion. Education should include the understanding of the benefits that financial services can bring about. Benefits such as cheaper payments, safekeeping of any excess liquidity and the ability to borrow are just a few of the services that are of benefit to everyone. Furthermore, the skill to be able to see the cost of being unbanked versus having a bank account can create a substantial incentive. It's cheaper to send money through a digital wallet than through an intermediary.

In parallel to the benefits of banking, the risks of banking should also be well understood. Understanding these can help users in two ways. Firstly, making users aware of the risks of a banking product – especially when matched to an understanding of benefits – can make the identification of the product that best meets their needs more straightforward.

About 30 per cent of respondents in the World Bank research mentioned previously state distance from the bank as an issue. Anecdotally, unbanked and underbanked individuals that see the lack of branches as an issue in getting a banking or payment account are often those that would benefit from education on the benefits of digital and mobile banking – as we said the majority of the unbanked have access to mobile phones.

Identification and authentication is and can be a real issue when applying for a bank product. New residents and existing residents sometimes do not have access to the right type of identification or they cannot meet some of the authentication requirements for a bank account, such as regular income or a fixed address. The rules for these requirements are changing across the globe and across different products – for example, a digital wallet can deliver most of the services of a bank account with often less complex ID and authentication requirements. Being aware of these options is an important factor for any unbanked individual.

Lastly, there is a lack of understanding among some end-users of the actual cultural and religious barriers to taking on certain types of financial products, the providers and their communities within which they operate. Religious financial education should be a key component of any financial services education programme.

All the players in the banking ecosystems should realize that the lack of financial literacy is a major barrier to ending financial exclusion. This should become a key focus of all initiatives aimed at tackling this fundamental social, economic and financial issue impacting economies across the globe.[18]

Conclusion

Access to banking service in today's society is becoming increasingly central to the wellbeing of most people. Banking in itself is not the goal – the real goal is what it enables us to achieve. Every human should have the right to earn a living, ask for a loan and protect their financial surplus. Digital banking initially exacerbated the difference in access offered to some versus what others could get. As the presence of digital devices became prevalent, providers started seeing the benefits of providing digital financial services. Regulators started warming up to fintech innovations and providers started to increasingly offer efficient and effective products. Users are starting to see that the 'bank in your pocket' may be the answer to making financial exclusion nothing more than a bad memory for all of us.

Notes

1 J Weinberg (2010) The great recession and its aftermath, Federal Reserve History. www.federalreservehistory.org/essays/great-recession-and-its-aftermath (archived at https://perma.cc/K9F9-HAH5)
2 European Central Bank (2021) SEPA, European Central Bank. www.ecb.europa.eu/paym/integration/retail/sepa/html/index.en.html (archived at https://perma.cc/3HNN-Q8FV)
3 G Garvy (1972) Banking under the tsars and the Soviets, *The Journal of Economic History*, 32 (4), 869–93. doi.org/10.1017/s0022050700071187 (archived at https://perma.cc/6DN2-UKG4)
4 J Nellis (1991) Improving the performance of Soviet enterprises, World Bank Discussion Papers
5 G Grossman, V G Treml and N Malyshev (1985) The second economy in the USSR and eastern Europe: A bibliography, Defense Technical Information Center. https://apps.dtic.mil/sti/tr/pdf/ADA269615.pdf (archived at https://perma.cc/MTU9-RSG6)
6 European Commission (2021) European digital identity, European Commission. commission.europa.eu/strategy-and-policy/priorities-2019-2024/europe-fit-digital-age/european-digital-identity_en (archived at https://perma.cc/5U5P-KPFV)
7 S Roy (2022) Preventing mis-selling and protecting customers in financial institutions, Central Bank of Bahrain. www.researchgate.net/publication/361438735_Preventing_Mis-Selling_and_Protecting_Customers_in_Financial_Institutions (archived at https://perma.cc/8K8G-84VY)
8 A Demirgüç-Kunt, L Klapper, D Singer and S Ansar (2022) *The Global Findex Database 2021*, The World Bank
9 V Eaton (2022) 8 oldest insurance companies in the world, Oldest.Org. www.oldest.org/structures/oldest-insurance-companies-in-the-world (archived at https://perma.cc/S624-APYH)
10 B Mock (2015) Redlining is alive and well – and evolving, Bloomberg. www.bloomberg.com/news/articles/2015-09-28/eight-recent-cases-that-show-redlining-is-still-alive-and-evolving (archived at https://perma.cc/RDW3-NDXV)
11 IDB Invest (nd) Uncovering the hidden cost of gender biases in lending to women, IDB Invest. idbinvest.org/en/blog/gender/uncovering-hidden-cost-gender-biases-lending-women (archived at https://perma.cc/9G9K-66A5)
12 GOV.UK (2022) Divorces in England and Wales, 2022, ONS. www.ons.gov.uk/peoplepopulationandcommunity/birthsdeathsandmarriages/divorce/bulletins/divorcesinenglandandwales/2022 (archived at https://perma.cc/ZE2Y-YU6F)
13 C Price (2021) Banking on loyalty: Are we more loyal to our banks than our spouses? The Drum. www.thedrum.com/opinion/2021/10/20/banking-loyalty-are-we-more-loyal-our-banks-our-spouses (archived at https://perma.cc/CB4W-V8N3)

14 Persistence Market Research (2024) Refurbished and used mobile phones market size, share and growth forecast for 2025–2032, Persistence Market Research. www.persistencemarketresearch.com/market-research/refurbished-and-used-mobile-phones-market.asp (archived at https://perma.cc/E2JB-CR29)

15 W Jack and T Suri (2011) Mobile money: The economics of M-Pesa, National Bureau of Economic Research. dx.doi.org/10.3386/w16721 (archived at https://perma.cc/J5FE-E3DC)

16 World Bank (2022) Financial inclusion, World Bank. www.worldbank.org/en/topic/financialinclusion/overview (archived at https://perma.cc/HK8U-RL69)

17 World Bank (2021) The Global Findex Database 2021, World Bank. www.worldbank.org/en/publication/globalfindex (archived at https://perma.cc/3P47-F65L)

18 United Nations Economic and Social Commission for Asia and the Pacific (2017) Financial regulatory issues for financial inclusion, United Nations

4

The importance of payments and the birth of the current account

The role of payments

Even before the beginning of recorded history, the most basic form of payment was barter. A person could pay for a cow by giving four sheep to the owner of the cow. This was a transparent but complicated transaction. The person needing a cow had to find someone that needed four sheep. They would have had to manage the logistics of the barter transaction, from the physical transport of the sheep to the assessment that the four sheep were of good enough quality to be of equal value to a cow.

In time, this type of transaction was replaced by money. One party would offer an agreed number of shells, a large stone 'donut' (also known as rai in Micronesia) or a number of metal coins and the other party would happily surrender the cow for the value of the currency they were receiving. The acceptance of this currency was due to the fact that both parties agreed that the currency changing hands was worth a cow. The seller was happy to exchange their asset for three coins – because they knew that they could exchange these for the four sheep they actually needed.

The creation of currency slowly led to the creation of all the financial products we are familiar with today. The concept that an intermediate item could be a store of value and that this value could be exchanged for a valued good or service was a fundamental change for society, dramatically reducing the complexity of trade.

To oversimplify a very complex journey, the creation of currency led to a variety of innovations on the sheep-for-cow model. It led to cheques, bank transfers, card payments, mobile payment and eventually cryptocurrencies – all aimed at offering easier, efficient and more useful ways for value to change hands, as shown in Figure 4.1.

Beyond cash

In the past, wealthy individuals gave banks their excess cash for safekeeping. In return, they were issued certificates of deposit. This was a primitive form of the modern-day current account. Where allowed by the local laws and customers, these individuals were not only promised the security of their deposits, they were often also given interest for their deposits. Sometimes when they were short of liquid cash these customers would need to withdraw some cash.

FIGURE 4.1 Means of payment: Their evolution and enablers

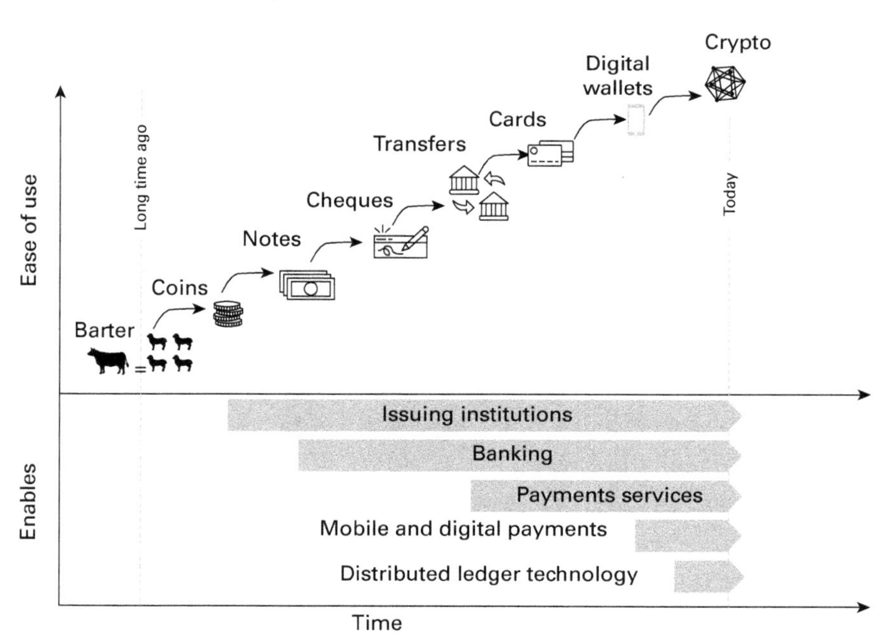

SOURCE The Pacemakers Ltd, 2024

These certificates allowed them to do so – all they had to do was go to the bank, show their deposit certificate, identify themselves and withdraw the funds they needed. This ongoing need to go to the bank became tedious, leading to the creation of what was called a bill of exchange in Europe, or Suk (better known today as Sukkuk in its plural form in Shariah finance) in the East. The first recorded version of Suk (or صك) was in the 8th century in the Abbasid Empire. The word derives from the Persian language and eventually evolved to become the world cheque or check. This was a piece of paper, with data that allowed the bearer to receive payment from the bank without the account holder present.

The cost of issuing and processing the cheque was sometimes free but often earned a processing fee for the bank. One of the most important components of the current account, the ability to move money in and out of it without the need to physically go to the bank, transformed the global financial system.

With the advent of communication technology, a new version of remote payments emerged when banks started allowing their customers to replace sending physical cheques with the ability to 'wire' funds. The term wire of course refers to the fact that these transactions were cleared when an authorization was sent through wired communication devices – the telegram, the telex and eventually the fax machine, all of which use wired communication networks. These transactions were again simply the transfer of money from one financial institution to another based on mutually agreed principles.

As payments and technology evolved, we saw the emergence of charge and credit cards. These were initially designed as a product for the affluent (paying for expensive restaurants was the first use case). The first modern payment card was the Diners Card launched in the USA in 1950. This was followed by American Express in 1958. The first card schemes, a technical and commercial arrangement that provides the legal, organizational and operational framework for customers holding a card to initiate payments, was initiated in the US when several regional banks came together to create the Interbank Card Association, launching what eventually became Mastercard. The convenience of using a payment card slowly replaced the use of cheques for everyday transactions – even though cheques remain popular today in countries like France and the USA.

With the advent of the internet and ecommerce, cards were the prevalent means for sending payments in exchange for goods and services. But slowly a new type of payment has emerged – the digital wallet. The first digital wallet was issued by the Coca Cola Corporation in 1997 in Helsinki, Finland where the company installed two vending machines that allowed users to pay for drinks through a text message. A year later PayPal launched in San Jose, California. Users could load their PayPal wallet and send money from it to another wallet across the globe. In turn, the recipient could withdraw the payment as cash using their bank. The service used the card schemes to create a much more efficient way to process payments than cheques, bank transfers or cards allowed. The digital wallet user experience became the prototype for the digital bank account launched by both incumbent banks, challenger banks and fintechs.

The latest innovation in payments is cryptocurrencies. These take many forms, and we will discuss their intricacies in more detail in Chapter 15. There are many versions of what we would term cryptocurrencies, but the three principal ones are:

1. **Payments cryptocurrencies:** These operate as a means of transfer of value and their value is defined entirely by the market. Examples: Bitcoin, XRP.
2. **Stablecoins:** The value of Stablecoins is guaranteed by the issuer, usually by using another asset (hard currency, a commodity, etc) as validation of the currency's worth. Examples: Tether, Binance USD.
3. **Central bank digital currencies (CBDC):** The digital version of a country's national currency. They are issued by central banks, mostly still in the experimental phase and a lot of controversy surrounds them, especially from the privacy perspective. Examples: eYuan, eNaira.

CBDCs are being considered by almost all major economies worldwide. What is distinctive about all CBDCs is that their value will be set and guaranteed by a state central bank – the Federal Reserve, the Bank of England and the European Central Bank are all considering their version of CBDC. This would make them as close as possible to an electronic version of fiat currency. They will by and large operate like the US dollar, the British pound or the euro. That said, their introduction is not free from opposition from financial institutions happy with the status quo, and with experts concerned about the potential risks that a badly designed CBDC could introduce to individuals' rights to privacy and data protection.

Payments exclusion

Today there are millions of unbanked and underbanked people who do not have access to most of these payment options and therefore they cannot benefit from the capabilities each offers.

If a person only means to send and receive payments is cash they are impacted in several ways.

ACCESS

We all know that across the globe, from the more developed economies to the developing ones, cash is slowly being withdrawn from use.

On the spend side, buying large-value items with cash has always been difficult. Attempting to buy a car or real estate in cash is highly unusual and would *ad minimum* attract scrutiny as a possible attempt at money laundering. Paying for smaller items – groceries, local transport, etc – should be easy with cash. But the introduction of innovative means of payment that are as simple as cash for smaller items has been changing this landscape. When paying with a phone tap became as easy as paying with bills and coins, without many of the risks associated with keeping cash – from storage to security – businesses selling small ticket items also started to move away from cash. This was of course accelerated with the increase in digital payments due to the Covid pandemic in 2020–21.

Beyond physical stores, dependence on cash excludes access to online transactions. This results in being excluded from a wide range of choice and often it means being unable to benefit from better-priced goods and services available on the web. But the issues associated with smaller purchases are practically insignificant when compared with larger ones. The ability of an individual that only has access to cash to make larger purchases (an automobile, housing, etc) is impacted by the logistics and risks associated with moving large amounts of cash.

Receiving money (when being paid a salary, for example) is also extremely difficult for cash-only individuals. Most employers, especially larger ones, are uncomfortable paying their employees' salaries in cash as the administrative costs and risk of not being compliant are high. Unbanked employees paid with cheques are obliged to use various cheque cashing services that can charge high fees to process these payments.

Only being able to pay in cash, and not using cheques, transfers, cards, mobile payments and the like, excludes an individual from a large number of optimal situations. Online payments become largely impossible. Large payments are difficult to make, and they expose the payer to transactional risks running from theft to fraud.

Lastly, cross-border payments become expensive, lengthy and uncertain. Sending money abroad affordably is a real issue for many of the underbanked. Many belong to what is called the 'new to market' demographic. They often need to send money abroad, and by being unbanked they are obliged to use more expensive cross-border payment providers or sometimes informal payment options that are often not only more expensive than bank transfers but also less secure.

SECURITY

Using cash for payments can also be dangerous. Using cash as a means of payments – as recipient or sender – results in an individual being in possession of sums of money for a certain amount of time. They could become crime targets in that period. Fraud or crime based on cash changing hands is much harder to stop or reverse than one involving a payment-processing organization. Receiving a salary directly in a current account is less of a security risk than receiving an envelope with the same amount but in the physical, tangible and untraceable form of banknotes and coins. Once the payee receives a cash payment, what are their options in protecting their funds from theft before they spend them?

Reliance on cash on payments requires the customer to store cash physically. According to the Institute for the Study of Labour (IZA) in Germany, the introduction of cashless benefit payments in the US state of Missouri in the 1990s resulted in a 9.8 per cent reduction in crimes such as burglary and assault.[1]

COST

This is not only the cost of transacting, but also the cost of goods that can be purchased by individuals that only have access to cash. Being obliged to rely only on cash has a premium that increases every year. In a world where the internet is allowing all of us to source better-priced goods using the internet, being solely reliant on cash makes it very hard to benefit from the advantages of ecommerce.

Cash usage effectively imposes an indirect tax that disproportionately affects the unbanked, creating a significant financial burden. According to the FDIC, 4.2 per cent of households (approximately 5.6 million) in the US do not use banking services, while an additional 14.2 per cent (approximately 19.0 million) are underbanked.[2] Common fees include those for services like cheque cashing, payday lending and buy-here-pay-here auto loans. Additionally, unbanked individuals in the US are five times more likely to incur fees when accessing cash through payroll and electronic benefit transfer cards.

In a recent study, Pockit, a digital current account provider serving nearly half a million customers in the UK, focused on quantifying the additional financial burden faced by unbanked individuals.[3] Pockit analysed official data and pricing details to determine what they call the ‘banking poverty premium’. In their analysis, Pockit examined costs associated with electricity, gas, mobile data, broadband and the interest on a 52-week loan of £300. They found that the average annual cost for these services for individuals with a bank account amounted to £1,118. In contrast, for those without a bank account, the total annual cost was significantly higher at £1,603.

This difference of £485 can be attributed to several factors. For instance, providers of services like energy, broadband and mobile phones typically offer discounts and more favourable terms to customers who pay via direct debit. Such savings are not accessible to individuals only using cash.

How to make digital payments more inclusive

Payments are the underlying component of all financial products. Arguably, banks were created as a means of dealing with payments more efficiently. Access to payments is the first and most important step to make financial products and banking available to everyone. Until the introduction of digital payments, access to cash was sufficient to allow everyone to be able to pay and to be paid. This allowed anyone with access to cash – including anyone that did not have access to financial services – not to be financially harmed if they were unbanked. They would not have access to all the range of financial products and services that banks could provide, but they were not excluded from the financial world altogether.

Modern digital banking was the direct result of digitally transferable money. Digital payments provide a more efficient and less expensive means for almost everyone to gain access to a better and wider range of financial and non-financial services. But they also create a very big access problem for certain segments of society. To use physical cash, no special effort was necessary – to access digital money several factors need to align. First, the end-user needs to understand how digital money works and how they can use it. Secondly, the user needs access to a service where they can receive, store and send the digital cash. This does not always mean owning a digital device (see the homeless in China receiving donations from the public using a QR code printed on a paper card), but it can certainly help.

Let us examine some of the most successful challenges to the incumbent banks' inability to enable the billions of unbanked and underbanked individuals gain access to payments in the digital age (or their lack of interest in doing so).

QR CODE MOBILE PAYMENT

The adoption of digital payments is almost universal in China. According to the World Bank's Global Findex Database, 82 per cent of Chinese adults made a digital merchant payment in 2021.[4] That figure is more than double the global average. Many millions of digital payments in China are processed using Quick Response (QR) code payments. QR codes became popular in China because they enabled merchants to accept digital payments through their customers' mobile phones without having to have an expensive point of sale (POS) device. QR code payments, now broadly available across the country, were initially introduced by Alipay in 2011. As China is fast becoming a cashless economy, it is becoming very difficult for unbanked individuals to get paid.

To tackle issues of financial exclusion among homeless communities in large urban areas in an environment dominated by digital payments, WeChat and Alipay sponsored an initiative that allowed the unbanked to receive digital payments through QR code payments. It worked by giving them a QR code often in the form of a plasticized card. This QR code could be used by anyone with an Alipay or WeChatPay app on their phone to transfer money to the QR holder's digital account. The user could then go to any retailer accepting QR codes to pay for goods or even to simply withdraw the cash.

In its simplest form, this solution does not even require the receiver to even have a smartphone. The user can get a QR code at a local authorized reseller simply by identifying themselves. This system is not problem-free, but it has resolved part of the financial exclusion of the less affluent members of Chinese society. The use of QR codes in payments is also very prominent in countries like India, Indonesia and the Philippines, as it enables smaller and less sophisticated merchants to accept payments.

MOBILE WALLETS

Mobile wallets are powerful tools in enabling the unbanked to access modern payments networks. Most of these wallets initially catered to the more affluent parts of the economy and mobile phones were not necessarily widespread worldwide. As mobile adoption became less exclusive across the globe, the phone became a channel for financial services, especially for the more excluded sectors of society. As of 2021, close to 6.1 billion people had a bank or mobile money account and at the same time 6.94 billion had access to a smart or mobile phone.[5]

The following examples discuss some of the more successful mobile money solutions worldwide. Most were not designed to address financial exclusion; they were created to address opportunities created by the fact that local banks were not able to use technology to address their clients' evolving needs, desires and expectations.

M-Pesa The integration of technology in the banking sector has been exemplified remarkably in Kenya and Tanzania, primarily driven not by a start-up but by a telecommunications company. In 2007 Safaricom, the Kenyan subsidiary of global telecom giant Vodafone, launched M-Pesa, a money transfer that uses simple mobile technology to transfer money from one mobile account to another. M-Pesa originated to serve unbanked customers who lacked conventional financial services. The concept of M-Pesa was born when Safaricom realized that many of their urban customers were transferring mobile phone airtime minutes to their rural family members. These would then exchange these minutes for cash – resulting in the equivalent of an instant and free money transfer from the city to the village. Safaricom simply formalized this process by creating a mobile wallet.

M-Pesa allowed the transfer of funds to remote areas without significant costs, barring minimal airtime purchase fees. The success of this model is evident in M-Pesa's contribution to the Kenyan financial market, accounting for approximately 10 per cent of total commercial bank revenues in 2015–16 and generating over 10 times growth in revenues for Safaricom between 2011 and 2023.

Research by Tavneet Suri and William Jack at MIT indicates that from 2008 to 2016 M-Pesa played a substantial role in enhancing per capita consumption levels and elevating approximately 194,000 Kenyan households, equating to 2 per cent of the population, out of poverty.[6] M-Pesa has a customer base of close to 60 million people across Africa.

M-PAiSA A few years later, a parallel development occurred in Afghanistan with Roshan, a local telecommunications operator (also affiliated to Vodafone), which implemented M-PAiSA, a variant of M-Pesa. M-PAiSA was used to streamline police salary payments. Prior to this, salaries were distributed in cash by police commanders to their officers, which often resulted in incomplete payments.

The direct disbursement of salaries via M-PAiSA led many officers to mistakenly believe they had received a raise, when in fact they were receiving their full salary for the first time, as the process had eliminated the physical intermediaries that each charged a fee when conveying the cash salaries to the officers. In an interview, Karim Khoja, CEO of Roshan, recounted an instance where 250 policemen expressed their gratitude for what they perceived as a pay increase, highlighting the profound impact of this financial technology on reducing corruption and ensuring fair compensation. At its peak in 2021, there were 1.7 million people using M-PAiSA in Afghanistan. More recent data suggest that, due to local political unrest, this number has since fallen.

bKash bKash was launched in 2010 by BRAC Bank in Bangladesh. In its first incarnation, it was accessed by unbanked individuals through mobile (not smart) phones. The user would visit a bKash agent with a form of ID. The agent would verify the account and register the user's mobile number. Thereafter the user was able to receive payments from other account holders or load their own account with cash at a bKash agent.

In 2018 this system was complemented by an app for smartphone users and enabled users to be offered several banking products – even a formal bank account. Over the years, bKash has built a network of nearly 330,000 agents and 550,000 merchants across the country. bKash also integrated with banks, financial institutions and service providers to strengthen the cashless digital financial ecosystem of the country. As a result, bKash is now a trusted platform with a customer base of more than 70 million previously unbanked Bangladeshis.

PayTM PayTM stands for 'pay through mobile'. It was created by visionary entrepreneur Vijay Shekar Sharma in 2010 in India as the means for owners of prepaid mobile phones to load their mobile wallets without having to go to a store. PayTM allows the end-user to open an account on their phone then go to affiliated banks or to a PayTM member retailer to deposit cash. To meet AML (anti-money laundering) regulation, without ID the PayTM wallet is operational but only up to ₹10,000 (Indian rupee) (approximately $120). Once the customer has been authenticated, they can have access to higher limits, a wide range of financial services and more.

PayTM became a preferred channel for some of the Indian government's push to modernize the country's payment systems. These efforts led to the memorable 'demonetization' day on 8 November 2016. On this day the Indian government declared that the ₹1,000 and ₹5,000 notes would no longer be legal tender, making 86 per cent of the country's cash unusable. This was meant to push all transactions online, to drive better compliance with the national tax requirements. The event created great difficulty in an economy that was predominately cash-based, even for larger transactions. But it did largely achieve its desired effect. According to the Reserve Bank of India (RBI), the number of digital transactions in India grew from 2.8 million in November 2016 to 40.1 million in November 2020, an increase of over 1,400 per cent. A big beneficiary of this initiative was (and is) PayTM. Today they have over 330 million users, almost double the number they had in 2016.

FINTECHS AND BANK CHALLENGERS

An interesting alternative to the traditional bank accounts is the bank accounts provided by the fintechs, or the more aptly named bank challengers. These can be offered by new banks (confusingly called challenger banks), or by tech platforms working with incumbent banks and e-money wallets (also known as prepaid cards). What unifies these groups is that they believe that they can do banking better than the incumbent banks, lowering the barriers to entry for the unbanked and underbanked while remaining compliant to regulation and (often) profitable.

Most countries have several bank challengers. The list is long, and the names are known to all: Revolut in the UK, Nickel in France, Postepay in Italy or Chime in the US. These players enable previously excluded customers to gain access to their country's payments networks by not only receiving and sending funds, but also safely storing them. Once these deposits are in place, if they are a bank, they can offer savings accounts earning the customers a return and they can also offer their new customers credit. When these bank challengers are not banks, such as tech companies, they provide these services and more by partnering with local banks that hold regulated licences.

Across the globe, the majority of these bank challenger account providers created their offering to initially serve the digitally savvy customers that were banked but were looking for a better way of paying and being paid. These innovative providers were able to differentiate themselves from the incumbent banks by creating and consistently delivering payment processes that offered better and cheaper outcomes than the incumbents could deliver. This was achieved largely by new technology, better internal processes and better user experience. The ability not to be constrained by the legacy issues (technology, process, culture and offering) of the incumbent banks was at the core of this success.

TABLE 4.1 Comparing a bank account and an e-money (pre-paid) account

	Incumbent bank account	Bank challenger account
Account opening	Usually heavier ID requirements Often requires branch engagement	Lighter ID and usually remote or through intermediaries (post office, retailers, etc)
Fees	Free to open – product fees are often higher	Often account opening fee but lower costs for other products
Payments	Access to all payment networks – sometimes not accepting new payment channels (e.g. mobile payments)	Access to all payment networks and accepting most new alternative payments

(continued)

TABLE 4.1 (Continued)

	Incumbent bank account	Bank challenger account
Overdrafts	Yes, at a fee	No spending beyond the loaded amount for e-money accounts
Loading	In branch (cash or cheque), ATMs or by bank transfer	Multiple digital transfer choices and at different intermediaries such as local stores and post offices
Fraud protection	Yes, often as required by the regulators	Yes, often as required by the regulators
Interest	Sometimes interest rates are paid on deposits	No interest paid on deposits in e-money accounts
Credit	Negotiated credit is often offered	No credit offered in e-money accounts
User experience	Often driven by legacy – converting branch experience online	New user experience designed to benefit from new technology
Branches	Often need branch visits to operate	Almost always remotely managed

What also distinguished bank challengers is their ability to onboard potential new customers more efficiently than most incumbent banks, making them very well positioned to also serve the unbanked and underbanked. Overall:

- The fact that they were simpler to use made it easier for users who were less educated in the complexities of banking.
- The fact that they required simpler ID validation made it easier for many of the underbanked segments – especially the 'new to country' segments. These include expats, immigrants, students and more.
- The fact that they didn't not have to rely on a branch network had two benefits:
  - greater access, as banks often do not maintain branches in less affluent areas where the unbanked often reside;
  - less bias, as less-affluent customers are often parts of communities that can sometimes be discriminated against by branch staff.

> The e-money accounts became an ideal vehicle for the unbanked to obtain what was, from many functional and operational perspectives, a bank account.

Bank challengers and fintechs worldwide initially had a mixed relationship with regulators. The initial reaction of the regulators worldwide was that of hesitation. This attitude changed quickly after the 2008 financial crisis. Regulators started thinking that the financial services industry could benefit from more competition. So – especially in the EU, UK and China – attitudes changed, becoming more supportive of new financial services players by creating better dialogue between them and the banks. A good example of this change in attitude is the proliferation of 'innovation sandboxes' where fintechs and challengers are invited to get the regulators' opinions before launch. According to a Bank for International Settlements study, more than 50 countries have established financially focused sandboxes designed to enable companies to build and regulators to learn from new financial propositions with a strong focus on payments.[7]

The regulators also started several initiatives that forced the banks to be more collaborative with their new challengers. The most important legislation that affected this was the introduction of the EU's second Payments Services Directive (PSD2) and the UK's Open Banking Standards. Both regulations went live in January 2018, forcing hundreds of incumbent banks in Europe to allow third parties to access customers' account data safely and securely at their request, offering a big opportunity for fintech companies like bank challengers to plug into traditional banks and build new services for consumers.

This also coincided with a huge flow of investment into the fintech sector, with billions in hard currency being made available to entrepreneurs building these new banks. According to KPMG, from 2017 to 2023 close to $1.1 trillion has been invested in fintech in the form of venture capital, private equity or merger and acquisition (M&A) activity in the sector, as shown in Figure 4.2.[8] These monies were not intended to invest in inclusive finance. Rather, inclusion was a side

FIGURE 4.2 Total global investment activity in fintech (venture capital, private equity and M&A)

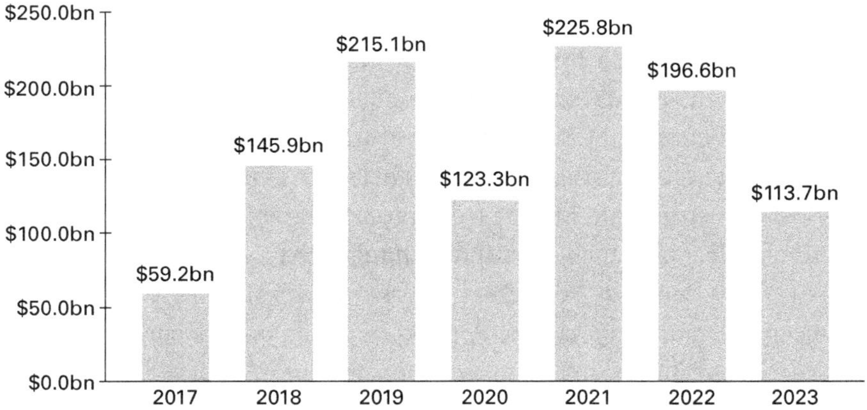

$250.0bn
$200.0bn
$150.0bn
$100.0bn
$50.0bn
$0.0bn

2017	2018	2019	2020	2021	2022	2023
$59.2bn	$145.9bn	$215.1bn	$123.3bn	$225.8bn	$196.6bn	$113.7bn

SOURCE KPMG, Pacemakers

effect of investing in the innovation of an industry that is so important to everyone's lives.

Access to a digital wallet or account was a necessary component in modernizing payments. As mentioned previously, one of the earliest bank challengers was PayPal. It was created to make it easier for its users to process payments online – not only for consumers, but also for businesses. The proposition eventually became the prototype of many digital wallets and current accounts.

PayPal's founders, Max Levchin, Peter Thiel and Luke Nosek, eventually joined by Elon Musk, were benefiting from a set of transformational changes coming together: technology, customer demand, regulatory support and access to capital. The creators of wallets such as PayPal had a vision that eventually not only transformed an industry, it also changed everyone's needs and expectations from their payments provider.

These new bank challengers built their offering to serve a tech-savvy, banked and often relatively affluent customer base in developed, but also in less developed, economies. This better way of paying opened doors for new customers that were not well served by the traditional ways of banking their providers were offering. Many of these new customers were unbanked and underbanked. A product made for the better-off became an entry point for the less affluent.

Outlook

Overall, digital payments are the single biggest tool in making banking inclusive. They are replacing what was considered the most egalitarian way to transfer value ever conceived – physical cash. Thinking back to the past, a rich person could transfer value to a pauper and vice versa using cash. At the same time, the rich person had access to a much wider set of payment options (cash, cheques, bank transfers, credit, etc) than the pauper had, and their money was safer because they did not have to store it physically. Their friendly banker was there to help them.

Historically, the less affluent segments have been excluded from financial services for several reasons – but the most important is commercial. Financial institutions thought (and many still do) that they could not serve them profitably. And, truth be said, before the introduction of digital wallets and digital banking, the reality is that many could not.

FIGURE 4.3 Digital payment transactions and unbanked individuals worldwide

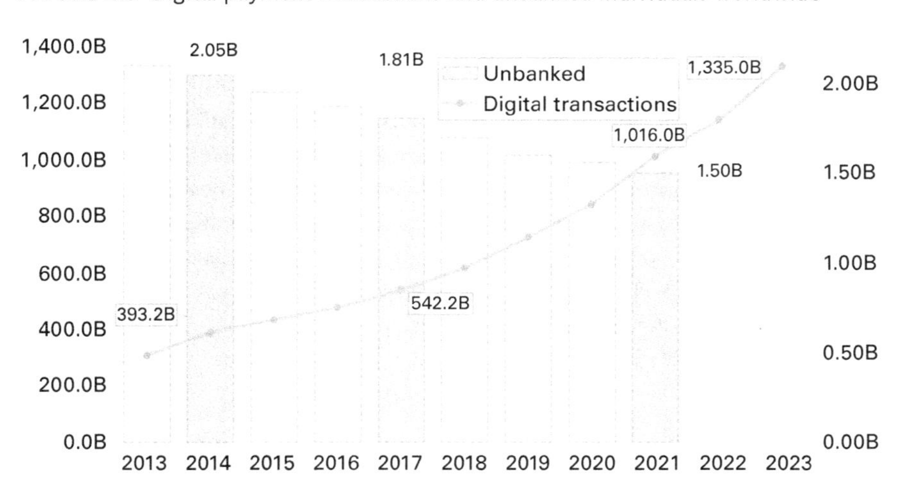

SOURCE Statista, World Bank and Pakemakers analysis

As finance (and the rest of society) digitized, innovative financial players dramatically reduced the cost of serving customers. This growth of digital banking slowly improved the ability of all people to seek and be provided with the financial products they need. The massive adoption of mobile phones and smartphones powered this revolution and as access to and understanding of how to access digital banking has grown, so has financial inclusion.

The growth of digital payments has been a fundamental factor in reducing financial exclusion. This and the resulting gradual displacement of cash as the primary means of exchanging value has driven many to seek access to digital wallets. The initial nuisance for many unbanked and underbanked individuals eventually led to a huge number seeking digital wallets and eventually gaining access to banking services. Growth in digital payments is closely correlated in the reduction in financial exclusion.

As with the creation of banking a few millennia ago, payments are at the core of financial services. And today the importance of e-money and digital payments is becoming increasingly evident as the foundation through which technology is democratizing finance.

Notes

1 R Wright et al (2014) Less cash, less crime: Evidence from the Electronic Benefit Transfer Program, SSRN Electronic Journal. papers.ssrn.com/sol3/papers.cfm?abstract_id=2492429 (archived at https://perma.cc/V2B8-JWVM)

2 FDIC (2023) 2023 national survey of unbanked and underbanked households. www.fdic.gov/household-survey (archived at https://perma.cc/6H5P-BZGM)

3 R Jones (2019) Britons without a bank account 'pay a £485 poverty premium', *The Guardian*. www.theguardian.com/money/2019/apr/22/britons-without-bank-account-pay-poverty-premium (archived at https://perma.cc/6BQ5-KHSL)

4 World Bank (2021) The Global Findex Database 2021. www.worldbank.org/en/publication/globalfindex (archived at https://perma.cc/8EN4-QZEB)

5 World Bank (2021) The Global Findex Database 2021. www.worldbank.org/en/publication/globalfindex (archived at https://perma.cc/N9LM-TE3J)

6 W Jack and T Suri (2011) Mobile money: The economics of M-Pesa, National Bureau of Economic Research. www.nber.org/papers/w16721 (archived at https://perma.cc/6F5X-HKR3)

7 G Cornelli and S Doerr (2020) Regulatory sandboxes and fintech funding: Evidence from the UK, BIS Working Papers No 901, Bank for International Settlements. www.bis.org/publ/work901.pdf (archived at https://perma.cc/BN4H-4HHD)

8 A Ruddenklau (2024) *Pulse of Fintech H2'23*, KPMG. assets.kpmg.com/content/dam/kpmg/xx/pdf/2024/02/pulse-of-fintech-h2-2023.pdf (archived at https://perma.cc/73KV-UYT2)

5

The role of credit

Affordable lending as a change agent

After payments, credit is the most important financial service. Ideally, it is the transfer of capital from an individual or entity to another with the agreement that the borrower will return it with some provision to compensate the lender for the effort and risk. Credit is important because it allows the borrower to benefit from their potential to succeed. When a person is able to secure a loan they are not only being recognized as a trustworthy individual by their creditors, they are also being offered the opportunity to build something with resources (capital) that they did not previously have access to. At the core of credit is hope for a better life, desire for greater welfare and the means to build a better future for the borrower and their extended ecosystem. Unbanked individuals are denied this dream.

Introduction

Let us take a quick look at the history of credit. The first instances of lending occurred even before the invention of money, when farmers lent other farmers seeds with the agreements that the borrowing farmer would return them to the lender with a little surplus after the next year's harvest. After this form of barter credit lending then grew across the globe, with all cultures recognizing its value and many religions frowning upon the concept of excessive interest or usury.

Most of the global economies are now comfortable with some sort of lending proposition. Even in countries that are governed according to Islamic law, which prohibits the charging of interest, communities are finding creative ways of compensating the lender for taking risks with the borrower.

Ideally the purpose of credit is to improve the borrower's circumstances, helping them to do something for which they do not have enough liquidity but which they could pay for if this cost is affordably spread through time. Implicit in the credit agreements are several factors:

- The borrower is able to return the borrowed amount in the future.
- The lender believes in the creditworthiness of the borrower and that the borrower is able to return the capital as promised.
- The regulatory, legislative and enforcement frameworks in place make sure all parties are protected and that the agreement shared between the two parties is safe, fair and reasonable.

A loan is an agreement between two parties. One has a financial need that can be addressed with access to liquidity. The other has the capital and is willing to take the risk of offering the liquidity needed in exchange for getting back a bit more than they lent. Described in this way it all seems very simple. But there are concerns to address to make this simple model work. Let's look at it from both parties' perspectives.

The borrower

For the borrower, the benefits of credit are substantial. Being able to get a short-term line of credit means that the borrower can weather a cash flow shortfall such as temporary unemployment or an unexpected expense due to some unforeseen event. A personal loan also means that a borrower who is also an entrepreneur can start a business. If successful, this venture could then attract a business loan to be able to grow and generate even more value to the borrower, the lender and society as a whole. And if the borrower needs to acquire an asset such as a piece of equipment, a car or real estate – like a family home or a farm – the borrower can share the ownership of the asset with the lender to mitigate the risks they would undertake. All in all, credit is about hope and aspiration. The unbanked and underbanked are being denied the ability to achieve these outcomes through means that are fair and sustainable.

By being excluded from the normally fairer credit options offered by regulated lenders, the unbanked are exposed to informal lenders ('loan sharks') that will impose pricing and conditions that are often unaffordable and detrimental to them. The unbanked in need of credit face two very negative scenarios. On one side, they are unable to resolve a compelling need by receiving an honestly priced loan from a trustworthy provider. On the other side, their only option left is to engage with informal lenders, often finding themselves in even more extreme financial situations. A perfect lose–lose situation.

The importance of financial education comes to the forefront at this stage. Overall, borrowers should have enough awareness about financial services to know what products and services could suit their needs, have an idea of what fair terms and conditions should be and, importantly, know that the provider that they are considering is trustworthy, reliable and supervised. The borrower should know enough about credit to be able to have a view on these core points:

- Who is the ideal lender for them?
- What credit product is best suited to their needs?
- How should they ask for the right credit?
- What are the terms and conditions that they could live with?

To answer these questions, the borrower needs to be able to do several things – they must have a vision of what they need and be able to illustrate it in such a way that a possible lender is able to see the purpose of the credit, and the borrower's ability to benefit from the liquidity to such an extent that they will be able to repay the loan. The lender needs to be able to validate their current situation and status (identification, credit history, guarantors, etc), their plans with the new liquidity and how they will be able to repay it.

Fundamentally, a potential borrower will also need to be able to know how *and* who to ask for the credit line. To be able to benefit from credit, the borrower needs to have access to information and know-how that is often not available to all borrowers – especially if unbanked and underbanked. The way to address lack of information requires effort from many parties involved: the lenders, the borrowers, media, governments and more. The topic of how financial education can play a fundamental role in financial inclusion is discussed in Chapter 17.

The lender

Very simply put, providing credit is about the opportunity to benefit from excess liquidity. Lenders are individuals and organizations that aim to generate a return from their monetary assets by providing a loan to borrowers. The core consideration of this activity is the likelihood of being repaid. This depends on the profile of the borrowers and the credibility of what they are going to do with the capital. Ultimately the lender is taking an intelligent bet.

To be able to justify this 'gamble', first and foremost the lender has to feel comfortable with and believe in the purpose of the loan. Data points such as identity and financial history are good ways for the lender to determine the likelihood and ability of the borrower to repay a loan – defining the riskiness of the borrower. The other component of a credit assessment is the purpose of the credit ask. If the borrower is asking for a personal loan, the only guarantee for the loan is the creditworthiness of the borrower. If the borrower is seeking financing for a business venture, the creditworthiness of the borrower is combined with the lender's assessment of the likelihood of success of the venture. Loans that are based on assets (car loans, mortgages or equipment financing) can give the lender some form of recourse by being able – in case of default – to liquidate the asset.

The unbanked customer often has a hard time delivering this information in a way the lender can use.

Another factor that defines the lender's attitude is competition. The lender of course usually wishes to maximize their returns, as most banks are for-profit organizations. The mitigation of these returns are determined by several forces. Seeing that the borrowers have little choice in finding lenders often leads lenders to offer more onerous conditions. Lack of choice is a real problem for the unbanked and underbanked, often pushing them to resort to informal lenders who tend to offer much more onerous conditions than the more established lenders.

The attitude of lenders towards the unbanked or underbanked is also defined by a number of additional factors. First and foremost in importance is regulation to which lenders are subject and by which the borrowers are affected. Regulation is the result of a number of pressures but ultimately they aim to create the best possible balance between the needs of the lenders, the borrowers and society. Regulation responds also to factors such as ensuring fairness.

This is even more important today, as social media has created a transparency in everyday life that makes it hard for unethical lenders to get away with poor (but not necessarily illegal) behaviour. The collapse of Wonga, the UK and Australian PayDay lender focused on the 'employed underbanked' market, was triggered by a close media scrutiny eventually revealing a number of shortfalls that led to the firm closing in 2018.[1] Also, the recent investigation by the UK Treasury Committee into the closure of 141,620 SME accounts in 2023 by the eight major banks including Barclays, HSBC, TSB, Lloyds, Santander, NatWest, Metro Bank and Handelsbanken was similarly triggered by social media requests.[2] It emerged that the banks were not breaking regulations or charging excessive fees – they simply felt that closing these accounts was easier than upping their technical and operational capabilities in serving them. This did not go down well with the banks' customers, investors and employees.

The credit decision

A credit decision is dependent on a number of data points. To understand how credit can become more inclusive, we need to look at these points. In order to extend a loan, a lender needs to validate the following factors for the borrower.

Identity

We have already discussed the relevance of identity in financial inclusion. What is embedded in the identity process is the ability of the lender to validate the data that they are being provided by the borrower.

A few other perspectives are embedded within the concept of identity. The lender must have recourse in case the borrower does not honour their part of the borrowing contract. In these cases, address, employment, birth details, full names and the like are data points that would potentially allow the lender to engage with the borrower more directly. The inability of some of the underbanked to provide broad identity information (employment, physical address, birth certificates) is a key factor in the provision of credit.

Also, identity is what allows the borrower to reach out to regulators and law enforcement if something goes wrong. It would be very difficult for a lender to seek recourse on a loan gone bad without a clear set of data on who the borrower is. Not being able to identify oneself is a key cause behind many individuals not only being unbanked but also being underbanked. Not being able to provide a clear and trusted ID makes it practically impossible for an individual to get credit.

Credit history

If lending is about the lender believing the narrative of the borrower, then being able to know how the borrower has been earning and spending their money in the past is a key source of information. Providing proof of past behaviour, especially if validated by a trusted third party, enables the lender to evaluate the risk of a loan more accurately. This is not simply a binary yes or no decision from the lender. The provision of financial information enables the lender to introduce pricing and conditions that best protect them from a possible default by the borrower.

Frequently, an unbanked or underbanked individual cannot provide this information. In the past, the borrower could sometimes refer to a guarantor. This person would provide their guarantee that the borrower would be able to repay the loan. This is still common practice in some countries, where first mortgages are often guaranteed by the parents of the borrower. In most cases the guarantor becomes liable for the loan's default. So, in fact the lender is lending to a borrower with better financial history and can expect to be paid by both the borrower and by the guarantor if things go wrong. This would allow the lender not only to agree to offer the loan but also to – ideally – propose better terms and conditions.

Solidarity banking, a modern version of this approach, has grown in popularity in developing economies. This is a loan that is provided to a group and not an individual. Under this system, would-be borrowers form groups (usually of between three and six), within which each member agrees to guarantee the loans of the others in the group. If any one individual member defaults on their loan, the other members of the group are required to cover the shortfall. Solidarity lending dramatically decreases the cost of access to credit, particularly where institutional infrastructure is weak and borrowers' projects are small.

In addition, microfinance, a form of solidarity banking, has revolutionized the way in which credit is provided to the rural poor.[3] Grameen Bank, founded by Nobel Prize winner Muhammad Yunus in Bangladesh in 1976, is a good example. They provide loans to groups of people. These are people living in the same community that specifically must not be related to each other. These individuals – usually not more than five – provide personal guarantees for the loan, all being liable for any default. Grameen has over two million members in Bangladesh spread over 35,000 villages, 94 per cent of whom are women. This approach has achieved loan recovery rates above 90 per cent consistently and has had a positive impact on rural wages and poverty reduction. Grameen is now expanding internationally: Grameen America was established in 2008. Today they are focused on underbanked female entrepreneurs; as of their 2023 annual report Grameen USA had lent $4.7 billion to more than 211,000 women entrepreneurs.

Credit score

Many lenders – especially in the more developed economies – rely on credit scores to make their credit decisions. Credit scores are created by specialist credit bureaus (also known as consumer reporting agencies in the United States and credit reference agencies in the UK). They are the evolution of state credit registries. Historically, many countries created public databases where large loans and mortgages were registered. Credit bureaus evolved by complementing this information with other data such as domicile, income and financial history.

They provide a score on the individual asking for credit. This score makes it faster and safer for lenders to decide whether they wish to extend a loan. The credit score is 'earned' by the borrower through years of recorded good financial behaviour. A default on a loan can have a long-term effect on the credit history of an individual even if they have recovered from the difficulties that resulted in the default. In addition, a lack of historical data can make it difficult for an individual to receive the credit score they deserve based on their current financial circumstances.

This affects several unbanked and underbanked segments in countries where credit scores are used as a creditworthiness assessment tool. Individuals that are new to market, new to work, have had legal issues in the past or have had financial defaults will have difficulty in being given the credit scores they deserve. Lastly, recently created businesses will have difficulty in achieving reasonable credit scores, forcing the owners of the firms to provide personal guarantees which in turn reduces their access to growth capital. According to consulting firm Oliver Wyman, 19 million people in the USA do not have a credit score.[4]

One interesting underbanked segment is the new to market group. These are people moving from one country to another and finding out that their new home considers them unbanked even though they have a solid credit history in their country of origin. These included immigrants, professionals, students and even pensioners retiring to a sunnier climate. Banks have realized that this is a very interesting segment. Businesses like Nova Credit in the USA and QuadFi in

Canada have create compelling cross-border credit scoring models to address this need.

The value of collateral

The most straightforward way to get a loan is to guarantee it with an asset with value and liquidity. These can be in the form of real estate, equipment, jewellery, art or something along these lines. This can be an issue for the underbanked and unbanked for the obvious reason that many may not have access to assets to use as collateral.

There is another issue for the unbanked. Often, the assets that could be used as collateral are also the main source of income for the borrower and their family. A defaulted loan would not simply result in financial loss, it would also have the effect of the borrower losing their livelihood. The risks involved in using collateral as a guarantee for a personal or business loan are sometimes not clearly understood by borrowers. The fear of losing what you have is often mentioned by the unbanked as a key reason not to work with banks. This is understandable when we see that in 2023 in the USA lenders filed 180,000 foreclosures.[5]

Vision

Vision is a shortcut way of describing more complex issues. We previously said that part of the reason why a lender will extend a loan is the belief in a story that is presented by the borrower. In this story, the borrower outlines a situation where the credit line will enable them to benefit from the facility and that they will thereafter have all the requirements to be able to honour the conditions put forward by the lender.

This is in fact the borrower sharing a vision with the lender in a way that is credible and truly desirable for the lender to extend the loan. The borrower needs to provide enough narrative to not only validate the other data points gathered by the lender but also potentially make them feel confident enough to even agree on small shortfalls in expected scores or financial parameters.

In banks of today, where human interactions are replaced by digital algorithms, there is little opportunity to provide a vision to the banker and to get a positive buy-in. So, the vision that we need is one where the borrower knows the size and type of credit facility they require, and they also know who is the most likely lender that will provide it.

One of the most difficult issues to resolve in addressing financial exclusion is that unbanked individuals often feel that banks cannot help them because the banks:

- will take advantage of them
- will not be able to offer the service that they need
- will not want to lend to them

The lack of awareness of what banks can do and what they need from borrowers to be able to provide their services is a major barrier to financial inclusion. Not having a vision of what benefits access to finance can provide is an important challenge in addressing financial exclusion. The findings of the 2023 The FDIC National Survey of Unbanked and Underbanked Households in the USA eloquently illustrates these points:

- 40.1 per cent of unbanked households said that they 'Don't have enough money to meet minimum balance requirements'.
- 33.0 per cent said that they 'Don't trust banks'.
- 19.2 per cent said that 'Banks do not offer services needed'.[6]

Table 5.1 shows some of the most common credit products and identifies the level of relevance of identity, history, credit rating, collateral and vision for each. The importance of these requirements may not be surprising but it is interesting to see them on the same table. But if you look at them from the perspective of an unbanked individual it becomes clear that they are at a real disadvantage.

There are numerous challenges for the unbanked and underbanked to obtain fair and affordable credit. The main issue in obtaining credit from a legal source remains the lack of identity validation. Not

TABLE 5.1 Common credit products

Type of credit product	Assessment metrics				
	Identity	History	Credit rating	Collateral	Vision
	Confirmation that the customer is who they say they are	Past financial transaction history at a bank or financial institution	Assessment of creditworthiness by a third-party specialist	Liquidation value of assets used as security to obtain a loan	Belief that the client will be able to repay the loan (e.g. a degree or a business plan)
Overdraft	Required	Desirable	Desirable	Not required	Not required
Credit card	Required	Desirable	Desirable	Not required	Not required
Personal loan	Required	Required	Desirable	Not required	Not required
Car loan	Required	Desirable	Desirable	Required	Not required
Mortgage	Required	Required	Required	Required	Not required
Student loan	Required	Desirable	Desirable	Desirable	Required
Business loan	Required	Desirable	Desirable	Desirable	Required

SOURCE The Pacemakers Ltd, 2024

having some form of ID exposes the unbanked to predatory lending practices. These are provided by entities and individuals that not only offer extortionate rates and conditions, but who also are not constrained by legal means in securing the repayment of their loan.

The World Bank's ID4D (Identification for Development) survey found a strong correlation between the lack of ID and financial exclusion.[7] A national ID system is a service that should be provided by the state, but due to economic and political issues many countries are not delivering on this fundamental national service. The lack of a simple government offering that allows every citizen to be able to validate who they are is preventing billions of people from accessing credit from legal and trustworthy providers, forcing them into situations and circumstances that are hard to emerge from unscathed.

Conclusion

Access to credit is a key benefit of banking. This is as true today as it was when the first banks were conceived. The ability to access capital on the back of an individual's potential is at the core of credit. This may sound a bit lyrical, but access to credit is to be given the ability to dream of a better future. Sadly, for reasons we discussed in this chapter, billions of people are denied this dream.

Notes

1 Money Marketing (2018) Wonga: A recent history of the UK payday lender. www.moneymarketing.co.uk/news/wonga-recent-history-payday-lender (archived at https://perma.cc/9WZY-QDJF)

2 Treasury Committee (2024) New de-banking figures show more than 140,000 business accounts closed by major banks, UK Parliament. committees.parliament.uk/committee/158/treasury-committee/news/200127/new-debanking-figures-show-more-than-140000-business-accounts-closed-by-major-banks/ (archived at https://perma.cc/M57G-XZ2N)

3 J Jaffer (1999) Microfinance and the mechanics of solidarity lending: Improving access to credit through innovations in contract structure, SSRN Electronic Journal. doi.org/10.2139/ssrn.162548 (archived at https://perma.cc/YSD7-VXYY)

4 T Burke, B Sobolewski and A Mar (2023) 5 themes to watch as the ACA heads into its second decade, Oliver Wyman. www.oliverwyman.com/our-expertise/perspectives/health/2023/dec/5-themes-to-watch-as-the-aca-heads-into-its-second-decade.html (archived at https://perma.cc/JYJ6-7WM8)

5 ATTOM (2023) Foreclosure activity in first half of 2023 ticks upwards toward pre-Covid levels. www.attomdata.com/news/market-trends/foreclosures/attom-mid-year-2023-u-s-foreclosure-market-report (archived at https://perma.cc/3U49-AWYF)

6 FDIC (2023) 2023 national survey of unbanked and underbanked households. www.fdic.gov/household-survey (archived at https://perma.cc/R3E5-6SLQ)

7 World Bank (2024) Digital ID: A critical enabler for financial inclusion. blogs.worldbank.org/en/psd/digital-id-critical-enabler-financial-inclusion (archived at https://perma.cc/AMF2-SFTG)

6

Protection

From savings to investments, pensions and insurance

Introduction

Another fundamental component of everyone's basic banking needs is the ability to 'protect' our assets. Protection services encompass a comprehensive suite of financial products that range from savings to insurance, pensions and, of course, investments. These services enable all of us to prepare ourselves for the unexpected; they empower us to manage risk, build resilience and try to build future financial stability.

As we navigate the rapidly evolving role of fintech in financial inclusion, it is crucial to recognize the transformative potential of protection products. By enabling individuals to protect themselves against unforeseen circumstances, these products create more resilient individuals and businesses. This, in turn, contributes to overall economic stability and growth, as individuals are better equipped to weather financial storms and continue participating in the economy. Financial protection products are not just beneficial for individuals, they're also essential for the social, economic and financial stability of all economies.

Access to savings, investments, pensions and insurance is a powerful tool in breaking the cycle of poverty. When low-income individuals can protect their assets and build a financial cushion, they're less vulnerable to financial shocks such as losing a job or facing an unexpected financial demand. Moreover, these products empower marginalized groups, particularly women, by giving them greater financial resilience if facing financial challenges and difficulties.

While the potential is immense, we must acknowledge the challenges. Affordability, accessibility and financial literacy remain significant hurdles. The industry must work collaboratively with governments, regulators and consumer groups to address these issues.

As we move forward, the focus should be on developing sustainable, customer-centric solutions that leverage technology to reduce costs, using data responsibly to better understand and serve customers, and prioritizing financial education. The importance of financial education is greater in the case of protection products and services, as these are often more complex than financial products such as payments and credit.

At the core of protection products is the ability offered to any person or business to protect and grow any liquidity they have in excess of their immediate needs. When anyone benefits from a surplus of liquidity they inevitably look for ways to be able to use it against future downturns in income or increased financial demands. The options available to individuals and firms in such a situation can be grouped into the following categories.

Savings

When trying to protect any surplus liquidity the unbanked have few choices. The traditional method of the unbanked to keep funds safe is to hide them – physically. This is obviously a very inadequate solution. Even if hiding money does provide easy access it also exposes the user to theft (with the associated physical risks) and actual damage of the physical currency, and, importantly, it generates no return.

In an ideal safekeeping arrangement money is handed over to a trusted third party where in exchange for leaving the capital with them they will provide the customers with security and possibly a return, usually in the form of an agreed rate of interest and terms of access to the funds. The options available to the financially excluded segments of society are very limited in this area.

Beyond physical storage, the unbanked have a limited number of choices. These are divided into major categories: services that offer safekeeping at a fee, and safekeeping that provides a return.

Mobile wallets and digital accounts

These accounts, offered by fintech companies and mobile network operators, provide a way for the unbanked to store and save money digitally. All digital wallets allow their users to store money. The amounts that can be stored vary from wallet to wallet based on the level of authentication and KYC provided by the user.

Most wallets only provide storage services. A number of wallets have begun providing savings accounts in partnership with banks or by becoming banks themselves. India's PayTM (an acronym of pay through mobile) is a good example of this approach. They began as a pure payments company founded in 2010 and went public in November 2021, at the time becoming the largest ever initial public offering (IPO) in India. PayTM declared 100 million active customers in 2024. To cater to this huge customer base, it initially aimed at partnerships with the likes of Mastercard and Citibank, and eventually launched its own bank, PayTM Payments Bank. This decision was when things went wrong, with its inability to remain compliant – leading to the Reserve Bank of India, the banking regulator in India, ordering PayTM Payments Bank Ltd to stop the bulk of its activities from 29 February 2024.[1]

Savings banks

The historical solution to providing savings products to the unbanked was the creation of 'savings banks'. These were aimed at the less affluent, creating the means through which an unbanked individual could store excess liquidity safely while earning a small return. In the developed economies these organizations evolved to normal banks, regulated as banks and called savings and loans associations only in name. The savings and loans crisis of the late 1980s also contributed to their evolution into regulated banks.

At their inception, these institutions were created as the means for the less affluent (usually unbanked) to be able to benefit from simple savings accounts and mortgages. By maintaining a network of local branches, savings banks facilitate access for individuals living in less affluent or rural locations. They also have a much simpler range of products than traditional banks and often engage with local communities, developing trust and providing information about their services, enhancing the financial literacy of the community they operate within.

Savings groups

A similar initiative in scope to the savings banks of the 19th century is informal savings groups, such as rotating savings and credit associations (ROSCAs) or accumulating savings and credit associations (ASCAs). These allow their members to pool their money and take turns accessing the funds. For example, an organizer could set up a 10 member ROSCA in India to raise ₹50,000 ($600) for their community. The organizer could then gather nine more trusted individuals and ask each of them to contribute ₹5,000 to the fund monthly. At the end of the first monthly cycle one of the members of the ROSCA would take home a lump sum of ₹50,000. The recipient could be chosen through several processes, including a random selection, a financial bidding system or another mechanisms agreed by the group. Each member would take the lump sum only once in each cycle. This would continue until everyone has had a turn with the proceeds. At the end of the 10 months, when everyone has had a distribution, the ROSCA would either disband or begin another round. The benefits to the members is a hybrid credit and savings solution. The members have both kept their funds safe and have earned an interest-free short-term loan of varying duration. The latter is an important fact in many predominantly Islamic countries where paying interest is not Sharia law compliant.

ROSCAs are present across the globe, each with their own distinct name and cultural characteristics. Some examples are shown in Table 6.1.

TABLE 6.1 Rotating savings and credit associations

Region	Country	Name
Africa	Cameroon	Jangui
	Democratic Republic of Congo	Restourne
	Egypt	Gama'yia
	Ethiopia	Equub and Idir
	Francophone W Africa (e.g. Benin, Senegal, Togo)	Tontines
	Ghana	Susu
	Kenya	Chama or Itega
	Nigeria	Esusu or Ajo
	Somalia	Hagbad or Ayuuto
	Sudan	Sandooq
Americas	Bahamas	Sousou
	Barbados	Lodge
	Haiti	Sol
	Jamaica	Partner
	Mexico	Tanda
	Peru	Juntas
	Trinidad	Susu
Asia	India	Chits, Kitties or Kuris
	Indonesia	Arisan
	Japan	Kou
	Pakistan	Community
	South Korea	Kye
	Sri Lanka	Cheetu
	Vietnam	Hụi and Họ

ROSCAs are sometimes regulated, but most are not regulated by government. As they are based on social connections and bonds of the members of the communities, they are often regulated and supervised by the communities they serve.

Government savings bonds

Some governments offer savings bonds or certificates that can be purchased without a bank account. These provide a safe, low-risk way to save money over the long term. Unfortunately, as the concerns about money laundering have increased in recent years, most government bonds now require identification and bank accounts, thus putting this product increasingly out of reach for the unbanked in many countries.

Postal accounts

Postal accounts, traditionally more marginal government savings banks, have retained their status of gateway to banking by the underbanked. Post offices have traditionally worked with global money transfer organizations like Western Union and MoneyGram to enable people in developing countries to receive remittance payments from friends and family working abroad. These services have frequently naturally led to the provision of postal current accounts and eventually to postal savings accounts. In many developing countries the post offices provide banking services to the unbanked that the banks are unable or unwilling to provide.

But postal banks are not a solution only suited to the developing world. In her testimony before the United States Congress hearing on 'Banking the Unbanked' in 2021, Professor Mehrsa Baradaran from the University of California, Irvine School of Law, said:

> More than 40 percent of Americans do not have even $500 in savings and would need to borrow if they had a shortfall [...] Having a safe, low-cost, and easy savings account could lead to more savings, which could diminish the need for payday loans when families hit a snag. When individuals can dip into savings, they are less likely to need payday loans. A Postal Savings Account made possible through a local postal branch could significantly ease the burden on many families leading to more savings.[2]

Investments

One way of describing investing is that of using capital to take part in activities that take on a risk with the promise of offering a higher return than other options available. These can be funds, shares and any other vehicle that generates higher returns with higher risks than savings accounts. Investing in growth opportunities is a possibility many banked individuals can opt for – this is very hard for the unbanked. The options available to the unbanked are:

- **Direct investment:** This is the transfer of capital (usually cash but also digital wallet transfers) to entrepreneurs with the expectation of getting the capital back plus upside if the venture goes well. It is often done informally and as such the lender may not be protected from various types of payment defaults.
- **Liquid assets:** A well-trodden path for unbanked individuals is to purchase assets that will gain value in time. These can be jewellery, gold or even livestock. Compared to cash hoarding, these assets can gain in value, but as with cash they are liable to being stolen, lost or damaged.
- **Real estate:** This is one of the most desirable types of investment for most individuals, banked or unbanked. For the unbanked, these property acquisitions are almost always full-price cash purchases without the ability to benefit from loans or mortgages.
- **Peer-to-peer lending:** This is a potential option for the underbanked investor but not unbanked individuals. It offers an irrefutable opportunity for both the borrower and lender underbanked to benefit from lower credit of cost and higher returns on capital. That said, regulatory requirements across the world require the lender to be banked, and in most countries the borrower needs to have a bank account.

Pensions

Across the globe, a number of pension options are available to the underbanked. These are usually state funded, and very few options are available for unbanked individuals to top these up. Pension options available to the unbanked are as follows.

State pensions

These are issued by the government to older individuals on the basis of specific parameters including age, sex and work history through which the individual made contributions to their pension through taxation. In developing countries, the impact of state pensions can be dramatic, and beyond the positive impact on the individual they affect the recipient's household. A study conducted by the OECD on the impact of pensions in Africa found that:

- Pensions reduce the poverty gap ratio by 13 per cent in South Africa and increase the income of the poorest 5 per cent of the population by 50 per cent.
- In South Africa, families receiving a pension are 11 per cent less like to become poor.
- In Tanzania, where there is no pension, out of 146,000 children orphaned by HIV/AIDS, only 1,000 attended secondary school, because grandparents could not afford the fees.
- In Zambia, a pilot cash-transfer scheme to older people caring for orphans has improved school attendance.
- In South Africa, girls living in a household with an older woman who receives a pension are 3–4 centimetres taller than girls in households with older women who do not receive a pension.[3]

Private pension schemes

These are schemes provided by NGOs where individuals not formally employed can make a regular contribution that will lead to a pension when they reach retirement age or when they become unable to work. In some countries like India and Rwanda the local government makes contributions to the schemes. In most other countries, including those

FIGURE 6.1 Protection risks and rewards for the unbanked and underbanked

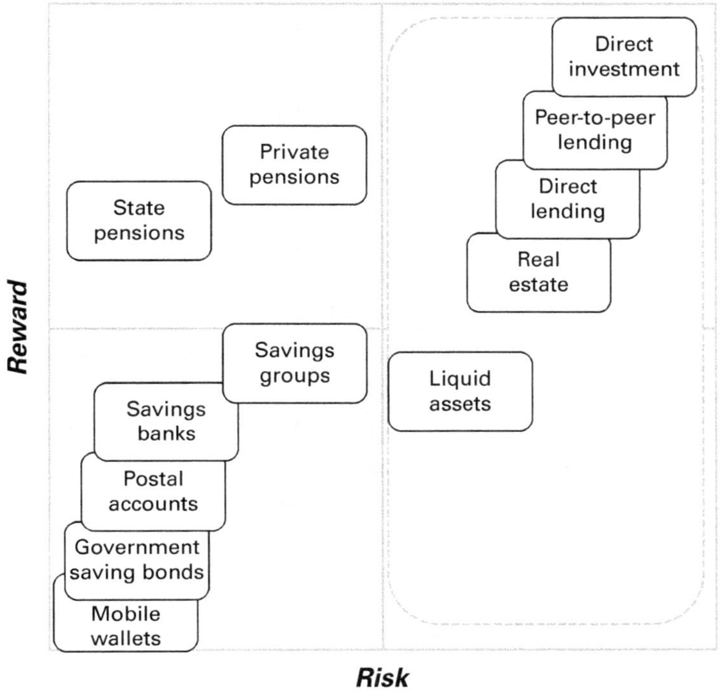

Direct investment
Peer-to-peer lending
Direct lending
Real estate
Private pensions
State pensions
Savings groups
Liquid assets
Savings banks
Postal accounts
Government saving bonds
Mobile wallets
Reward
Risk

SOURCE The Pacemakers Ltd, 2025

in developed economies, private schemes are funded by the individual with the occasional tax incentive placed on the treatment of the pension contribution (see Figure 6.1)

Insurance

Insurance products are another means of wealth preservation and protection. But they offer a different risk reward profile compared to the other protection products. They have no return if the event that one insures against does not happen, but they have a substantial benefit if the insured event takes place.

The types of insurance most taken on by the unbanked populations around the world tend to focus on affordability, accessibility and relevance to their daily lives and risks. These insurance products are often designed to be low-cost and easy to understand and purchase, especially for those without traditional banking relationships. Here are some of the most common types of insurance for the unbanked.

Microinsurance

Microinsurance is designed specifically for the low-income market, offering coverage for health, life, property and agriculture at very low premiums. It's tailored to be accessible and affordable for people with limited financial means, often using simplified policies and claims processes. Just like all classical insurance systems, microinsurance works with the principle of risk mutualization among a great number of individuals. This mutualization allows a protection against any low-frequency or high-intensity claim. The service is provided in return for a regular premium payment that is proportionate to the probability of the risks concerned. The most common types of microinsurance include:

- **Life insurance:** Life insurance emerges as a pivotal element within the financial ecosystem, frequently integrated with loan offerings by microfinance institutions (MFIs). This product amalgamates a life insurance policy, effective in the event of the policyholder's demise, with a savings component, applicable during the policyholder's lifetime. Additionally, it offers the option to incorporate various supplementary coverages, including those for loans and funeral expenses.
- **Funeral insurance:** In Sub-Saharan Africa, the financial burden of funeral expenses significantly surpasses the average household income, presenting a substantial economic challenge. In South Africa, the funeral insurance market is particularly robust, with an estimated 10 million adults benefiting from such coverage, underscoring its critical importance in the region.

- **Property insurance:** This insurance variant offers coverage for fire and various accidents, catering to a wide range of risks including personal, professional and agricultural. It is designed to provide financial protection in the event of loss or damage to property.
- **Agricultural insurance:** Acknowledging the vital importance of agriculture for rural communities, agricultural insurance is poised for substantial expansion. Prominent international organizations, such as the World Bank and the United Nations Food and Agriculture Organization (FAO), in collaboration with insurance companies, are spearheading initiatives to develop climate-related insurance projects across continents including Africa, South America, Europe and Asia. This sector also encompasses specialized products like crop and livestock insurance, addressing the specific needs of agricultural activities.
- **Health insurance:** In many countries across the globe, the unbanked do not need health insurance as the state provides national health services. Most European countries, most of North America (except the USA), the largest countries in South America, most of Asia and many African countries provide some form of national health service where most of the cost is borne by the state. The unbanked in countries where there is no national health service have limited options.

  A country where healthcare is an issue for the unbanked is the United States. In the US unbanked individuals have the following options in seeking health insurance – the US federal government required that insurance companies should accept 'paper checks, cashier's checks, money orders, replenishable prepaid debit cards, electronic funds transfer from a bank account, and an automatic deduction from a credit or debit card', opening the way for unbanked US residents to buy health insurance.
- **Embedded insurance:** These are insurance products embedded inside the purchase of another service. These products can be accessed as an addendum to a service contract offered to the unbanked user and as such does not require a banking relationship to be activated.

- **Mobile insurance:** With the rise of mobile phone usage among the unbanked, mobile insurance has become more popular. It often covers the loss or theft of, or damage to, mobile phones. This type of insurance is often bundled with the mobile phone contract and as such does not require a bank account to pay the premium.
- **Remittance insurance:** Some insurance products are tied to remittances, where migrant workers can purchase insurance coverage for their families back home as part of the remittance process. This type of insurance covers the risk of loss of remittance due to various reasons, such as political unrest, currency fluctuation or the untimely demise of the remitter, and it is covered by the remittances fees

These insurance products are often distributed through innovative channels that bypass traditional banking and insurance systems, such as mobile money platforms, microfinance institutions and community groups. By leveraging technology and alternative distribution networks, insurers can reach unbanked populations with products that meet their specific needs and constraints.

Conclusion

Access to the means of protecting any excess liquidity in view of future need is a very complex area for the unbanked. Protection services are not easily accessible to many of the unbanked, especially if they live in underprivileged or isolated areas. In the event that some protection products are available, these are often not trusted or understood by the unbanked and underbanked individuals. Many can refer to instances – sometimes inaccurately – where inappropriate, ineffective, mis-sold and/or ill-explained protection products such as insurance, pensions or investments have resulted in poor financial outcomes to them or to people they know. This factor is of course also due to a lack of financial literacy on the subject by many of the unbanked.

Lack of trust is something that could benefit from both tighter and more innovative financial regulation and enforcement. The first would affect the proliferation of badly designed or even fraudulent protection propositions leading to greater levels of trust in the unbanked; the second would support the growth of new products aimed at better addressing the needs of the unbanked.

The ability to protect one's wealth, no matter how small, is a fundamental need of all individuals and firms, banked or unbanked, that needs to be addressed in making sure financial exclusion is a thing of the past.

Notes

1. T Pathe (2024) India's RBI orders PayTM Payments Bank to halt banking services by end of February, Fintech Futures. www.fintechfutures.com/2024/02/rbi-clamps-down-on-paytm-payments-bank (archived at https://perma.cc/N53Z-H5PB)
2. Subcommittee on Consumer Protection and Financial Institutions (2021) Banking the unbanked: Exploring private and public efforts to expand access to the financial system, US House of Representatives. www.govinfo.gov/content/pkg/CHRG-117hhrg45508/html/CHRG-117hhrg45508.htm (archived at https://perma.cc/N56T-DGSA)
3. F Stewart and J Yermo (2009) Pensions in Africa, OECD. doi.org/10.1787/227444006716 (archived at https://perma.cc/VS8Q-KCUV)

7

Regulation

How regulation can be the means to eradicate financial exclusion

Introduction

Regulation is about setting the rules of the game. It is about creating the right engagement framework for different entities working with each other to ensure – as far as possible – that a fair and expected outcome is assured for all participants. This is absolutely the case in financial services, which we will explain in this chapter. Regulators take these goals very seriously. Universally, all regulators see themselves and are seen by the ecosystem as the supervisors and protectors of the market and of the financial services industry they are responsible for.

This mission statement outlined by the Financial Conduct Authority, one of the UK's financial regulators, illustrates this perspective very clearly:

> Financial markets must be honest, competitive and fair so consumers get a fair deal. We work to ensure these markets work well for individuals, for businesses, and for the growth and competitiveness of the UK economy.
>
> [...] We focus on reducing and preventing serious harm, setting higher standards and promoting competition and positive change.[1]

At its core, the role of the financial regulators is to ensure the stability of the markets they supervise by supporting the creation of a financial services sector that delivers what the country and the economy requires. Regulators aim to make sure that the new products and services on offer do not create any undue harm to the people and businesses using them and that the providers are able to provide these products in ways that are sustainable in the long term. To make sure that the market remains efficient, regulators must also make sure that no provider dominates the market, hindering the emergence of competition from challengers and innovators. The strategic objectives of the financial regulators can be summarized as follows:

- guarantee fairplay
- define boundaries
- support competition
- promote the welfare of all participants
- ensure stability and growth of the financial ecosystem and of the economy

In pursuing these strategic objectives, regulators can have both deeply positive and negative impacts on financial inclusion.

On the one hand, regulators have the opportunity to become promoters of inclusion by making it mandatory to offer bank accounts to all. On the other hand, they could impose such high security, identity and authentication demands that less affluent, homeless or new to market users could not be legally offered banking services.

Globally, regulators are considering a number of ways to support financial inclusion, which we will discuss in more detail. In order to support financial inclusion, regulators have a number of different options. Below we examine some of the steps regulators can take to further financial inclusion.

Make it easier to open an account

One of the ways regulators could encourage financial inclusion is by simplifying bank and wallet account opening processes. Many

FIGURE 7.1 The financial regulation life cycle

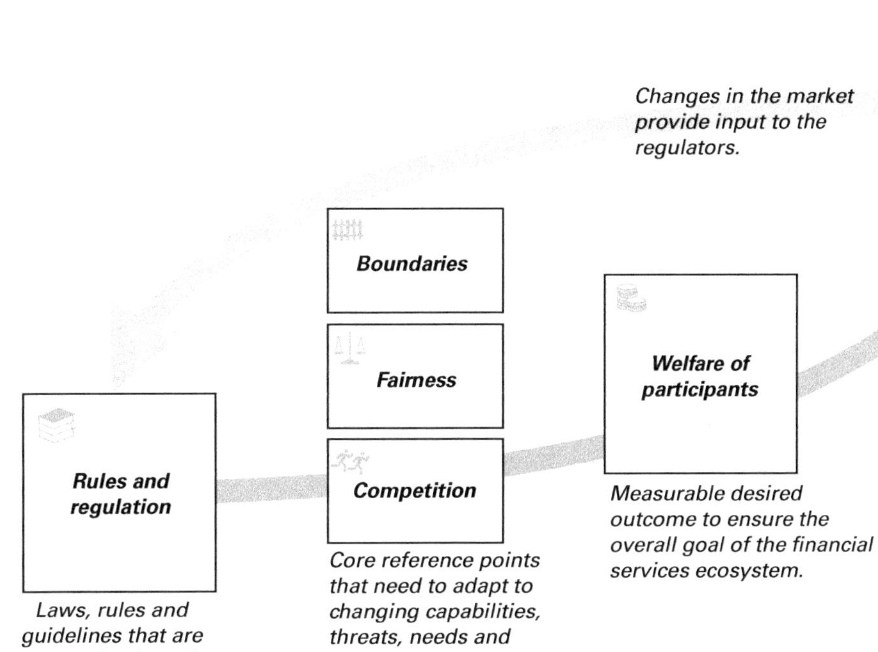

SOURCE The Pacemakers Ltd, 2024

providers decline unbanked users due regulatory KYC and authentication requirements that can be discriminatory towards certain segments of society. The application of the authentication requirements and the interpretation of the KYC/identification regulation can be arbitrary. Across the world, the interpretation of the authentication and ID requirements to open an account can often vary from bank to bank. Today many banks continue to exclude certain users based on their own interpretation of regulatory requirements.

Most regulators mandate the collection of a number of data points before they allow a provider to offer a banking product. Data to be collected can include items such as the identity of the customer, the fact that they are not on any sanctions list, their ability to afford the product being offered and the like. These requirements were often defined when access to a bank account was only needed by the more affluent and the majority of the population did not need a bank account to run their daily lives. This changed with the digitalization of banking, and those without bank accounts found themselves badly affected by their inability to move from a cash-based economy to one based on digital finance.

Today many financial institutions still demand validation of factors that many of us cannot readily provide. Many of the unbanked are unable to provide traditional proof of identity, some do not have a fixed address or a consistent source of income. Many would have a hard time addressing these without access to financial services. The answer is not to eliminate the basic requirements expected by the banking regulators, but to make sure that these are still appropriate today and to see whether they should be replaced by new ones that reflect today's situation more effectively.

One interesting point to observe is that many new bank challengers, e-wallets and fintechs are able to offer their customers banking services that are denied to them by the incumbent providers. These new players are subject to the same rules as the older competitors but frequently they are delivering very different outcomes. The issue of the legacy application of banking rules by the incumbent banks should be an area that banking regulators examine further in order to support financial inclusion more broadly.

Why is it that – and this is my personal experience – when I (Alessandro) tried to open a bank account for a new business I had set up, the incumbent banks offered to open a bank account in two weeks while the online bank I subsequently approached opened an account for me in 10 minutes? They were both applying the same regulation but with very different outcomes. The incumbent bank required paper documents to be sent to the branch. The online bank allowed me to submit the required documents digitally.

Regulators should make it their responsibility to explore why this is happening. To fight financial exclusion, banking regulators should look at fighting legacy implementation of rules by some of the larger providers in the market. One way of doing this could be the regulator to promote the creation of simpler, more affordable 'no-frills' banking products aimed at the unbanked.

The EU and the UK have already engaged in this approach by mandating the creation of the 'basic bank account' aimed at the unbanked and underbanked customer.[2] A basic bank account is an account that covers standard transactions that we all use in our daily lives, such as:

- receiving payments
- making payments (for example direct debits and card purchases)
- making deposits
- withdrawing cash
- the provision of a payment card that can be used both online and in stores
- some access to other banking services

Where available, the banks are asked to include access to online banking services with this account. However, they do not always have to automatically include an overdraft or credit facility. In some EU countries, your bank might still charge you an annual fee for this basic payment account. But this fee is monitored by regulators to ensure it remains reasonable. In many countries, alternatives to the basic bank account are digital wallets. These are more lightly regulated by the financial authorities and cannot pay interest on deposits or offer credit directly, but they do provide many of the features of the basic banks account.

Make banking feel safe

One of the major reasons for people not opening bank accounts is that they do not feel that their money and their data is safe with banks. According to the 2021 FDIC National Survey of Unbanked and Underbanked Households, the second and third most frequently mentioned reason why individuals do not have bank accounts are concerns about privacy and trust.[3]

This lack of trust can be powerfully addressed by regulation. There are many ways that regulation can help increase trust among banking customers.

Control costs

Regulations that mandate clear disclosure of fees and interest rates protect consumers from predatory practices and encourage their participation in the formal financial sector. Most countries have laws against usury, unfair customer treatment and predatory pricing. However, the fact is that many unbanked and underbanked individuals are unaware that these are in place, nor do they understand what they can do if they are treated unfairly.

The provision of basic bank accounts is meaningless if they are priced beyond the means of the unbanked. Arguably, a large part of the success of the M-Pesa wallet in Sub-Saharan Africa was that it was perceived as being free, because the cost of storing value in your M-Pesa wallet was covered by the already existing telephony agreement with the mobile provider.

But banks sometimes hide charges for other services. An important function of the bank account is the ability to send and receive funds. In countries with big international diasporas the extortionate fees charged by the banks in processing transfers are often unaffordable for the less affluent. That is what is behind the success of cash-based cross-border processors such as Western Union and Moneygram or informal payment processors such as the Hawala processors, a trust-based money transfer method that allows the transfer of funds without the physical movement of money.

Today cross-border payments are regulated with a focus on preventing money laundering and fraud. Costs are less of a focus. The fact that bank transfers are so much more expensive than cash-based or informal transfers is, in the eyes of many unbanked, evidence that banking is too expensive. By taking a closer look at the costs of transfers, regulators could provide a helping push to stopping financial exclusion.

Privacy and data protection

Strong privacy and data protection laws build trust in digital financial services, a critical factor for their acceptance and use among the unbanked or underbanked populations. In Europe the General Data Protection Regulation (GDPR) is a comprehensive European Union law that regulates the processing of personal data, including financial data, by organizations. When it was introduced in 2018, many feared that its requirements would badly affect the growth of digital services in the EU. This has not been the case and many global technology, social media and financial services have reluctantly adopted its requirements with little downside in the adoption of their services by end-users. If anything, many European users feel more comfortable in sharing their personal data online as they know that they have to approve the use of their data in all instances.

The situation is different in the United States. The USA has various federal and state laws that cover different aspects of data privacy, like health data, financial information or data collected from children. Although data privacy in the United States is notably different to that in the European Union, some states have passed their own comprehensive data privacy laws that have drawn comparisons to the EU GDPR system. Since data collected by many companies is unregulated in most states, these companies can use, sell or share data without notifying their US customers. This lack of safeguards on personal data use by the banks is a major issue for many unbanked individuals in the USA, according to the 2022 report *Unbanked in America* by the Federal Reserve Bank of Cleveland,[4] as shown in Figure 7.2.

The main exception to this rule is the state of California. In 2018 California passed the California Consumer Privacy Act (CCPA) act, the strictest data privacy law in the US, which applies to businesses that collect personal information about consumers and outlined specific rights consumers have. The CCPA allowed consumers the right to know what personal information a business collected and to whom it was sold, the right to delete personal information collected by the business, the right to opt out of the sale of personal information and the right to non-discriminatory treatment for exercising privacy rights.

The CCPA was updated with a second act – the California Privacy Rights Act (CPRA) – which was passed in 2020. Together, the CCPA and CPRA form a comprehensive data privacy framework that gives Californian consumers significant control over their personal information collected by businesses.

China has implemented a variety of legislation dealing with privacy in financial services. The one most relevant to underbanked individuals is the Personal Information Protection Law (PIPL). Often called China's version of the GDPR, the PIPL regulates the collection, use, processing and transfer of personal financial data. It imposes strict requirements around consent, data localization and cross-border data transfers for financial institutions.

India's response to the need for privacy of financial data is the introduction of the Digital Personal Data Protection Act (DPDPA) in 2023. As with GDPR, DPDPA covers 'personal data' relating to an identifiable natural person. But, unlike the GDPR (which applies to all personal data, digitized or not) DPDPA applies only to personal data that is in digital form or is digitized after its collection.

In addition to DPDPA, the Reserve Bank of India (RBI) has issued specific regulations requiring banks and payment service providers to store all payment system data within India, with limited exceptions for the foreign leg of international transactions.

FIGURE 7.2 Reasons given by the unbanked for not having a bank account

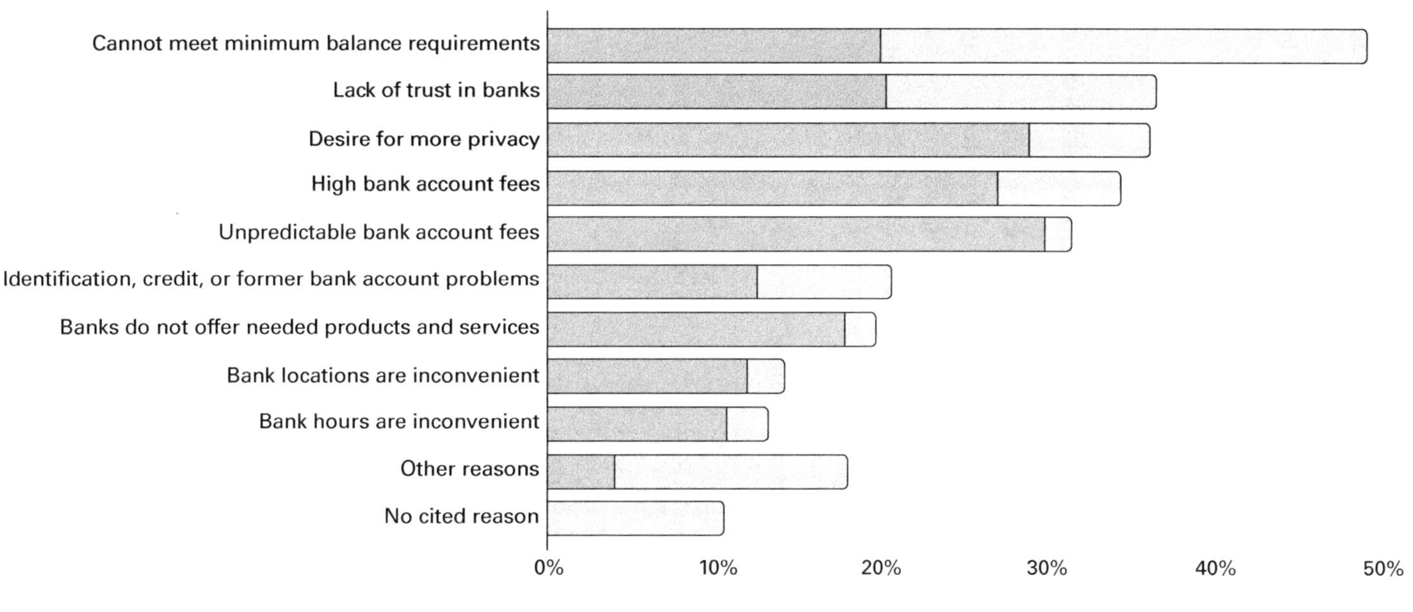

SOURCE Federal Reserve Bank of Cleveland 2020 and The Pacemakers Ltd analysis

Regulators worldwide should mandate that customer data held by financial services organizations is secure and that it cannot be used to the detriment of account holders. Such a provision by regulators across the globe will go a long way toward increasing the confidence of the unbanked in the banks.

Encourage competition and innovation

One of the stated goals of most regulators is that of maintaining a competitive market. In today's fast-changing technology banking landscape and with the emergence of innovative new players, it is important that regulation does not become the means through which established legacy players stop challengers from entering the market. Many of the regulators worldwide have noted this risk and are creating the means for them to achieve two things:

- support challengers and the incumbent in developing new capabilities while remaining fully compliant in meeting regulatory requirements
- evolve financial regulation to meet the new customer needs and expectations brought about by digital innovation and to make sure that the regulator is able to understand and supervise innovative providers

There are many potential areas of focus for financial regulators looking to promote financial inclusion through a competitive marketplace.

Launch regulatory sandboxes

A regulatory sandbox is a framework set up by a financial sector regulator to allow small-scale, live testing of innovations by private firms in a controlled environment under the regulator's supervision. These allow fintech companies to test new financial products, promoting innovation that can lead to more inclusive financial services.[5]

According to the World Bank, 57 countries had introduced regulatory sandboxes to foster financial innovation by 2020.[6] Of the 73 sandboxes set up in these jurisdictions, 23 were related to financial inclusion or financial inclusion themes. Also interesting in the World Bank report is the distribution of the sandboxes, with the vast majority of regulatory sandboxes located in the Middle East and Africa. The striking point was the relatively low presence of sandboxes in North America.

Support digital identity

Difficulty in identification/authentication is one of the most mentioned reasons by the unbanked for not having a bank account. In reality this issue could be addressed through the intelligent use of digital identity. Financial regulations that are supportive of the use of digital IDs can make financial services more accessible to individuals who lack traditional forms of identification.

In some countries national ID schemes are seen as a potential risk to the freedom and anonymity of their citizens. Financial regulators could work with other governmental entities to create digital ID solutions. Creating digital IDs that are designed to guarantee anonymity and security, are secure and are widely accepted requires a smart regulatory framework.

In order to attain widespread adoption of a digital ID system a number of characteristics are key. Standardization of the ID system would reduce compatibility and interoperability issues between the holder of the ID and the issuer of the financial services. Clear guidelines to financial services providers to enable or even mandate the acceptance of digital ID would make widespread adoption easy. Finally, key to the success of the digital ID scheme is the implementation of stringent rules and guidelines that make the providers of the financial services accountable for any misuse of the digital ID – including privacy, data integrity and technological vulnerabilities of their own systems.

Expand regulators' knowledge base

Regulators have deep knowledge of the traditional financial services world. They sometimes have a less in-depth awareness of the latest innovation in the financial services industry. To keep up with the rapid pace of digital innovation, regulators employ a variety of strategies.

International collaboration

Collaboration and partnerships with other regulators is a good approach that regulators use to make sure they are able keep up with a fast-evolving industry. The Global Financial Innovation Network (GFIN) is one example of numerous such collaborations. It comprises over 70 organizations and is dedicated to fostering financial innovation for consumer benefit. It offers a streamlined method for innovative firms to engage with regulators and facilitates their expansion across multiple countries, easing the process of scaling up new ideas. Innovative firms can apply to participate in pilot programmes that allow them to test innovative products, services or business models in more than one jurisdiction. GFIN aims to become a new framework for collaboration among financial services regulators on topics related to innovation, exchanging insights and perspectives on dealing with new financial technologies and practices.

Talent acquisition

Financial service providers and regulators are often talent pools for one another. It is not unusual for an ex-banker to become a regulator and vice versa. A quick browse through the careers of members of all financial regulators reveals a clear pathway from financial services to regulation. What is changing is that recently we are seeing regulators increasingly hiring talent from challenger financial services firms rather than incumbent ones.

Review and revise existing regulations

Regulators continuously update their rules to accommodate new technologies while safeguarding consumers. A few examples of these changes include:

- The Securities and Exchange Commission (SEC) in the USA has been actively engaging with issues around cryptocurrencies and initial coin offerings (ICOs).

- With the rise of digital finance, there is an increased focus on cybersecurity. Regulations like the Digital Operational Resilience Act (DORA) in the EU are being introduced to set standards for ICT risk management and incident reporting.
- Regulators need to expand their focus on inclusion-friendly financial products. In particular, microfinance and social lending firms would benefit from supportive regulation, enabling them to continue being reliable sources of credit to underserved populations without compromising the stability of the financial system.
- Regulators are modernizing macroprudential policies to prevent systemic risks in the financial sector due to the fast growth of fintech. The shift to cloud computing has created a renewed focus on this, as the collapse of one of the large cloud providers could potentially have a substantial impact on the stability of a country's financial services infrastructure.
- The growing interest in banking, payments, credit and other financial products by the global Big Tech firms is leading to an increased push for cross-industry regulation that captures the risks from the significant interconnection among different entities within Big Tech groups.[7] Many unbanked individuals are users of the services provided by the global Big Tech firms, potentially making Big Tech a good partner in helping the eradication of financial exclusion.[8] Making sure that the financial services regulation applicable to Big Tech firms is protective of the needs of the unbanked and underbanked individual should be a key goal of regulation going forward.

Strengthen financial literacy

As we have said previously, lack of financial education is a major barrier for the unbanked to understand how banking could help them improve their lives. Regulators are increasingly active in leading and participating in initiatives that improve financial literacy in the markets they focus on.

These are a few example of financial regulators supporting initiatives aimed at enhancing the financial literacy of the public:

- The European Commission, in collaboration with the OECD International Network on Financial Education (OECD-INFE), has developed dedicated financial competence frameworks for adults and for children and young people. These frameworks aim to improve individuals' financial skills and knowledge, enhancing financial literacy across different age groups.
- The Financial Conduct Authority is supporting the Strategy for Financial Wellbeing initiative by the Money and Pensions Service. This 10-year framework aims to improve the financial literacy and wellbeing of UK citizens. The strategy sets measured goals to bring benefits for individuals, their communities and wider society, focusing on increasing the number of children receiving meaningful financial education among other objectives.
- The Reserve Bank of India, as the money market and the banking regulator, has launched basic financial education as well as sector-focused financial education. These include financial literacy guides, diaries and posters covering the tenets of financial wellbeing, such as savings, concepts of interest, time value, inflation, etc. Other subjects covered include supporting businesses, ATMs, payment systems, Ponzi schemes and financial awareness messages.
- The US SEC hosts investor education events and provides resources through its Office of Investor Education and Advocacy. Its website at investor.gov delivers information (not advice) on investment.
- The Central Bank of Nigeria (CBN) has developed a National Financial Literacy Framework to improve financial literacy across Nigeria. This framework is part of a comprehensive agenda for implementing the Nigerian Financial Inclusion Strategy, aiming to reduce poverty, improve income and facilitate development through enhanced financial literacy.
- The Investor and Financial Education Council (IFEC) in Hong Kong, supported by the Education Bureau and other financial regulators in Hong Kong, has developed and led the implementation

of the Financial Literacy Strategy 2019. This strategy aims to improve the financial literacy of the Hong Kong population by working with different stakeholders.

- Bank Negara Malaysia, Malaysia's central bank, provides financial education through social media, mobile applications and outreach programmes such as road shows and financial carnivals. These efforts are part of a comprehensive strategy to improve financial literacy in the country.

Financial regulators play a fundamental role in ensuring that financial operators in their markets are supportive of eliminating financial exclusion. Across the globe, regulators realize their role and, to varying degrees, they are trying to make changes to the ways they implement their rules and supervise their implementation. Through targeted and thoughtful regulation, governments and regulatory bodies are directly impacting the accessibility, affordability and appropriateness of financial services for the broadest possible population.

Notes

1 Financial Conduct Authority (2016) About the FCA. www.fca.org.uk/about/what-we-do/the-fca (archived at https://perma.cc/43M4-TL9S)

2 European Union (2024) Bank accounts in the EU. europa.eu/youreurope/citizens/consumers/financial-products-and-services/bank-accounts-eu/index_en.htm (archived at https://perma.cc/TN2W-K5ZY)

3 Federal Deposit Insurance Corporation (2021) 2021 FDIC national survey of unbanked and underbanked households. https://www.fdic.gov/household-survey/2021-fdic-national-survey-unbanked-and-underbanked-households (archived at https://perma.cc/AH9Y-SCX5)

4 Federal Reserve Bank of Cleveland (2022) *Unbanked in America: A review of the literature*. www.clevelandfed.org/publications/economic-commentary/2022/ec-202207-unbanked-in-america-a-review-of-the-literature (archived at https://perma.cc/N5V7-FUBS)

5 G Cornelli, S Doerr, L Gambacorta and O Merrouche (2023) Regulatory sandboxes and fintech funding: Evidence from the UK, *Review of Finance*, 28 (1). academic.oup.com/rof/article-abstract/28/1/203/7140150 (archived at https://perma.cc/8RPU-YU5W)

6 M S Appaya, H Gradstein, H Luskin and M Kanz (2020) Global experiences from regulatory sandboxes, World Bank. documents.worldbank.org/curated/en/912001605241080935/Global-Experiences-fromRegulatory-Sandboxes (archived at https://perma.cc/6WZR-8D8E)

7 J C Crisanto and J Ehrentraud (2021) The Big Tech risk in finance, International Monetary Fund. www.imf.org/external/pubs/ft/fandd/2021/05/big-tech-fintech-and-financial-regulation-crisanto-ehrentraud.htm (archived at https://perma.cc/Q2DK-5KC5)

8 J Ehrentraud, J L Evans, A Monteil and F Restoy (2022) *Big Tech Regulation: In search of a new framework*, Bank for International Settlements. www.bis.org/fsi/fsipapers20.pdf (archived at https://perma.cc/9FCX-LGEH)

PART TWO

How do we fix finance?

8

The role of fintech

How fintech is fighting social exclusion and what more it could do

Introduction

As we said previously, when fintechs started challenging the financial services incumbents, their primary targets were not the less affluent or the unbanked. They principally targeted digitally affluent younger customers who would be comfortable with using their smartphone to send and receive money, buy shares or even get an overdraft instead of going into their bank or talking to their broker. These were not unbanked individuals, they were fully banked, relatively affluent people who wanted a user experience that was more similar to their favourite ecommerce sites than what their bank was willing or able to offer.

Fintech pioneers like PayPal, eTrade and Klarna allowed their customers to open an account with them, but these were enormously limited until the user was able to connect their bank account to authenticate themselves, to pay into their wallet or to withdraw funds. Fintech was a developed world proposition for the relatively well-off, replacing the bank and the broker with something better.

As an ex-PayPal employee, I (Alessandro) had a very clear notion of what the firm's ideal customer looked like. During a trip to Tanzania, I remember being utterly surprised to see that so many people were able to make and receive payments without a bank account simply by using M-Pesa on their mobile (not smart) phone. The realization that technology was able to make a difference for the unbanked suddenly dawned on me during that trip.

In exploring how fintech can rewire banking to make it more universal, it would be useful to see how different players are tackling specific issues faced by the unbanked and the underbanked.

Let's take a closer look at the creativity and vision fintechs are showing in tackling financial exclusion.

Helping customers without bank accounts

The entry point into financial services is often opening a bank account at your local friendly bank branch. But what if there are no banks in a 50-mile radius around where you live, or the bank has told you that you are not eligible or that you need to pay fees you cannot afford? Fintechs around the world are addressing this issue. One of the more interesting such fintechs is MoMo in Vietnam.

MoMo

Vietnam remains one of the most unbanked countries in the world; only 31 per cent of the population has a bank account, while 66 per cent have access to the internet.[1] MoMo was founded in 2007 and has the goal of transforming Vietnam's financial landscape.

Nguyen Manh Tuong, MoMo's CEO, articulates their mission: 'MoMo is dedicated to releasing a future where digital payments are embraced wholeheartedly, empowering every Vietnamese citizen to reap the benefits of the digital economy, regardless of their circumstances.'

They want to build a world where the unbanked can seamlessly participate in the digital economy, where financial transactions are no longer hindered by physical limitations, inappropriate processes or outdated systems. MoMo's vision is to empower every Vietnamese citizen, from the big cities to the most remote villages, to embrace the convenience and security of mobile digital payments.

Today, MoMo customers can access a wide range of financial opportunities on their phones, unlocking the potential for economic growth, entrepreneurship and personal empowerment. The firm sees itself not as just a payment platform but also as a catalyst for social and economic transformation, breaking down barriers and fostering a more inclusive society.

They could be described as a 'super app' that acts as a single destination[2] through which its customers can access:

- bill payments
- peer-to-peer transfers
- cash deposit and withdrawal
- offline payments for in-store purchases
- insurance products
- savings and investments
- buy now, pay later (BNPL) and short-term loans

Today MoMo is one of the fastest-growing Fintech companies in Vietnam. It has over 31 million users and more than 50,000 domestic partners and over 140,000 payment acceptance points nationwide in partnership with 70 banks. It is the leading mobile payments app with 68 per cent market share.

In 2019, the FIS Global Payments Report found that 85 per cent of Vietnam's point-of-sale (POS) transactions by value were in cash. Since then, the Vietnamese government and the State Bank of Vietnam have strongly promoted the use of digital payments. By the end of 2027 the number of cash transactions is by value expected to fall to 24 per cent.[3]

Building a credit history

Being underbanked is another manifestation of financial exclusion. The underbanked often do not have a credit history, and as such they are unable to access the banking services they need and should be eligible for. 'Credit builders' are a specialist kind of fintech whose goal is to allow underbanked (and in some instances unbanked) individuals to create a credit profile or to improve an existing one. In doing this, they enable their users to become eligible to be offered the financial services that they need by banking and finance providers.

A good example of credit builders is US-based fintech Grow Credit.

Grow Credit

Grow Credit aims to lower the barriers to entry for millions of people in the USA by helping them establish and strengthen their credit profiles through subscription payments. Its users can pay for their favourite streaming services like Netflix, Hulu and Spotify through a virtual Mastercard, all while simultaneously boosting their credit score. Grow Credit's ingenious platform integrates subscription payments into a powerful credit-building tool, at costs much lower than traditional credit cards.

Its understanding of the processes used by credit score builders such as FICO helped it put together an approach that allows it to build a credit history for its clients much more quickly and cheaply than other solutions. At the core of its approach lies a deep understanding of the intricate – and often inappropriate for the less affluent – processes that shape a credit score.

Its offering brings together a recurring payment processing and a credit line – both key contributors to building a credit score. Grow Credit reports the monthly repayments made by its customers to the three major US credit bureaus to improve their credit repayment history.

Grow Credit also allows existing financial institutions to access a 'credit-building-as-a-service' solution through white-labelled application programming interfaces (APIs) for banks, insurance carriers, fintech firms and subscription-based businesses. In 2024 Grow Credit announced a partnership with Wells Fargo Bank to support its drive in promoting financial inclusivity.[4]

Help in making the right financial choices

We mentioned earlier in this book that one of the most common reasons cited by the unbanked or underbanked is not knowing what the banks can do for them. What if there was a business that could help you find what you need to do? Personalized insight on your money is a great tool to get the unbanked to engage with the world of finance. A great fintech operating in this sector is Wagestream.

Wagestream

Wagestream, an employee platform dedicated to frontline workers, offers solutions based around early access to pay, specifically access to accrued pay at any point in the month, budgeting and microsavings, shift tracking (enabling customers to know exactly how much they are owed, and to review historic earnings to ensure income is maintained at the right level), as well as educational tools around financial wellbeing, including personalized financing coaching. Its goals are clear: 'We're on a mission to bring better financial wellbeing to frontline workers. We do that by providing a set of fairer financial services, designed for them, through their employer.'

This is how it operates: on enrolling, the customer allows the employer to send their shift/salary data which automatically gets added to the app once submitted and approved. They then receive a number of services, including the following:

- **Flexible pay access:** Employees can access a portion of their earned wages at any time during the pay cycle. This flexibility can help manage unexpected expenses and reduce reliance on payday loans or credit cards.
- **Financial tracking and planning:** The app includes tools for tracking earnings and spending, helping users budget more effectively. It also features financial coaching and educational resources to improve financial literacy.
- **Savings features:** The platform includes automated features to help users save money, known as Build Pots, which facilitate setting

aside funds for future requirements without the need to manually transfer money.

Wagestream, founded in 2018 in the UK, has since expanded into the US and Spain. It partners with large employers such as the NHS, Hilton Hotels, Pizza Hut, Burger King and the Co-op.[5]

Benefiting from social banking

Historically, in areas where access to financial services is limited, communities often come together to form rotating savings and credit associations (ROSCAs). These are akin to informal versions of credit unions. In previous chapters we described how ROSCAs operate across the developing world, providing badly needed means to save and to borrow. Most ROSCAs are informally organized but some are slowly embracing the potential of technology. One of these is a company that has become one of Egypt's most successful fintech unicorns – Money Fellows.

Money Fellows

ROSCAs have existed in Egypt for a long time, where they are known as Gama'ya. Money Fellows is an innovative digital Gama'ya.

The genesis of Money Fellows can be traced back to the personal experiences of its founder and CEO, Ahmed Wadi. While studying in Germany, Wadi encountered financial difficulties and leveraged the Gama'ya system to manage his finances. This experience inspired him to create a digital platform that would facilitate similar community-based financial support but on a broader scale.

Despite the promise of his idea, Wadi faced significant hurdles in introducing this concept to a German audience, who were unaccustomed to and sceptical of sharing financial details within personal networks. The cultural barriers proved too steep, prompting Wadi to pivot towards markets with a cultural affinity to Gama'yas. He eventually launched Money Fellows in Cairo in 2016, after initial challenges in the UK market as well.

This platform exemplifies how cultural insights, coupled with technological innovation, can transform traditional financial practices into dynamic, scalable solutions.

Money Fellows has created a more sophisticated and safer version of the ROSCA. It is supervised by the Egyptian regulator, the General Authority for Investment (GAFI). It also works with large employers. Some of the key services it provides are:

- **Digital money circles:** Money Fellows allows users to join digital money circles, where they can contribute a certain amount each month. Each member takes turns receiving the total amount contributed by the group, which can be used for various financial needs.
- **Flexible payment options:** The platform offers multiple payment methods, including credit card, salary deduction, direct debit, Fawry payments (a leading digital payments services platform in Egypt) and cash collection, catering to the diverse needs of its users.
- **Guaranteed payouts:** Money Fellows guarantees payout dates and amounts, ensuring that users receive their money even if other members are late or miss their payments.
- **Smart credit scoring:** The platform employs a smart credit scoring system that allows users to build their creditworthiness over time, unlocking higher payout amounts.
- **Corporate benefits:** Employees of corporate partners can enjoy additional benefits, making the platform attractive for businesses looking to offer financial solutions to their workforce.

Money Fellows has primarily operated in four major Egyptian cities: Cairo, Alexandria, Mansoura and Damietta. Looking ahead, the company is preparing for both local and international growth. As Money Fellows is fully Shariah compliant, targeting Muslim countries could be a very smart strategy. In an interview in early 2024 the founder, Ahmed Wadi, said, 'Saudi and Morocco are the two most exciting countries that we're looking into now, I believe by the end of this year, we'd definitely be at least in one of them.'[6] In the near future we can be sure to find digital ROSCAs in many more countries.

Affordable regional cross-border payments

Whenever payments in the developing world are discussed, the focus seems to be on remittances, described as sending money from developed countries to less developed ones. Remittances is a relatively well-served segment addressed by many successful challengers like Remitly, Currency Cloud and WorldRemit, and incumbents such as Moneygram and Western Union. The segment that is still woefully underdeveloped is cross-border payments within developing countries. One of the more interesting businesses in this sector is ChipperCash, serving Sub-Saharan Africa.

ChipperCash

The concept at the centre of the ChipperCash proposition is that cross-border payments often operate in corridors, and one of the least-served corridors is the one connecting the largest economies in Africa.

The business was founded in 2018 by Ham Serunjogi and Maijid Moujaled, who recognized the need for more affordable and efficient cross-border payment solutions in Africa. It has five million registered users in seven countries, including Uganda, Ghana and Nigeria, with operations also in the USA and UK. It offers not only low-cost money transfers but bill payment, crypto trading and the ability to buy US stocks. Excluding crypto transactions, ChipperCash took in more than $75 million in revenue in 2021, compared with $18 million in 2020.

ChipperCash was one of the most successful African unicorns, being valued at $2.2 billion in November 2021 and was able to boast investors such as Jeff Bezos's Bezos Expeditions. The years after 2021 were not too favourable to it, following the global fintech valuations slump of 2022. Like many businesses in the industry, it had to go through major restructuring while continuing its growth trajectory, but with much leaner organizations having closed both their expensive US and UK operations. ChipperCash co-founders reiterated in 2024 that Chipper is 'doing well' and is looking ambitiously to the future.[7]

Access to financial education

One of the most common causes of financial exclusion is often identified as a lack of financial education. Put simply, this is not knowing what financial product to look for, not knowing how banking and finance can help and, of course, thinking that banks are too expensive or even dangerous. These attitudes and mindsets are due to lack of information (and sometimes misinformation) – fintech firms are well positioned to help.

Financial education fintechs have different splinter groups. The major ones are:

- **Youth education:** Focusing on the young, potential financial services customers, aimed at demystifying and explaining the banks' offerings.
- **Unbanked and underbanked education:** These are activities undertaken by financial services providers aimed at helping users make smarter decisions with their money.

An interesting example of youth education-based fintech is Greenlight in the USA, which is educating young people on banking by working with their parents.

Greenlight

Greenlight was founded to help young people understand how finance works. According to CNBC, a recent survey revealed that 83 per cent of US residents believe that it is the parents' responsibility to teach children about finance. In the same survey 31 per cent of surveyed parents said that they have never spoken about finance with their kids.[8] In another survey, 73 per cent of teens said they wanted more financial education. So to address this issue Greenlight created an app to be shared between parents and their children so that they can be introduced to finance in a gradual, monitored manner. Its offering provides a prepaid card that children can use instead of cash. The card is loaded with cash by the parents.

Greenlight also provides a number of services to help kids understand basic services like saving and investing – although no credit product is yet in the pipeline. It allows children to save (earning interest) and even invest – again under full supervision of the parents. In 2023 it also launched a product aimed at helping teenagers build a credit history to support them in the future.

It is also partnering with banks to enable them to offer their Greenlight account for children that would normally not be eligible for a standard bank account. As of mid-2024, the company boasted over six million users, comprising both parents and children.

Greenlight has successfully raised a total of $556.5 million over six funding rounds. The latest funding round was a Series D that raised $260 million in April 2021, led by Andreessen Horowitz. This funding round nearly doubled Greenlight's valuation to $2.3 billion. The company has seen rapid growth, more than tripling its year-over-year revenue. However, Greenlight was affected by the global fintech contraction, and laid off 20 per cent of its staff in 2023 to address concerns on operating costs.

PayTM Money

Financial education of the unbanked and underbanked is the most complex area to tackle by fintechs, but several are doing a good job, nevertheless. One market that is showing a great promise with fintechs educating the underbanked is India.

PayTM Money is a division of the renowned PayTM banking service provider. It delivers a seamless mobile app experience, offering investment and wealth management services. With a focus on user education, it provides comprehensive resources and tools to demystify various investment avenues and financial planning strategies. These include the PayTM Financial Literacy Programme, a volunteering initiative through the PayTM Foundation aimed at empowering women with financial knowledge; and the PayTM Wealth Academy is a fin-ed-tech providing webinars covering various financial topics in multiple languages.

PayTM is a leading Indian payments app. It serves over 20 million merchants and businesses and over 300 million consumers. Its aim is to bring 500 million unserved and underserved Indians to the mainstream economy.

PayTM has been backed by major investors such as Alibaba, SoftBank and Berkshire Hathaway, and went public in 2021 with India's largest IPO at the time. However, in 2024 it faced regulatory challenges, particularly with its payments bank operations, leading to a strategic shift towards new banking partnerships to ensure continuity and compliance.

BANKIT

BANKIT's stated mission is to address the financial needs of the underbanked and unbanked segments of the population, particularly in India's rural and semi-urban locales by creating an intuitive mobile app and network of correspondents and agents that act similarly to how bank branches used to do in urban setting. The company strives to offer a limited range of products that are simple, clearly understood by the end-user and delivered digitally. It sees itself as a B2B2C business, where the second B is its agents. The network of over 70,000 correspondents and 50,000 agents plays a pivotal role in explaining how these products operate, stopping short of providing financial advice.[9]

At its core, BANKIT is driven by a vision of financial inclusivity, striving to equip every Indian with easy-to-use, affordable banking and financial solutions through cutting-edge fintech capabilities. The delivery of these services through correspondents and agents addresses the lack of bank branches in rural areas. Could technology be the best way to deliver financial services through direct person-to-person interactions innovatively and efficiently? The success of its model seems to suggest the answer is yes.

Access to religiously compliant finance

One of the issues affecting unbanked communities is the lack of cultural awareness of the banks' offerings, especially when addressing the needs of communities that have special moral, ethical or religious needs. The most compelling and complex of these situations is how to deliver modern financial products that are compliant with Islamic law.[10]

In keeping with the requirements of the Quran, some practising Muslims are unable to benefit from some of the most common bank services like borrowing or receiving interest. To address this issue Shariah-compliant banks do not charge interest but use equity participation systems instead – these are a form of profit sharing with the borrower. When a Shariah-compliant bank lends money to a business, the business will pay back the loan without interest and instead give the bank a share of its profits. If the business defaults or doesn't earn a profit, then the bank also doesn't get paid. Also, any investments involving items or substances forbidden in the Quran – including alcohol, gambling and pork – are prohibited.

Not being able to access Shariah banking products forces certain communities to be underbanked. Several fintech companies have found ways of using technology to address this issue.

Nomo

UK-based Nomo Bank is one of the first completely digital Shariah-compliant digital banks in the world established as part of the Bank of London and the Middle East plc (BLME), which is a subsidiary of Boubyan Bank from Kuwait. Nomo combines traditional Islamic banking principles with modern digital banking technologies. It provides a quality digital banking offering to the Shariah-compliant community of the UK.

Overall, Nomo represents a blend of Islamic banking principles and modern financial technology, aimed at providing a seamless banking experience for people who need to manage their finances in a Shariah-compliant manner. It is an example of an established player using technology to reach a set of customers with specialist financial needs quickly and effectively.

Zoya

Zoya is a US-based business designed for investing, enabling users to find Shariah-compliant stocks and exchange traded funds (ETFs).

Its app is a non-custodial platform that offers the means for portfolio tracking, Zakat calculation, and connects users with a community of Muslim investors (Zakat is an Islamic finance product referring to the obligation that an individual must donate a certain proportion of wealth each year to charitable causes).[11]

To ensure adherence to Islamic ethical standards, Zoya utilizes the Accounting and Auditing Organization for Islamic Financial Institutions (AAOIFI) screening methodology and consults with Shariah advisors. AAOIFI is provided by a Bahrain-based not-for-profit organization specifically established to maintain and promote Shariah standards for Islamic financial institutions, participants and the overall industry.

Zoya has over 200,000 investors using its platform and through its integration with a number of global brokers it is able to operate in 30 countries including the USA, Canada and the UK.

Pfida

Pfida is an ethical fintech company that provides finance products and services designed to be fair, equitable and free from debt and interest, adhering to Shariah-compliant and halal principles. It has created several creative solutions that enable Shariah-compliant individuals to access financial services. It offers:

- **Home financing:** It offers a mortgage replacement product that is based on a partnership model where the buyer contributes a minimum of 15 per cent equity and Pfida helps finance the rest.[12]
- **Savings:** Pfida provides various savings accounts that offer ethical returns by investing in property purchases that help people own homes debt-free.
- **Investment:** Investors become shareholders in a ring-fenced entity, Pfida Finance PLC, which owns the assets directly.

Overall, Pfida's mission is to reshape the finance world by providing alternatives to conventional banking methods that often lead to debt. Its products are designed to be beneficial, fair and accessible to all, promoting a more ethical and equitable financial environment.

Fintechs need to redesign banking for the unbanked

Fintechs are increasingly adopting a customer-centric approach to enhance financial inclusion by focusing on the specific needs and barriers faced by underserved or excluded groups. This approach will not only increase loyalty and market share, but it will also address the fundamental issues that contribute to financial exclusion. Here's how fintechs are implementing customer-centric strategies to foster financial inclusion.

Understanding and addressing specific barriers

Fintechs begin by identifying the barriers that lead to financial exclusion, such as a lack of internet access, the absence of a valid government ID, inadequate credit scores, high fees or poor financial literacy. By understanding what is lacking, fintechs can develop targeted solutions that address these specific barriers, potentially through new distribution channels, innovative technologies or new business models.

Customer segmentation

Instead of adopting a one-size-fits-all approach, fintechs need to focus on defined unbanked and underbanked customer segments. This segmentation involves dividing potential users based on characteristics that reflect their specific financial needs and the barriers they face. This tailored approach allows for the development of personalized products and services that are more likely to meet the unique needs of each segment, thereby enhancing financial inclusion.

Utilizing human-centred design

Human-centred design (HCD) is a framework that integrates the human perspective in all steps of the problem-solving process. Fintechs use HCD to ensure that their products and services are designed with a deep understanding of their customers' lives and financial needs. This approach helps in creating solutions that are not only effective but also user-friendly and relevant to the target audience. This is a fundamental distinguishing factor when the targeted segment is a minority.

Fintechs are committed to inclusivity, ensuring that their services are accessible to all, including those with limited access to traditional banking facilities. This involves creating user-friendly interfaces that cater to people with varying levels of financial literacy and digital skills.

Applying the jobs-to-be-done framework

The jobs-to-be-done (JTBD) framework focuses on understanding the customer's needs in terms of the 'jobs' they are trying to get done when they use a service or product. This framework helps fintechs to design solutions that are precisely aligned with what customers aim to achieve, thereby increasing the usefulness and adoption of financial services. This also reduces unnecessary complexity and costs.

By utilizing advanced technologies, fintechs can lower the cost of delivering financial services, making them more accessible to a broader audience. This is particularly important for reaching low-income individuals who may not be able to afford traditional financial services.

Fintechs continuously gather feedback from their users to refine and improve their offerings. This iterative process ensures that the financial products and services evolve in response to the changing needs and circumstances of their customers, thereby maintaining relevance and effectiveness.

Conclusion

By adopting more customer-centric strategies, fintechs are not only enhancing their business performance but are also playing a crucial role in reducing financial exclusion and enabling more people to access essential financial services. This approach is fundamental in creating a more inclusive financial ecosystem that supports the broader economic empowerment of underserved communities.

Notes

1 Fintech News Singapore (2021) Vietnam, Philippines, Indonesia among top 10 most unbanked countries in the world. fintechnews.sg/53303/financial-inclusion/vietnam-philippines-indonesia-among-top-10-most-unbanked-countries-in-the-world (archived at https://perma.cc/FH48-HNAS)
2 Mizuho Financial Group (2023) Mizuho Bank supports MoMo, Vietnam's leading financial platform. www.mizuhogroup.com/digital/momo (archived at https://perma.cc/TZ23-3SGJ)
3 Worldpay (nd) *Global Payments Report 2024*, Worldpay. worldpay.globalpaymentsreport.com/en (archived at https://perma.cc/PK24-HLEQ)
4 Media Feature (2024) Grow Credit expands banking relationship with Wells Fargo to support its financial inclusion capabilities, Newsfile. www.newsfilecorp.com/release/194930/Grow-Credit-Expands-Banking-Relationship-with-Wells-Fargo-to-Support-Its-Financial-Inclusion-Capabilities (archived at https://perma.cc/R5TW-JE5P)
5 Wagestream.com (2018) Our mission: Improving financial wellbeing for all workers, Wagestream.com (archived at https://perma.cc/8JX2-GBRX)
6 S Khouri (2024) Money fellows founder, Ahmed Wadi, discusses digitizing Egypt's money circles, Forbes Middle East. www.forbesmiddleeast.com/money/fintech/ahmed-wadi (archived at https://perma.cc/78BP-5ZFF)
7 K Abuya (2023) Exclusive: Chipper Cash cuts 15 jobs in fourth round of layoffs, TechCabal. techcabal.com/2023/12/11/chipper-cash-cuts-15-jobs (archived at https://perma.cc/7ZG8-CFND)
8 M Fox (2022) Who should teach kids about money? Americans say parents, but many don't talk to their own children about it: CNBC + Acorns survey, CNBC. www.cnbc.com/2022/04/06/americans-think-parents-should-teach-kids-about-money-yet-many-dont.html (archived at https://perma.cc/G3L5-D3M2)
9 J Jain (2023) BANKIT success story: Banking, financial and payment solutions startup, StartupTalky. startuptalky.com/bankit-success-story (archived at https://perma.cc/8NVH-L7EA)
10 Accounting and Auditing Organization for Islamic Financial Institutions (AAOIFI) (nd) Why practical law? Westlaw. content.next.westlaw.com/practical-law/document/I3f4a4355e8db11e398db8b09b4f043e0/Accounting-Auditing-Organization-for-Islamic-Financial-Institutions-AAOIFI (archived at https://perma.cc/4AGJ-MWQE)
11 D Liberto (2008) Zakat: The basic rules for one of the five pillars of Islam, Investopedia. www.investopedia.com/terms/z/zakat.asp (archived at https://perma.cc/82R4-GMXC)
12 Pfida (2024) Apply for halal mortgage. Pfida.com (archived at https://perma.cc/HH2D-5K7A)

9

Open banking and APIs

Introduction

Open banking, open finance and open APIs are the technical building blocks to solving financial inclusion by creating innovative, easy-to-access and lower-cost financial services products and advice through data sharing, payment innovations and building upon open APIs from financial institutions.

In this chapter we will explore the three concepts of open banking, open finance and open APIs by providing a definition of each, identifying how each has improved financial inclusion, reviewing the challenges and/or limitations and exploring a selection of tangible use cases in the retail and micro, small and medium enterprises (MSME) sectors.

Open banking and open finance

At a conceptual level, open banking is the exchange of payment account data between financial institutions and third-party providers (TPPs) with a customer's consent, via APIs. According to the European Commission's Mairead McGuinness, 'the purpose of sharing our financial information is to give us access to new and different services based on the information we share'.[1]

This is echoed by Open Banking Limited, which defines open banking as 'a secure and simple way to help you understand your finances more effectively – from borrowing to savings, from credit scores to switching – and inform your financial decision-making', with many regulators sharing a similar definition.[2]

The Saudi Arabian Markets and Authority (SAMA) states, 'Open banking is a banking practice to enable customers of financial institutions to share their financial data securely with third-party providers, which in turn provide new and innovative financial services and products for customers.'[3] Another facet of open banking is payment initiation or account-to-account payments. With payment initiation services, customers can connect their banks and authorize a third-party provider to pay directly from their accounts. They are safer and cost less than a card payment.

Open banking refers to distinct definitions at the national or regional regulatory level. Around the globe, regulators are establishing open banking frameworks, mandates and guidelines to standardize and facilitate data exchange between banks and TPPs, or fintechs, and approaches tend to be regulatory-driven or market-driven. Open banking regulation generally focuses on account information access, with payment initiation regulation as a further stage in promoting innovation and fostering competition.

Suppose open banking is exclusive to payment account data. In that case, open finance is about sharing 'other' data, such as sales and expense data from SMEs, investment data from retail consumers, insurance data for consumers and SMEs, and pension data from consumers. Furthermore, open finance encompasses sharing this 'other' financial data with non-banking, fintech or regulated TPPs. For example, a consumer is looking to secure a rental contract. To prove their net or gross salary, they can share their payment account data with a non-regulated platform, such as a rental platform or agency.

Challenges and considerations

A core challenge of open banking is data standardization. While far from perfect in many markets, the ambition to standardize user data allows fintechs playing in the lending and savings spaces to serve their customers through streamlined data. Furthermore, standardized data and data-sharing protocols lower the barrier for fintechs to enter a market, creating greater competition and allowing them to offer products and services where traditional banks have failed or are underserved.

As previously discussed, at the heart of open banking and open finance is the ability for a user to share their payment account or other financial data. This inherently makes the impact of open banking in its current form negligible for the unbanked but potentially groundbreaking for the underbanked. According to CGAP:

> a recent UK report found that those 'on the margins' of financial inclusion (with no account or only a basic account) are likely to pay less in fees with open banking – saving the equivalent of 0.8 per cent of their income. Open banking would save those who are 'overstretched' (with account(s) and heavily indebted) the equivalent of 2.5 percent of their income.[4]

The educational component of open banking also poses a significant challenge for supporting the underbanked, specifically around consent and data management. Most open banking consumers are younger, digitally savvy individuals with high financial literacy. More must be done to promote awareness and education and ensure users can trust open banking and finance-powered services and companies, especially those who are underbanked and lacking financial literacy. The incentives need to be explicitly called out for underbanked individuals to trust these services to access the benefits. Consent information, specifically how to manage consent and outlining what data is being shared, needs to be communicated in a simple-to-digest manner.

Open APIs outside open banking

Open banking regulation and market-driven open banking are not prerequisites for third parties to build products and services via consuming banking APIs. In fact, before and in the absence of regulation of open banking, the supply and demand of APIs from traditional banks has been a catalyst for innovation and fintech development, shaping a mature, open finance ecosystem. This is especially true in Southeast Asia where traditional banks in Singapore, Indonesia and beyond offer extensive API catalogues, via developer portals or API marketplaces that allow fintechs, telcos, super apps and other providers to create products and services utilizing payment rails, ATM networks, account opening, cards and other services.

The opening up and consumption of APIs provide the greatest opportunity for inclusive fintech and serving both under- and unbanked customers. According to Florent Ogoutchoro, founder of Moneex, 'The power of open banking in Africa goes beyond the regulation of payment account information and is found in the provision of new products for underserved customer segments. The first wave of fintech in Africa focused on B2B, but now we see more fintechs using bank and telco APIs to build new products and services.'[5] Djiba Diallo, Ecobank's fintech lead, believes within Africa a critical part of an open banking strategy allows third parties to build on top of banks' infrastructure. She stated, 'It's about connecting the bank's services or enabling fintechs to connect with the bank's services, be it for enabling payment, be it for collecting money, [opening] accounts or to create tokens to withdraw money on our ATMs.'[6]

The telco or mobile money operator, a historically key player in fighting financial inclusion in Africa and other markets, could unlock the power of open banking and APIs in driving financial inclusion. Ogoutchoro states that 'open banking in Africa may not always look like open banking in Europe. Most Africans have a mobile money account rather than a bank account. Mobile money providers should open up their APIs.'

With additional banks opening their APIs, telcos can continue to partner with established banks to offer products and services beyond payments and accounts, such as savings and loans. Beyond Africa, the case for allowing non-banking brands and companies already serving the informal economies, rural areas and unbanked to create regulated financial services via consuming bank APIs is also valid.

Use cases and case studies exploring how fintechs and non-bank entities use traditional banks' APIs are explored in other chapters, specifically in Chapter 9.

Selected use cases and case studies

Use case 1: Personal finance management – subscription monitoring, wage advances, budgeting, micro-investing, accounts transparency

One of the primary pockets of innovation from open banking is providing services to help users better manage their finances. By aggregating one or more payment accounts within these fintechs, customers can obtain a comprehensive view of all their financial data. Furthermore, these fintechs typically provide tips, recommendations and rules to manage their spending habits better and facilitate the creation and management of savings goals. A handful of providers go one step further by offering 'round-ups' on transactions and 'squirrel' this money into a low-cost exchange-traded fund (ETF), bringing individuals who cannot afford the minimum deposit for traditional brokerages into the investment space.

An evolving use case under open-banking-powered money management is receiving a pay-day advance if the app or platform detects the user may run out of funds before their next pay check. For users living pay cheque to pay cheque, an unexpected cost or bill can harm their financial health. Furthermore, these customers are often caught in a cash-rich and cash-poor cycle, depending on the day of the month and how this aligns with their payday. Historically, underbanked customers faced expensive alternatives, namely payday loans, one of the most predatory lending methods because they have high fees and short repayment terms.

Australian fintech Beforepay uses account aggregation via open APIs powered by Basiq to 'detect pay schedules and expenses'. Once a user connects their bank account, Beforepay analyses the transaction history to determine when a user gets paid and what they spend. The user then indicates how much they need, with a maximum of

$2,000 of the user's wages. The user pays a 5 per cent fixed transaction fee and can repay the amount in up to four pay cycles. In addition to a payday advance, Beforepay also helps users understand their income and spending habits and provides bespoke budgets based on their account transaction history.

Another use case for open banking to help the financially vulnerable is in the overdraft prevention, subscription and bill monitoring and reduction spaces. In the UK, overdrafts before 2021 were often predatory products for the unbanked and financially vulnerable. According to the FCA, 'overdrafts offer a convenient way to help some people manage temporary cash flow issues. But some banks were charging more than 80 per cent APR (annual percentage rate) on arranged overdrafts, once fees and charges were factored in.'[7]

One fintech operating in this space is Snoop, a free money management and budgeting tool, allowing UK users to track their spending, reduce the amount spent on bills and control finances. One of the core features of Snoop is the ongoing bill-tracking feature. By aggregating existing current accounts and credit cards, users can understand how their monthly subscription services and bills compare month on month and access special offers and a dedicated switching service. Snoop also uses past and upcoming account and credit card data to warn users when they cannot cover a bill, helping them avoid late payments and overdraft fees. Snoop also provides money-saving services and tips without aggregating a bank account.

Emma helps users avoid going into overdraft and find and cancel subscriptions. Emma also allows users to track debt and save money. Emma has 1.6 million customers in the UK and expanded its product offering to support boosting a user's credit history by reporting rent payments.

Use case 2: Faster, cheaper, targeted lending for consumers, MSMEs and SMEs

Perhaps one of the most exciting use cases for open banking is the impact of providing access to credit for underbanked individuals and micro-businesses or SMEs. Through open banking, lenders can access

TABLE 9.1 Selected personal finance management, savings, payday lending, and micro-investing fintechs

Fintech	Market	USP (according to the provider's public website or Crunchbase)	Website
Beforepay	Australia	Transparent salary advances with tailored budgets and education.	beforepay.com.au
Cleo	UK	AI is fighting for the world's financial health, providing personalized advice and products.	meetcleo.com
Deciml	India	Allows users to round up online transactions made via UPI or other online payment methods.	deciml.in
Emma	UK	Financial app advocates to help users avoid overdrafts and wasteful subscriptions and control their finances.	emma-app.com
Opportun	USA	A finance app that analyses your spending habits and automatically saves the perfect daily amount.	oportun.com
Pearler	Australia	Low-cost ETFs and share trading automatically roundup and invest spare change from purchases.	pearler.com
Piggyvest	Nigeria	A savings app that allows users to save money for specific goals. It uses open banking to connect users' bank accounts and automatically transfers money to their savings goals.	piggyvest.com
Plum	UK, Europe	Personal savings assistant solutions for customers.	withplum.com
Trim	USA	Analyses transaction data and negotiates better utility deals.	asktrim.com

real-time financial data from applicants, allowing them to better understand a retail customer's financial standing, including critical data points such as income, expenditure and business sales, expenses and capital expenditure. This data has the power to provide more accurate and personalized lending products, providing greater accuracy and richness than traditional credit bureaus.

Open banking data also allows lenders to better mitigate risk with existing loans, allowing them to pre-emptively support customers who may struggle to make repayments. This is especially critical for low-income borrowers who are establishing their credit history, a large cohort in several developed and developing markets. For example:

- Nineteen per cent of American adults do not have a conventional credit score. This includes 28 million adult Americans who are credit invisible and 21 million who are unscoreable. An additional 57 million have subprime or below credit score.[8] Open banking and APIs can reduce this number by utilizing existing transaction history from their bank account rather than relying on traditional credit bureaus.
- The Central Bank of Nigeria estimates that the MSME funding gap is 48 trillion Naira ($62 billion). Regardless of the market, MSMEs and SMEs are underserved regarding access to credit because of limited credit history, poor credit rating and operating in informal economies. MSMEs and SMEs can access quicker, more personalized capital by sharing sales and financial information in several clicks.
- Within Southeast Asia, a funding gap is faced by 39 million of over 70 million MSMEs, estimated to be worth as much as $300 billion. According to the Center for Impact Investment and Practices, the primary challenges Southeast Asian MSMEs and SMEs face for financing include a lack of collateral, scarce transaction history and inadequate record keeping. Here, as well as in Africa and Latin America, open finance can play a critical role by extracting data from non-banking providers, namely telecom providers.[9]
- One example of a fintech using open APIs is Autochek, an African fintech operational in Nigerian and Ghana that makes it easier for people to get auto loans and carry out servicing and transactions around automobiles. They partner with Okra, which provides open APIs, allowing Autochek to verify customers' identities, ascertain their creditworthiness based on bank account data and facilitate loan payments. Using the Okra APIs, Autochek has

reduced the time to loan processing from one week to one day. Core to this reduction is the ability for Autochek to verify a user's bank statements digitally rather than requiring the customers to visit a branch to print and certify statements. The service is available to consumers, MSMEs and SMEs.

- In Chile, Floid, an open banking and finance provider with the ambition to 'change the information market to make it more inclusive' partnered with Banco Estado, a traditional bank with over 13 million customers, to launch an open finance solution to better assess the risk of SMEs that apply for loans with the Guarantee Fund for Small and Medium Enterprises, also known as Fogape. The scheme is an economic support measure to support MSME and SMES in refinancing debts.

TABLE 9.2 Selected fintechs powering open banking lending

Fintech	Market	USP (according to the provider's public website or Crunchbase)	Website
Abound	UK	Provides affordable loans based on transaction history instead of credit bureaus.	getabound.com
Autochek	Pan-Africa	Transparent salary advances with tailored budgets and education.	autochek.africa/ng
Indicina	Nigeria	Leverages open banking to help banks and lenders better understand their customers through the credit risk lifecycle.	indicina.co
Kontomatik	Central and Eastern Europe	Offers an open banking API enriched with analysis based on machine learning, providing lenders with the latest comprehensive view of clients' financial capacity, discipline, behaviour and more.	kontomatik.com
Tink	Europe	API provides real-time access to consumers' bank data to make better-informed credit and risk assessments.	tink.com

Use case 3: Making onboarding easier

A nascent use case in open banking is quicker, fully digital and less costly customer onboarding completed via using account information access and small payment initiation to fulfil KYC requirements. When a person or a legal entity provides account information access via open APIs or open banking, the user shares basic details of the user such as full name, date of birth, sources of wealth and transactional data. KYC and anti-money laundering (AML) specialists and software can use this data to fulfil their KYC and AML requirements to complete the onboarding of a new customer or entity.

By providing fully digital onboarding experiences and leveraging existing bank account data, customers or entities looking for new or complementary financial services providers can achieve easier, quicker access to platforms and products. In rural areas or for customers with lower financial literacy, the ability to simply 'share' existing financial and personal data via an open API to access more financial products and services is a potential game-changer.

Similarly to other use cases, this benefit can only serve those customers with an existing banking relationship. However, exploring this use case for the underbanked demonstrates huge potential in an open finance ecosystem should open banking and KYC/AML regulation expand to include telecom, social media, mobile money and other data types for formal identification.

One example of a fintech offering a fully compliant open banking-powered onboarding API is Klarna Kosma. It offers a range of open banking-powered products, including account verification and consumer identification. Via its APIs, Klarna Kosma allows any organization onboarding new customers in the EU to provide secure and compliant customer identification via open banking. The Kosma ID AML combines digital user ID and additional digital services to provide real-time digital identification.

Use case 4: Personalized insurance for retailers, MSMEs and SMEs

The case for using open banking to provide more personalized, relevant insurance coverage spans the retail, MSME and SME segments.

The MSME space is particularly ripe for innovation and could serve as a critical area for financially excluded individuals to protect their livelihoods better. The need is especially strong in markets heavily dependent upon agriculture and prone to extreme weather.

Insurance coverage of MSMEs tends to be low. For example, in Nigeria, where MSMEs comprise over 96 per cent of businesses and 84 per cent of employment, only 0.5 per cent of MSMEs have insurance coverage for events such as fire and flooding.[10] Traditional insurance products often have an analogue application process, requiring tedious information that wastes time for MSME owners to run their businesses. An opportunity for MSMEs to share their data around their financials, sales and geolocation data can pave the way for quicker and perhaps less costly insurance products.

Open banking APIs can allow insurance TPPs to access real-time data on a business's financial transactions, revenue and other relevant metrics to assess risk better and offer tailored insurance products that meet the specific needs of MSMEs – products such as fire, theft or flood insurance, health insurance for employees or other types of business interruption insurance. In addition, insurance TPPs could further customize underwriting by using factors such as type of business, geolocation data and other non-conventional data sources to ensure that the business gets the best rate possible. Applying this to the open finance space, underwriting can use non-financial data such as mobile app behaviour, harvest data and agronomic data to better serve those customers without a credit history or traditional bank account and subsequent transaction data.

Inspiration can be taken from the retail insurance space, particularly the partnership between Yapily and Certua. An embedded insurance enabler, Certua aims to create financial resilience by supporting brands and partners to embed innovative insurance products. By partnering with Yapily, a regulated TPP, Certua can use a customer's bank account information to access an individual's financial position and feed this into their underwriting for more accurate and personalized policies and recommendations. From the customer perspective, access to more relevant policies and products, in addition to the time reduction in providing data, allows those typically underserved to quickly and easily access the right products to protect their livelihoods or families.

Going beyond 'banking data'

While open banking holds immense potential in solving financial inclusion, the impact relies on users having basic access to a bank account. Open banking regulation is a technology primarily supporting the underbanked rather than the unbanked. However, this impact on the underbanked population has the potential to span across almost every financial product across retail, MSME and SME segments.

On the other hand, open APIs are increasingly becoming the building blocks of fintech and innovation within digital financial services. Combined with progressive regulation regarding KYC and AML, it can catalyse financial inclusion. Traditional banks offering access to their APIs via a developer portal or marketplace provide the basics to banking that could power fintechs to bring the unbanked into the financial services space. APIs focused on onboarding, basic accounts and local payments can allow digital fintechs and agency banking players to offer a digital tool for the unbanked.

In traditionally under- and unbanked markets, the mobile phone has become a catalyst for payments and financial inclusion. The next chapter will explore how traditional banks, banking-as-a-service and embedded finance companies harness open APIs to provide the regulatory, technological and product building blocks for innovative fintechs and brands to create digital tools to mitigate financial excursion.

TABLE 9.3 Open banking companies (for- and non-profit organizations)

Organization	Location	Objective	Website
CGAP	Global	CGAP is a global partnership of more than 30 leading development organizations that works to advance the lives of impoverished people, especially women, through financial inclusion.	cgap.org

(continued)

TABLE 9.3 (Continued)

Organization	Location	Objective	Website
Open Banking Exchange	Global	OBE helps regulators, self-regulated organizations and national communities implement effective, interoperable open solutions based on jurisdiction-neutral technology frameworks.	www.developmentaid.org/organizations/view/484602/obe-open-banking-europe-sas
Open Banking Limited	UK	The Implementation Entity described in the CMA Order provides the trusted framework to connect banks, fintechs, and technical providers.	openbanking.org.uk
Open Banking Nigeria	Nigeria	Backed by the Open Technology Foundation, an NGO, it builds a set of open API standards for banking in Nigeria by driving innovation and choice for customers, businesses, fintech companies, and banks with next-gen API standards.	openbanking.ng
Open Banking Project/TESOBE	Global	The leading open-source API solution for the financial services industry. They assist banks in executing effective API strategies by providing a battle-tested, feature-rich, and flexible API platform and an expert team of advisors.	tesobe.com

(continued)

TABLE 9.3 (Continued)

Organization	Location	Objective	Website
Open Banking Tracker	Global	Mapping the open finance and banking ecosystem, tracking 3,400+ banks, TPPs, regulations, use cases and open banking APIs.	openbankingtracker.com
Open Finance Brasil	Brazil	Information and directory for consumers, developers and participants from Banco do Brasil.	openfinancebrasil.org.br
Ozone API		Ozone API empowers banks and financial institutions to adapt and thrive in the new world of open finance. We provide technology that delivers compliant open APIs and goes beyond monetizing open banking globally.	ozoneapi.com

TABLE 9.4 B2B open banking/open API fintechs

Organization	Location(s)	USP (according to the provider's public website or Crunchbase)	Website
Banfico	Global	Plug-and-play open banking SaaS for regulatory compliance. Enterprise API platform complies with global open banking regulatory standards, and Banfico provide end-to-end delivery.	banfico.com
Basiq	Australia	An aggregation platform for acquiring financial data that provides access to financial institutions through APIs.	basiq.io
Floid	Latin America	An open data platform in Latin America, empowering people and companies to own their data for financial inclusion.	floid.ai/en/home
Moneyhub	UK	A data and payments fintech that provides open banking, open finance and open data solutions.	moneyhub.com

(continued)

TABLE 9.4 (Continued)

Organization	Location(s)	USP (according to the provider's public website or Crunchbase)	Website
Mono	Africa	Mono helps businesses to access high-quality financial data and direct bank payments. APIs power lending, financial management, account verification and payments.	mono.co
Okra	Nigeria	Access to financial data from banks and beyond with a single API to build financial products.	okra.ng
PayStack	Global, Nigeria	Modern online and offline payments for Africa. Paystack helps businesses in Africa get paid by anyone, anywhere in the world.	paystack.com
Plaid	Global	A data transfer network that powers fintech and digital finance products. Plaid's product, a technology platform, enables applications to connect with users' bank accounts.	plaid.com/en-eu
Prometeo	Latin America	API provides access to banking information and payment initiation in 10 countries in Latin America.	prometeoapi.com
SaltEdge	Global	API solutions enable access to 5,000+ banks globally.	saltedge.com
Stich	South Africa	A single, powerful, reliable API built on direct integrations with multiple banks and networks across South Africa, meticulously crafted to help businesses move money better and reach their goals faster.	stitch.money
Tarabut	MENA	MENA's first and largest regulated open banking platform (AISP and PISP) that connects a regional network of banks and fintechs via APIs.	tarabut.com
Token.io	UK, Europe	Account-to-account payment infrastructure powered by open banking.	token.io
TrueLayer	UK, Europe	Built off open banking, TrueLayer provides a payment network that connects banks, people, and brands across the UK and Europe.	truelayer.com
Yapily	UK, Europe	Connect to thousands of banks across 19 countries in minutes through Yapily's open banking API.	yapily.com

Notes

1. European Commission (2024) Keynote speech by Commissioner McGuinness at event in European Parliament 'From open banking to open finance: What does the future hold?'. ec.europa.eu/commission/presscorner/detail/en/SPEECH_23_1819 (archived at https://perma.cc/YKK7-4ETT)
2. Open Banking (nd) How open banking can help consumers. www.openbanking.org.uk/how-open-banking-can-help-consumers (archived at https://perma.cc/KQC5-JCDJ)
3. Saudi Central Bank (nd) KSA open banking program. openbanking.sa/index-en.html (archived at https://perma.cc/SZ9D-LV5K)
4. S Staschen and A Plaitakis (2020) Open banking: 7 ways data-sharing can advance financial inclusion, Cgap. www.cgap.org/blog/open-banking-7-ways-data-sharing-can-advance-financial-inclusion (archived at https://perma.cc/AQJ7-ST5Q)
5. Interview with author.
6. PYMNTS (2022) Open Banking APIs help Africa's mobile money fintechs expand services. www.pymnts.com/api/2022/open-banking-apis-help-africas-mobile-money-fintechs-expand-services (archived at https://perma.cc/M8MG-C5GH)
7. FCA (2023) Millions of customers together save nearly £1 billion due to overdraft rule changes. www.fca.org.uk/news/press-releases/millions-customers-together-save-nearly-1billion-due-overdraft-rule-changes (archived at https://perma.cc/V7ST-4R4L)
8. Experian (2022) Experian and Oliver Wyman find expanded data and advanced analytics can improve access to credit for nearly 50 million credit invisible and unscoreable Americans. www.experianplc.com/newsroom/press-releases/2022/experian-and-oliver-wyman-find-expanded-data-and-advanced-analytics-can-improve-access-to-credit-for-nearly-50-million-credit-invisible-and-unscoreable-americans (archived at https://perma.cc/RZ69-ZNJP)
9. CIIP (2022) First-ever impact-focused Southeast Asian financial inclusion report charts pathways to accelerate impact beyond access. ciip.com.sg/news-centre/media-release/Details/first-ever-impact-focused-southeast-asian-financial-inclusion-report-charts-pathways-to-accelerate-impact-beyond-access (archived at https://perma.cc/JN6D-XCNM)
10. Thisdaylive.com. (2024) Only 0.5 per cent of SMEs in Nigeria operate with insurance cover, says LCCI boss. www.thisdaylive.com/index.php/2022/11/07/only-0-5-of-smes-in-nigeria-operate-with-insurance-cover-says-lcci-boss (archived at https://perma.cc/695Q-PLF9)

10

Banking-as-a-service and embedded finance

Introduction

Banking-as-a-service (BaaS) and embedded finance (EmFi) are two global trends in digital financial services that have dominated innovation and the surge of fintech growth in the past decade. The core value proposition of the BaaS/EmFi model typically means easier access, greater customer centricity and lower costs to financial services, whether they be basic accounts, payments or micro-lending.

In mature markets such as Europe, BaaS and EmFi, like open banking, tend to favour the financially literate and included. Here, we see well-funded fintechs launch niche or entirely digital banking solutions via a BaaS partnership and well-established brands such as Apple, Samsung and others leveraging EmFi solutions to embed financial products into their platforms or hardware.

Looking to Africa, Southeast Asia and Latin America, the success of EmFi has taken place for almost two decades via the agency model approach. Recent partnerships and business models indicate a growing trend amongst commercial banks in Africa and Southeast Asia increasingly looking to take on the role of a BaaS provider, while newly established and existing BaaS and EmFi players in markets such as Nigeria and Indonesia are looking to power the next generation of fintechs to increase financial inclusion.

BaaS and EmFi have the power to reduce financial exclusion due to the inherent nature of the value proposition: lower transaction costs, API-first solutions that can integrate third-party information for a more inclusive KYC and lending process and a speedier, more flexible launch and platform. These benefits can mitigate the existing challenges in serving the un- and underbanked worldwide.

In this chapter we will primarily focus on the role of BaaS and EmFi in solving financial exclusion in Africa and Southeast Asia. We will, however, highlight relevant examples where appropriate in Europe. We will begin by defining both BaaS and EmFi and then deep dive into three approaches by which BaaS and EmFi have the potential to solve the financial inclusion problem. These include:

- BaaS offered by either pure-play BaaS providers or incumbent banks powering fintechs and digital accounts for the financially excluded.
- How agency banking is a quasi-embedded finance model to bring rural populations into financial inclusion.
- The potential embedding of finance into agriculture players to promote financial inclusion.

BaaS and EmFi: What's the difference?

To set the scene for this chapter, it is worth fully defining both BaaS and EmFi. At a rudimentary level, BaaS is when a financially regulated entity provides banking products to non-regulated or regulated entities via APIs. A BaaS offering can range from a complete 'bank in a box' solution, empowering fintechs, to an API marketplace or developer portal offered by a regulated financial institution, initially discussed in Chapter 12.

On the other hand, EmFi integrates a banking product or service into either an existing brand's frontend experience or within their operations. In developed markets this tends to focus on entirely digital solutions, using an API-first approach. However, in developing markets this manifests itself through agency banking and, to an extent, mobile money operators.

To demonstrate the various use cases of BaaS and EmFi, let's take Solaris (formerly Solarisbank), a mature BaaS and EmFi provider in Europe.

Use case 1: The foundation of fintech

Tomorrow, a digital account provider in Germany, targets consumers who want a sustainable financial relationship and partners with Solaris to offer a regulated financial app. Tomorrow cannot refer to itself as a 'bank' and offers investing capabilities as an 'agent' of Solaris. This direct fintech and BaaS model characterized the fintech boom of 2016–22 and is perhaps the most straightforward example of how BaaS can power fintechs.

Use case 2: Complementary business models and products for regulated entities

Financially regulated brands such as American Express and Bitpanda use Solaris to offer financial products and services. This relationship falls under the EmFi model. In the case of American Express, a BNPL solution offered by Solaris is integrated into the American Express platform, and a debit card offered by Solaris is integrated into the Bitpanda platform.

Use case 3: Embedded financial products into non-regulated entities

Solaris also partners with unregulated brands such as Samsung. In the case of Samsung, a debit card and BNPL solution are embedded within the device, providing a rare example of EmFi hardware. It also partners with automobile marketplaces, powering automobile lending branded by the marketplace and leading retailers.

Approaches to mitigating financial exclusion

Traditional BaaS

The traditional BaaS model sees a regulated entity offer the licensing and financial products to non-regulated (or regulated) parties. In general, there are three approaches to traditional BaaS.

The first and most notable are the fintech-first BaaS/EmFis. These original companies, which came to the forefront in the mid-2010s, only operate on a B2B basis, servicing fintechs and increasingly non-financial brands. They do not directly serve end-consumers and tend to be 'API-first'. The second, common in Southeast Asia, is the API portal/marketplace approach. In this model, banks offer product- or service-specific APIs to help fuel a particular product or experience in an application, typically consumed by super-apps and corporates. Some banks, such as BBVA, operate a hybrid approach where, when combined, a suite of APIs can power a fintech to offer an end-to-end regulated product.

Lastly is an approach in which an incumbent bank looks to replicate the fintech-first BaaS models and power fintechs and brands through APIs, allowing consumers of these APIs to passport the bank's licences and product offerings. Within the US and Africa, we tend to see regional and smaller community banks acting as 'sponsor banks' to power fintechs. Usually, the sponsor bank will work with a technical enabler to complete the BaaS offering.

Each model has pros and cons, but in all cases, end consumers must fulfil KYC and AML requirements, which typically involve having an identity document, a registered address and data. Therefore, the BaaS/EmFi models serve the underbanked rather than the unbanked. However, if operating as an agent, fintechs and brands using the BaaS model may have more flexibility in gathering the data required to fulfil customer onboarding requirements. Let's explore a few case studies to understand how this new business model is helping to fight financial exclusion.

Ukheshe

Ukheshe is a BaaS provider operating in 40 markets globally. As 'Africa's fintech enabler', it began its journey in 2018 as a digital platform to improve financial inclusion within South Africa. Today, it provides the technology for incumbent banks to operate a BaaS model. It partners with local or regional banks that 'bring the licence'. In contrast, Ukheshe brings the 'technology', allowing banks to offer a digital product or service for aspiring fintechs or non-financial brands.

In August 2023 it announced a partnership with Diamond Trust Bank (DTB), an East African bank active in Burundi, Kenya, Tanzania and Uganda. A fully regulated BaaS provider will allow fintechs and non-MNOs to compete with the dominant MNOs in the region, bringing more significant innovation competition and naturally supporting the un- and underbanked.[1]

Bloom Money

Bloom Money is a UK-based fintech that offers a digital platform for immigrant communities that traditionally use ROSCAs by providing ethical savings and community support. A ROSCA is an 'informal financial institution consisting of a group of individuals who make set contributions and withdrawals to and from a common fund'.[2] ROSCAs are most common in developing economies and among immigrant groups in the developed world, often used within Muslim countries and amongst women.

The app allows customers in three easy steps to set up a savings circle, add their bank account details and receive the payout when their time arrives. The objective of Bloom is to provide the foundation for helping UK communities build generational wealth.

Bloom partners with AF Payments, a UK-licensed electronic money institution (EMI) that provides payments to several fintechs. An entity operating on the BaaS model with an electronic money licence can offer payment, issuing and electronic money products to 'businesses and their customers seeking an experienced financial institution to assist with providing these solutions'.[3]

Fiberconnect

PT Bina Informatika Solusindo, commonly known as Fiberconnect, emerged in 2014 as an ambitious internet service provider in Indonesia with a mission to revolutionize the ICT industry. Its primary focus is expanding internet access, particularly in remote and underserved regions. In 2022, it integrated with BRIAPI, the API marketplace offered by BRI Bank in Indonesia, demonstrating a fantastic example of using incumbent bank APIs to embed financial products and services.

With over 12,400 villages having zero internet access, the Indonesian Ministry of Communication and Information Technology emphasized accelerating internet penetration. Fiberconnect's target audience consisted mainly of consumers in these remote and inaccessible regions. Initially, customers had to visit Fiberconnect offices for bill payments, a cumbersome and inefficient process for customers and partners. Moreover, the manual payment verification process was very inefficient and prone to errors.

Fiberconnect incorporated three essential BRIAPI products: BRI virtual account (BRIVA), account statement and account information. This integration paved the way for a digital payment system that significantly improved the customer experience. Today, 70 per cent of Fiberconnect's customers prefer BRIVA as their primary payment method, shifting from the need to pay in-store. Beyond customer satisfaction, BRIAPI also streamlined the payment reconciliation processes, reducing the time required for transaction confirmation, verification and reconciliation from 30 minutes to just one minute.[4]

OnePipe

OnePipe, based in Nigeria, is an embedded finance enabler targeting travel and mobility, fast-moving consumer goods (FMCG), fintechs and banks. Currently, the EmFi company offers two core products:

- PaywithTransfer offers virtual cards, accounts and cards.
- Pay4me offers credit products such as inventory finance, asset finance and short-term cash loans. It works with several partner banks which provide financing.

It partners with Motor Africa, a mobility and IoT infrastructure start-up in Nigeria, allowing Motor Africa to embed various products, including overdrafts and insurance. Motor Africa aims to 'help motorists in Africa unlock funding and optimize their mobility services' through access to funding and fleet management. The Motor Card includes credit line and fleet management, such as travel time reports, real-time daily fuel consumption analysis tracking and recommended workshops.

While such partnerships provide much-needed and valuable financing to gig-economy workers in Africa and other markets, economic and supply shocks such as fuel shortages can impact users' ability to make repayments. Edge cases and such macro and market conditions must be considered when launching an EmFi or BaaS solution in emerging or developing markets.

Agency banking

Developed in the mid-2000s to tackle financial exclusion, agency banking allows banks to distribute financial products and services to last-mile customers (or hard-to-reach customers) via permitted or accredited businesses (micro-businesses and SMEs) within their place of business, as opposed to a bank branch or mobile kiosk. While it is not EmFi in the traditional sense, it demonstrates how EmFi can be tailored to under- and unbanked populations.

The agency banking model provides one of the rare cases of embedded finance in a 'phygital' manner or a combination of physical and digital channels. Governments such as Indonesia, Nigeria, Mexico and Brazil promote and regulate the agency model as a means to combat financial inclusion. It is a fantastic example of how technology and a financial inclusion model can be tailored to developing markets.

Globally, agency banking is considered a successful tool to mitigate financial exclusion. In Nigeria, the EFInA Acess to Financial Services study shows that more than half of Nigerian adults (51 per cent) were using formal financial services such as banks, microfinance banks, mobile money, insurance or pension accounts. The 51 per cent was an increase from 49 per cent in 2018. In LATAM, Brazil maintains a network of agents that covers more than 99 per cent of the country's municipalities.[5]

BRI Indonesia

Indonesia's largest bank and microfinance institution, BRI, developed BRILink, an agency model aimed at servicing BRI customers who cannot easily access BRI branches via individual agents. The agents are customers of BRI and are selected based on their history with microloans. Agents serve customers with digital solutions, including card-reading machines and mobile apps. The agent's role is twofold: first, to gain customers' trust and demonstrate the benefits and safety of using digital channels for transactions; and second, to identify new entry-level borrowers and process financial transactions such as payments, loan installments and savings deposits.

Agents receive a commission and naturally see more footfall in their shops. The government of Indonesia has set a goal to obtain 90 per cent financial inclusion by 2024, which puts a special focus on agents of BRILink, viewing these agents as the drivers of Indonesia's economic strength and MSME development. The number of BRILink agents reached more than 503,000 with 929 million transactions in 2021, with the number of agents at the end of 2021 increasing to 600,000. BRILink agents recorded a strong performance in April 2022, with the sales volume reaching 433.75 trillion Indonesian rupiah ($29.59 billion) – an increase of 40.04 per cent compared to a sales volume of 309.73 trillion Indonesian rupiah ($21.13 billion) the previous month.[6]

A second initiative from BRI, which embeds financial services to support the financially excluded, is the partnership with Pegadaian, Indonesia's largest pawn lender, and PNM, Indonesia's largest group lender. The partnership aims to empower women, coming together to form one of the world's largest microfinance institutions, with a remit to bring 30 million customers out of poverty in four years. Pegadaian has over 18,000 branches across Indonesia and supports MSMEs, SMEs, farmers, fishermen and wet market traders to access financial services.

Agriculture

One primary cause of the significantly under- or unbanked population, is the lack of data on potential customers and consistent income. This holds especially true in rural populations, where industries like agriculture dominate the workforce. A strong focus on providing digital financial services integrated or highly targeted to the agriculture space, namely SMEs and SHF (shareholder farmers), can generate more data on individuals while also providing basic access to financial tools such as payments.

Embedded finance and BaaS offered in agriculture offer significant potential to increase financial inclusion across Africa, Southeast Asia and South America. Over 65 per cent of Africa's population is employed in agriculture. Historically, SMEs and smallholder farmers (SHF) have been underserved by traditional financial institutions due to their high-risk profile, driven by seasonality, volatile cash flows and a lack of financial infrastructure in rural areas.

While agritech and fintech companies have recently looked to fill the void, a high B2C customer acquisition cost (CAC) and a reluctance to invest from VCs and other institutional investors have proved prohibitive to significant strides in increasing the ease and access to financial services to those involved in rural and micro-agriculture. From the SME and/or SHF perspective, a lack of financial literacy and infrastructure, such as electricity and internet, have made it difficult for the ubiquity of digital services to reach some potential customers.

EmFi and BaaS can fill the traditional banking and fintech gap in bringing financial services to individuals and SMEs in agriculture. As stated at the start of this chapter, we outlined how BaaS and EmFi have the power to reduce financial exclusion due to the inherent nature of the value proposition: lower transaction costs, API-first solutions that can integrate third-party information for a more inclusive KYC and lending process, and a speedier, more flexible launch and platform. These benefits can mitigate the existing challenges in serving the under- and unbanked in agriculture worldwide.

One example of how banking products are embedded within agriculture is the partnership between Green Agro Solutions, an agribusiness solutions provider in Ethiopia, and the Commercial Bank of Ethiopia, the largest in the country. CBE Birr, the bank's mobile banking application and unstructured supplementary service data (USSD) service, is embedded within Green Agro Solution's digital platform Lesha. The platform provides rural farmers with digital access to information on agriculture practices. It supports the procurement of raw materials and machinery. The integration of CBE Birr allows the farmer to facilitate digital payments.

Looking forward

This chapter has illuminated the dynamic landscape of BaaS and EmFi and their potential to revolutionize financial inclusion. Success requires tailored approaches, understanding regulatory nuances and working within the constraints of digital infrastructure. While Europe's focus often gravitates toward the financially literate, our exploration has revealed the transformative power of these concepts when strategically applied in specific sectors and brands, with incumbent banks playing a critical role through partnering with BaaS enablers or through the opening of APIs.

Notes

1. Ukheshe (2023) Ukheshe partners with Diamond Trust Bank to deliver BaaS in East Africa. www.ukheshe.com/post/ukheshe-partners-with-diamond-trust-bank-to-deliver-baas-in-east-africa (archived at https://perma.cc/3HA7-AFFA)
2. J Chen (2024) Rotating Credit and Savings Association (ROSCA), Investopedia. www.investopedia.com/terms/r/rotating-credit-and-savings-association.asp (archived at https://perma.cc/AC3W-LTZZ)
3. Bloom (2024) A convenient, ethical money club for every community. bloommoney.co (archived at https://perma.cc/7VW9-79FA)
4. BRIAPI (2014) Fiberconnect-BRIAPI integration simplifies payments for customers. developers.bri.co.id/en/use-case/fiberconnect-briapi-integration-simplifies-payments-customers (archived at https://perma.cc/386J-GB53)
5. EFInA (2020) Access to financial services in Nigeria survey 2020. efina.org.ng/publication/access-to-financial-services-in-nigeria-survey-2020 (archived at https://perma.cc/5XAU-CKW9)
6. PT Bank Rakyat Indonesia Tbk (2020) BRILink agents continue to promote financial inclusion in Indonesia, PR Newswire. www.prnewswire.com/news-releases/brilink-agents-continue-to-promote-financial-inclusion-in-indonesia-301513926.html (archived at https://perma.cc/JCT8-QF8J)

11

Niche banking

Introduction

A niche bank is a financial services provider serving a particular subset of the population, and it is also often called community, vertical or affinity banking. The objective of a niche banking provider is to provide specific financial and non-financial solutions to the unmet financial needs of a particular group. Therefore, they naturally target under- and unbanked individuals or businesses. While the concept of niche banking is not new, it has been prominent in the fintech revolution, especially in the United States, mainly due to access to a range of BaaS providers, a catalyst we discussed in Chapter 10, and the sheer size of population and diversity of the country.

While most examples and initiatives we showcase in Part Two come from areas with high degrees of an under- or unbanked population, such as Africa, Southeast Asia and Latin America, the niche bank has thrived in North America, providing a targeted solution to underserved communities and groups. The technologies and business models used by niche banks are similar to those of neobanks, fintechs and greenfield banks from incumbent providers; however, the devil is often in the product and marketing details regarding niche providers. In this chapter, we will explore the role of niche banking in tackling financial exclusion, mainly through case studies. For each case study, we will identify the group or community marginalized from a financial perspective, give a general overview of the niche bank and highlight the details in their product mix that bring the excluded into the financial services system.

It is worth noting that we classify digital accounts using a BaaS partner as a niche bank despite not technically being banks.

Chickasaw Community Bank

Chickasaw Community Bank is a full-service community bank owned by the Chickasaw Nation in the US. It was built with a vision of creating a tribally owned bank that could serve the unique needs of the Indian community. Although Chickasaw serves all communities, its primary objective is to close the gap for the unbanked Native American Households. Sixteen per cent of Native American households do not have bank accounts, compared with 2.5 per cent of white households.[1] There are 20 Native-owned banks in the US, with more than 51 per cent of their voting stock owed by Native American or Native Alaskan individuals. Chickasaw and the 19 other Federal Deposit Insurance Corporation (FDIC) banks are often called 'financial oases in credit deserts'.

Chickasaw and other Native-owned banks aim to solve a significant barrier to Tribes regarding financial inclusion: the proximity of branches and banking services. The average distance from the centre of a Tribal reservation was approximately 12.2 miles to the nearest bank and 6.9 miles to the nearest ATM. In some extreme cases, banks and ATMs could be as far as almost 89 miles and 62 miles away, respectively.[2]

Another challenge Native American individuals and businesses face is lower-than-average credit scores. According to research from Investopedia, Native Americans who grow up on reservations have credit scores that are 10 points lower than the US average, have higher delinquency rates of up to 4 per cent and are 20 per cent less likely to have a credit report.[3] Credit is a problem amongst Native populations, and Chickasaw and other Native-owned banks put solving this problem at the heart of their solutions.

Greenwood

Greenwood was founded in Atlanta, Georgia, to serve the Black and Latino communities. It launched in 2020. The company differentiates itself by focusing on providing banking solutions that cater to the financial needs of its target demographics and address the historical gaps in banking services for people of colour. It operates on a BaaS model, with Coastal Community Bank as its banking partner as of Q1 2024.

A key aspect of Greenwood's offerings includes traditional banking services like debit cards and banking accounts and community-focused initiatives. For instance, it supports the Black and Latino communities through programmes like donating to non-profits such as United Negro College Fund (UNCF) and the National Association for the Advancement of Colored Peoples (NAACP) via spare change round-ups and small business grants to minority-owned businesses. Greenwood stands out for its commitment to no hidden fees, including the absence of overdraft fees and features like early pay options designed to foster financial prosperity within its community.

Majority

A 'bank for migrants', Majority is a digital accounts provider for non-US individuals residing in the US who need a US bank account. It aims to 'give the tools, resources, and support to thrive in a new country'. The US has over 11 million unauthorized immigrants in the US, who do not have the right to a Social Security Number (SSN). Although an SSN is not legally required to open a bank account, most US banks require one in the application process. A lack of an SSN is a root cause of financial exclusion for the migrant and immigrant community. As a result of a lack of access to essential banking services, the financially excluded are unable to build their credit score and face challenges when it comes to small business growth, home ownership and wealth creation.

The core value proposition behind Majority solves several challenges migrants face from a financial inclusion perspective:

- access to a bank account without an SSN
- access without a minimum deposit

- low-cost access to a basic bank account and fee-free transfers and payments.
- early access to salary
- cash deposit via significant retailers, mitigating the need to travel to access a branch
- financial support via an Advisors Program, a network of over 250 trained support staff throughout the US who are migrants themselves

In addition to low cost and streamlined access to accounts, payments and payday advances, Majority offers non-core financial services such as discounts on international calls, including free calls to more than 20 countries and the ability to send instant free mobile top-ups abroad.

Laurel Road

Laurel Road, operating under KeyBank, is a digital banking platform offering specialized services to enhance the financial wellbeing of healthcare and business professionals. It offers a range of banking and lending products, including loyalty checking, high-yield savings accounts, student loan cashback credit cards, student loan refinancing, mortgages and personal loans. These products are designed to offer a streamlined, personalized experience, aiding members in efficiently managing their financial journey and achieving their life objectives. Apart from targeting healthcare and business professionals, what makes Laurel Road a 'niche' provider is its focus on helping its customers with student loan repayment. It collaborates with GradFin, a leading Public Service Loan Forgiveness (PSLF) provider, to deliver student loan counselling services, assisting borrowers in understanding and managing their loan options.

For physicians and dentists, Laurel Road has developed Laurel Road for Doctors, a bespoke digital experience encompassing banking services, insights and exclusive benefits tailored to their financial needs at various career stages. In spring 2022, the company expanded its focus on healthcare professionals by introducing Loyalty Checking, the first checking (current) account created explicitly for nurses, showcasing its ongoing dedication to this sector.

Studio Bank and Karat Financial

The creator economy, which involves individuals and businesses that create digital content, could reach $480 billion by 2027. Historically, this segment has been underserved by financial institutions in several ways. Firstly, they need help to obtain credit due to their freelancer and self-employed statuses. Secondly, they experience irregular income payments, known as feast and famine. Personal finance management and monthly or bi-weekly salary tools provide little benefit. Lastly, payments are often delayed from TikTok, Instagram and YouTube platforms. Several fintechs and providers in recent years have targeted this highly lucrative yet very underserved segment, two of which are Karat and Studio Bank.

Karat offers specialized financial services for creators, including a custom credit card with rewards specifically customized to their unique needs, like higher limits based on the number of followers; unlike typical credit cards, it doesn't require a hard credit check, helping creators avoid the usual barriers to financial products. The leading message on Karat's website as of Q1 2024 was that 'Banks don't understand creators. We do.' It also provides dedicated bookkeeping and tax preparation services tailored to the unique financial dynamics of creator businesses. This approach addresses the financial exclusion often faced by creators in traditional banking systems, recognizing them as legitimate businesses with specific needs and contributions to the economy.

On the other hand, Studio Bank targets the broader creative community and offers both a digital platform and several branches, unlike Karat. Based in Nashville, Tennessee, its mission is to empower creators across various industries. It offers a unique blend of sophisticated financial services with the personal touch of a local bank, focusing on building community and providing hospitality-inspired banking experiences. Studio Bank offers a range of financial products, including commercial and personal banking, tech and start-up banking, credit and mortgages.

What sets Studio Bank apart from several fully digital plays in the niche banking area is its emphasis on empowering creators through resources such as capital, accounts, education, advice and management of finances. It views itself as part of the hospitality industry, aiming to create a banking experience that's both modern and human-centred. Studio Bank seeks to be a nexus point for people from diverse backgrounds and industries by prioritizing personal service and community building, fostering creativity and innovation.

Daylight and Zest Money

Not all niche banks and services have lasted. Two notable niche providers, Daylight (USA) and Zest Money (India), shut down in 2023. Zest's core objective was to bring short-term credit to the Indian consumer market via buy now, pay later. Amongst the objectives listed on its website were to 'make it possible to upgrade while keeping it affordable' and 'to make life more affordable for India using technology-led solutions'.

On the other hand, Daylight is a digital account provider targeting the LGBTQ+ community. It stood out by offering a key feature inclusive to trans and non-binary customers by issuing cards with their preferred name, even if they don't match the customer's legal identity. Personal financial management in Daylight was aligned with queer customers' distinct requirements around family planning, and it provided cashback when its customers shopped at shops that were LGBTQ+ friendly.

Daylight aimed to solve several challenges faced by the LGBTQ+ community. Many are forced to leave their homes due to rejection by their families, adding to their financial strain. Additionally, they often bear the costs of medical treatments, such as HIV/AIDS care, hormone therapy and fertility treatments, which can be substantial. A large portion of the queer community is drawn to expensive urban environments that are more inclusive and forward-thinking, yet this choice comes with higher living expenses. Furthermore, a notable absence of a support system, stemming from either a lack of familial backing or not having children to depend on, leaves many in the LGBTQ+ community without a financial safety net.

A short note on niche 'banks' targeting low-income and sub-prime consumers

Perhaps the most significant by-product of limited or no access to financial services or banking products is a lack of good credit. While this problem is at the heart of this book, and institutions targeting the issue are presented throughout the book, we wanted to highlight two strong examples of digital account platforms that specifically target consumers with bad credit. The core offering aligns more with the niche banking subset rather than a consumer-focused or B2B fintech. Dave and Chime in the US are two examples of niche banks supporting forward credit mobility. In the case of Dave, supporting upward credit mobility is done by offering a fee-free overdraft account and payday advances to avoid overdrafts and late bill payments. Apart from sub-prime friendly products, Dave offers 'side hustles', a jobs board available to customers, and access to take part in paid surveys. Dave is a consumer of BaaS products, with its partner as of Q1 2024 being Evolve Banking and Trust. Chime also operates on a BaaS model, partnering with Stride Bank as of Q1 2024. Like Dave, it offers fee-free overdraft protection and a payday advance service. Chime exclusively promotes the ability to 'Build credit history with no annual fees or interest'.

Conclusion

Reflecting on the examples provided throughout our exploration of niche banking, it's evident that many are US-centric. This focus is not by coincidence but instead reflects the fertile and ripe market for niche banking services within the country. The United States, with its vast and diverse population, presents a unique opportunity for niche banks to flourish, catering specifically to various ethnicities, communities and specialized needs that mainstream banking often overlooks.

This US-centric perspective underscores the significant impact of the BaaS model, which has been a pivotal catalyst in the proliferation of niche banking solutions tailored to underserved segments. Conversely, in Africa, the narrative shifts towards mobile money and remittance platforms as primary tools for financial inclusion, showcasing a different approach to bridging the financial gap among the underbanked and unbanked populations. The distinction between these regions highlights the adaptability and innovation within the financial sector, tailored to each area's unique needs and infrastructure.

Moreover, the reliance on a national credit score system, such as FICO in the US, establishes a framework that encourages the development of products and services geared towards upward credit mobility combined with a digital account offering. In contrast, regions without a clear path to credit mobility or a national credit score system tend to gravitate towards alternative credit methods for offering credit and lending products, as discussed in Chapter 5.

However, it's essential to acknowledge the changing dynamics of fintech funding, especially for challenger banks, which essentially niche banks are,[4] and the increasing pressure on profitability. These factors could lead to stagnation in the niche banking space or prompt a shift towards more contextualized or embedded financial service offerings. This adaptation could redefine the future of financial services, ensuring that the sector continues to evolve in response to economic pressures and the ever-changing needs of consumers.

In conclusion, while the examples highlighted are predominantly US-centric, they serve as a microcosm of the broader global potential and challenges facing niche banking. As the financial landscape continues to evolve, driven by technological advancements and regulatory changes, the lessons learned from these US-based case studies may offer valuable insights for other regions striving to enhance financial inclusion and cater to the unique needs of their populations.

Notes

1. Federal Deposit Insurance Corporation (2020) *How America Banks: Household use of banking and financial services 2019 FDIC survey*. www.fdic.gov/analysis/household-survey/2019report.pdf (archived at https://perma.cc/RJ2M-DXTE)
2. M Jorgensen and R K Q Akee (2017) *Access to Capital and Credit in Native Communities: A data review*, Native Nations Institute. www.novoco.com/public-media/documents/nni_find_access_to_capital_and_credit_in_native_communities_020117.pdf (archived at https://perma.cc/32CL-KZAT)
3. W Ward (2023) Native American-owned banks by state, Investopedia. www.investopedia.com/native-american-owned-banks-by-state-5085713 (archived at https://perma.cc/SH2V-H64F)
4. Deloitte (2023) Challenger banks: Profitability and cost efficiency in uncertain times. blogs.deloitte.ch/banking/2023/07/challenger-banks-profitability-and-cost-efficiency-in-uncertain-times.html (archived at https://perma.cc/RWQ6-9FXY)

12

Authentication and identification

Introduction

Authentication and identity are closely related and often discussed as one conceptual challenge when addressing financial inclusion. Identification is the first step towards and the foundation of financial inclusion. An identity is needed to bring an individual or business into formal financial services. It helps provide the right product or service mitigates risk when it comes to lending. An identity ensures that fraud does not occur and the users' account is not compromised.

Historically, identities have been proved physically, leading to costly products and services, and human error. The primary barrier to the formal financial services sector for many individuals is the absence of a physical identity document, whether this be a birth certificate, an ID, passport or land title. However, in the past 10 years, the rise of B2B KYC and AML fintechs has offered a digital, efficient and highly accurate mechanism for financial institutions to spend less investment and resources on identifying and authenticating customers. However, simply 'digitizing' the existing identity and authentication journeys does not address the root cause of financial inclusion, the inability to prove one's identity. This is where a government-led digital ID system is attractive, and it is increasingly at the heart of a financial inclusion strategy in many countries.

Creating a secure and inclusive system for identification and authentication requires a tailored approach; it cannot be one size fits all. This effort is crucial for combatting financial exclusion.

Therefore, it is imperative that governments, banks and private sector companies seriously address this issue. The numbers speak for themselves:

- The World Bank's Identification for Development (ID4D) initiative announced that one billion people did not have official proof of identity as of 2018.[1]
- Having an ID, however, does not automatically lead to inclusion, as some 3.4 billion people are still unable to make use of it online due to an inability to verify or authenticate their credentials.
- Only 3 per cent of developing countries have digital foundational ID schemes.[2]
- Digital ID is critical not just to financial inclusion but also to a strong economy. McKinsey Institute's research in seven countries (Brazil, China, Ethiopia, India, Nigeria, the United Kingdom and the United States) estimates that digital IDs could increase GDP from 3 to 13 per cent by 2030.[3]

Uncovering what is 'needed', 'required' or what 'should be done' from an identity and authentication perspective to combat financial exclusion varies from country to country. The key challenge in some nations and regions starts with the most basic requirement: registering individuals not currently in a formal government identification system. Implementing biometric authentication is seen as a mechanism to speed up the process of financial inclusion. On the other hand, in some markets, more advanced schemes and frameworks allow individuals to passport existing KYC data to access financial products and services.

Furthermore, regional hotspots of migration, namely Latin America, face challenges as to how to incorporate large proportions of migrants with or without foreign identity documents into their national identity schemes. Beyond this, these countries must facilitate such migrants to access basic financial services.

India and Estonia are leaders in implementing highly successful government-led digital ID schemes, leading to credible results in financial inclusion. Meanwhile, open banking holds an opportunity to bring easier access to financial products for those with an existing relationship with a financial services provider, as it allows individuals to passport their existing bank account information to fulfil KYC and AML requirements. At the same time, decentralized ID and self-sovereign identity (SSI) are two concepts currently being explored in parallel with decentralized finance and systems.

In this chapter we will define identity and authentication and highlight the role fintech can have in digitizing identity and KYC. Then we will discuss the role and requirements of a government-led digital ID system, highlighting the Indian and Estonian examples and their impact on financial inclusion. We will wrap up by exploring other methods, such as open banking-powered ID and the concept of a decentralized ID system.

Identity, authentication, fintech and financial institutions

In the simplest terms, identity refers to the attributes or credentials associated with an individual or entity. These attributes could be personal information, like name, date of birth, address, biometric data or any other specific information that uniquely identifies a person. Authentication, on the other hand, is the process of verifying the identity of a person or entity. It involves confirming that someone is indeed who they claim to be. This is typically done using one or more factors of authentication:

- Knowledge factors ('something you know'), like a password or a PIN.
- Possession factors ('something you have'), such as a security token or a smartphone.
- Inherence factors ('something you are') involve biometrics like fingerprints or facial recognition.

In financial services, identity and authentication processes are the foundational elements for financial inclusion by establishing trust between institutions and their clients. For financial institutions, ensuring the identity of their potential and existing clients is essential for three reasons:

1. **Preventing fraud and financial crimes:** The primary role of identity and authentication in financial services is to prevent fraud and other financial crimes. By accurately verifying the identity of customers, financial institutions can significantly reduce the risk of identity theft, money laundering and other illicit activities.
2. **Regulatory compliance:** Financial institutions are subject to stringent regulatory requirements, such as KYC and AML directives. Effective identity and authentication processes are essential for compliance with these regulations, helping institutions avoid hefty fines and legal repercussions.
3. **Cost to serve:** Efficient authentication processes also play a role in reducing operational costs for financial institutions. Streamlined processes minimize the need for manual intervention, reduce the time spent on customer onboarding and support and lower the overheads associated with customer management.

The rise of B2B fintechs such as IDNow, Jumio, Mitek, Yoti and OnFido has pioneered digital, less costly and more user-friendly experiences for identity and subsequent authentication. Used by fintechs and traditional banks, these fintechs have improved how financial institutions identify potential and existing customers. These fintechs tend to harness AI and machine learning; for example, both Jumio and OnFido use AI to verify the authenticity of government-issued IDs and compare them against facial biometrics from a real-time selfie. This helps in accurately verifying customers' identities. In addition, biometrics and liveness detection play a significant role. Jumio incorporates biometrics and liveness detection in its process. It is essential to ensure that the person completing the verification is present in real time and not using a pre-recorded image or video.

While these fintechs have improved the customer experience, reduced service costs and harnessed technology to mitigate violations of AML and KYC policies, not all fintechs practise a sound policy for onboarding, identifying and authenticating their users. This can be especially true for fintechs looking to bring the under- and unbanked onto their platforms. It highlights the challenges fintechs focusing on financial inclusion face in balancing user accessibility with the need for strong security and abiding by regulatory requirements.

One example of a fintech faced with KYC challenges is OPay, a Nigerian company. In 2023 it faced significant scrutiny due to concerns about its weak KYC system. This issue raised serious questions about the platform's vulnerability to financial fraud. OPay's registration process is notably simple, especially for the basic account type, which is a part of their strategy to attract unbanked users.

However, this approach has resulted in lax identity checks, making the system susceptible to misuse. Several tests have demonstrated that it's possible to register on the platform using minimal or publicly available information, even using details of well-known personalities, without thorough verification. This gap in the KYC process could facilitate illicit activities, posing a risk to the platform and its users. Recognizing these risks, the Central Bank of Nigeria has advocated stricter KYC measures across financial services to prevent fraud and ensure customer safety. OPay's situation highlights the challenges fintech companies face in balancing user accessibility with the need for robust security measures.[4]

Government digital ID systems

While B2B fintechs have provided the technology and tools for financial institutions to offer better identification and authentication experiences, these fintechs and initiatives tend to require the individual to access a government-issued ID document. As highlighted in the introduction to this chapter, many individuals still cannot formally identify themselves, and this is where government digital ID systems come into play as a method to quell one of the root causes of financial exclusion.

These systems are electronic forms of identity verification issued and regulated by governmental authorities. Unlike traditional physical identification documents such as passports or ID cards, digital IDs are stored in electronic formats accessible via smartphones, smart cards or web portals. They can be used online or in person. A hallmark of these systems is their use of advanced security measures for authentication, including biometrics (like fingerprints, facial recognition or iris scans), passwords, PINs or digital certificates, which enhance the integrity and security of the ID. GOV.UK defines a digital identity as a unique identifier allowing individuals to verify who they are without needing multiple documents as proof.[5] The identity will store various trusted sources of personal information called 'attributes', which a customer can choose to share with organizations.

As of 2020, 165 government-led partially digital or fully digital ID schemes existed. However, only a handful of programmes have reached mass adoption, with programmes often characterized by low use rates. Getting this right is not easy, but it has been done successfully in one of the largest nations, India, and one of the smallest, Estonia. The introduction and success of a digital ID system can mitigate some of the current challenges facing those financially excluded:

- A high cost-to-serve: As mentioned previously, the ability to quickly and efficiently prove one's identity reduces the cost-to-serve for banks and financial institutions. A digital ID opens the door to a fully digital, automatic identity verification for any individual looking to apply for a banking or financial service product, reducing operational costs. Ensuring applications with a digital ID can be done via smart and feature phones would provide greater inclusion and further reduce operational costs.
- Fraud: Digital ID systems, with their advanced security measures, offer enhanced protection against fraud compared to traditional identification methods. Crucially, by reducing the risk of fraud, these systems make financial services more accessible and appealing to the financially excluded. A trusted digital identity framework is instrumental in facilitating financial inclusion, especially for underserved populations, by easing the process of opening bank accounts and accessing financial services, often hampered by the stringent requirements and high costs associated with traditional identification methods.[6]

- Geographical barriers: One of the main barriers to financial inclusion is the lack of banking infrastructure in many rural and remote areas. In these regions, physical banks and ATMs are scarce, making it difficult for individuals to access basic financial services. A mechanism to digitally prove one's digital identity would, in theory, remove the need for branches and ATMs to prove the identity and facilitate transactions.

While digital IDs on paper appear to be a solution to the lack of formal identification, there are numerous challenges in launching a digital ID scheme and meeting the critical mass needed to make an impact for the under- and unbanked. The challenges to the implementation of a digital ID are numerous; however, a few stand out in terms of mitigating financial exclusion. These primary challenges must be addressed for any digital ID system.

- Trust: Fear and hesitancy around privacy, data protection, government surveillance and misuse. Trust is a foundation for interoperability and adoption by consumers and private organizations.
- Combatting financial and digital literacy: Closing the digital divide, ensuring those individuals in an area with limited internet access or lacking technology can be easily onboarded to the system.
- Creating a two-sided marketplace: Ensuring a system is not one-sided involves addressing challenges in adoption, interoperability and trust. The digital ID system should be compatible with various platforms and systems organizations use.
- Completeness of transactions: A digital ID scheme includes components such as signatures.
- Participation from the private sector: Collaboration between governments and private entities can help establish a universally accepted system, further encouraging organizational adoption.

It is worth looking at two successful digital ID systems, in Estonia and India.

Estonia

The Estonian digital ID system is a pioneering initiative in e-governance that has significantly improved financial inclusion in the country since 2001. Estonia has facilitated easier access to banking and financial services by providing every citizen with a secure digital identity, thus enhancing financial livelihoods. Over 98 per cent of Estonians own a digital ID card, and 70 per cent regularly use it to access public services. More than 1,300 new companies have been created, bringing an additional $4.6 million into the Estonian economy. The system has greatly streamlined government and financial services.

The system overcame challenges such as the digital divide by ensuring widespread internet access and digital literacy programmes. Trust was built through robust security and privacy features, while interoperability was achieved by integrating the digital ID with various public and private services. This high level of digital engagement has not only modernized identification practices but also improved the security and efficiency of online transactions, reducing the risk of fraud. Estonia's model, emphasizing mass adoption and integration with various services, serves as a blueprint for other nations seeking to enhance digital identity verification and foster financial inclusion through technology.

India

Aadhaar, India's biometric identity system, has also had a significant impact on financial inclusion and the delivery of government services. Launched in 2009, its primary goal was to provide a unique, verifiable identity to every Indian citizen. Aadhaar achieves this by collecting minimal yet crucial demographic and biometric data.

The success of Aadhaar lies in its simplicity and inclusivity. It allows for capturing either full date of birth or age when exact birthdates are unknown, ensuring no one is excluded due to lack of documentary proof. Additionally, the 'introducer' system enables residents without any documents to be enrolled by verified individuals, thus bridging the gap for low-income and vulnerable populations.

Aadhaar's impact extends to various sectors, significantly reducing the cost per transaction from around ₹1,000 to ₹30–40.[7] This cost-efficiency has led to substantial savings for the government in subsidy disbursements. By April 2017, over 1.13 billion members were enrolled, making Aadhaar the world's largest biometric ID system. The system has been instrumental in uncovering fraudulent activities in government schemes, and enhancing the efficiency of social welfare programmes.

The Aadhaar-enabled verification process has benefited the private sector, particularly in banking. It has bolstered confidence in retail loan disbursement and improved the reliability of employee and partner verification processes in various industries.

Despite its numerous advantages, Aadhaar has faced challenges, especially regarding privacy concerns. However, the Supreme Court of India upheld the constitutional validity of Aadhaar, recognizing its pivotal role in modernizing India's social and economic infrastructure.

In Table 12.1 we list a selection of other national digital ID initiatives.

TABLE 12.1 Selected national ID initiatives

Country	Regulation/law	Impact
Mexico	In 2017, the Mexican government issued a regulation enabling banks to perform biometric authentication.	Other banks now want to extend the programme to facial recognition and other more sophisticated proofs of life.
Philippines	In August 2018 a law was passed in the Philippines signing off a 30 billion peso ($563 million) project to create a digital ID.	Phil-ID will collect information and biometric data (including iris scans, fingerprints and facial images) of the 106 million Filipinos who make up the country's population. The digital ID card will grant Filipinos access to government services and ease the process of opening bank accounts and get jobs.
Thailand	In September 2018 the Proofing and Authentication of Digital Identity Bill – also known as the 'Digital ID Bill' – was approved in principle by the government's cabinet.	Similar to open banking powered KYC, the Digital ID system eliminates the need to undergo KYC checks continuously. However, in the context of financial inclusion it would require an individual to have the banking credentials and means to authenticate them.

Other approaches: Open banking and decentralized ID system

Similar to how cryptocurrency looks to upend traditional finance, two concepts (open banking and decentralized IDs) can potentially disrupt the traditional, centralized sense of identity. However, they are still nascent. Self-sovereign identity (SSI) and decentralized ID are intimately linked concepts in digital identity. SSI is a model where individuals have complete control over their digital identities, managing how, when and with whom their data is shared. This concept empowers users to be sovereigns of their digital identity, independent of centralized authorities. Decentralized ID, often enabled by blockchain technology, is the technological infrastructure that makes SSI feasible. In decentralized ID systems, identities are distributed across a network, enhancing security and privacy by mitigating central points of failure. The synergy between SSI and decentralized ID lies in the latter providing a secure, transparent and immutable framework necessary to realize self-managed digital identities.

Decentralized digital ID, a system where individuals have complete control over their data and how it is shared, offers several benefits over traditional centralized identity management systems. By leveraging blockchain and other decentralized technologies, these IDs can securely and efficiently verify identities without the need for traditional banking infrastructure or intermediaries.

Furthermore, decentralized digital IDs can enhance security and privacy for users, combatting the lack of trust in centralized and traditional systems. Unlike centralized systems, which are susceptible to hacks and data breaches, decentralized IDs distribute data across a network, making it significantly harder for unauthorized access to occur. This security feature builds trust among users, particularly in financial transactions, where the risk of identity theft and fraud is a concern.

In addition to facilitating access to banking services, decentralized digital IDs can unlock microfinance, insurance and investment opportunities. For small-scale entrepreneurs and farmers in developing countries, these IDs can be key to accessing microloans, crop insurance and investment in their ventures, contributing to economic growth and community stability. Lastly, it can play a crucial role in delivering government services and benefits. They can streamline the distribution of social welfare programmes, subsidies and direct benefit transfers, ensuring that aid reaches the intended recipients efficiently and transparently. This precision in targeting beneficiaries can significantly reduce leakage and corruption in the system.

Applying the concept of a decentralized ID to financial services, we would expect similar benefits to a fully digital ID: the automation and instant fulfilment of AML and KYC, reducing the operational costs for financial institutions and enhancing the security and efficiency of financial transactions. One of the practical examples of decentralized ID in action is Polygon ID, a blockchain-backed identity solution that uses zero-knowledge proofs. This solution illustrates the potential of decentralized ID in securing and simplifying identity verification processes across various industries.

Open banking-based authentication, while not necessarily a solution for the unbanked, could support underbanked individuals in accessing additional and relevant products and services. This type of authentication verifies a user's identity using their banking credentials. This concept is part of the broader concept of open banking, which we discussed in Chapter 9. Essentially, open-banking-powered APIs can allow a third party to access pre-verified data by the user's existing bank or fintech, including name, email, address and phone number, in addition to identity insights and users' activity patterns to detect fraudulent behaviour. This concept allows third parties to pass the already verified identity and data in previous KYC and AML flows. Similar to decentralized ID, this concept is still nascent but increasingly explored by banks, fintechs and other financial institutions.

The future is digital

The evolution of identity and authentication methods is crucial in addressing financial inclusion challenges. The shift from physical identity proofs to digital systems has opened significant opportunities for including more people in the formal financial sector, particularly those previously excluded due to lack of traditional identification.

The examples of India's Aadhaar system and Estonia's e-governance model demonstrate the effectiveness of government-led digital ID initiatives in enhancing financial inclusion. These systems show how digital identities can simplify access to financial services, but they also highlight the complexities involved in implementing such solutions. Key challenges include ensuring trust, bridging digital literacy gaps and fostering a conducive public and private sector participation environment.

Looking to the future, concepts like SSI and decentralized ID systems, often based on blockchain technology, represent an innovative approach to identity management. These technologies offer a more secure, user-controlled method of managing personal data, particularly relevant in financial services. By empowering individuals to control their own identity information, these models could significantly lower barriers to financial inclusion in the absence of a government-led digital ID initiative. However, to what extent traditional financial players can and would integrate with some systems is yet to be seen.

Additionally, integrating open banking with identity verification processes presents a promising development. This approach utilizes existing banking relationships and pre-verified data to streamline identity verification, potentially making financial services more accessible to underbanked groups.

The future of identity and authentication in financial inclusion balances technological advancement and practical implementation. Success in this area requires a collaborative approach, involving government authorities, financial institutions, technology companies and, most importantly, the end-users. The goal is to develop systems that are not only technologically advanced and secure but also inclusive and accessible to everyone, ensuring that financial services are available to all segments of society.

Notes

1. ID4D (nd) ID4D global dataset: Overview, World Bank. id4d.worldbank.org/global-dataset (archived at https://perma.cc/73DR-AJJW)
2. World Bank (2016) Enabling digital development, *World Development Report 2016*. documents1.worldbank.org/curated/en/896971468194972881/310436360_20160263021000/additional/World-development-report-2016-digital-dividends.pdf (archived at https://perma.cc/8RNH-5QFJ)
3. O White et al (2019) Digital identification: A key to inclusive growth, McKinsey Digital. www.mckinsey.com/capabilities/mckinsey-digital/our-insights/digital-identification-a-key-to-inclusive-growth (archived at https://perma.cc/XRQ8-9MZ3)
4. J Kaberia (2024) OPay introduces KYC requirements to prevent fraud, CIO Africa. cioafrica.co/opay-introduces-kyc-requirements-to-prevent-fraud (archived at https://perma.cc/T54U-KLVC)
5. GOV.UK (2023) Enabling the use of digital identities in the UK, www.gov.uk/guidance/digital-identity (archived at https://perma.cc/24D9-X78K)
6. IDEMIA (nd) Digital ID and eKYC: A catalyst for financial inclusion. www.idemia.com/insights/digital-id-and-ekyc-catalyst-financial-inclusion (archived at https://perma.cc/3CHG-JU3Z)
7. The Hindu Businessline (2018) Use of Aadhaar for KYC authentication will cut cost. www.thehindubusinessline.com/money-and-banking/use-of-aadhaar-for-kyc-authentication-will-cut-costs/article8490492.ece (archived at https://perma.cc/92VB-GV44)

13

Big data, alternative data and artificial intelligence

Introduction

While other chapters in Part Two discuss the implications of various technologies and their impact on creating financial inclusion, this chapter will focus on a aspect crucial to how well these technologies work: data. Data is often hailed as the new oil or gold, especially in banking and tech circles, and it is key to integrating the under- and unbanked into finance. As oil powers industries and gold holds intrinsic value, data is the foundation for crafting and elevating digital products and services.

This chapter will explore how data, specifically alternative and big data, is used for inclusive finance. Data and the use of artificial intelligence (AI) is worthy of its own book, let alone a single chapter. For this reason, we will primarily focus on how utilizing data and AI can create more financial inclusion within credit and lending. Credit is essential to any livelihood and plays an important role in modern society. When granted and used responsibly, credit and loans can open doors to opportunities for the individual, micro-SME and SME.

Wealthy markets or countries with low rates of financial exclusion typically have well-established credit bureaus, credit reporting systems and good digital infrastructures. However, even in wealthy markets, segments of the population can be underbanked or face barriers to accessing credit, often due to a lack of credit history, low income or other socioeconomic factors.

The lack of comprehensive and reliable credit information is a common challenge in less developed or poorer markets. These bureaus might not have detailed records for a large segment of the population, particularly those who are unbanked or underbanked. Furthermore, the credit challenge is compounded in markets with limited access to formal banking services, as informal credit systems often emerge. These can include local money lenders, community savings groups and other non-traditional forms of credit. While these systems provide access to credit, they typically do not match the scale and scope of credit formal financial institutions offer.

Financial data or history, a type of traditional data set, serves as the backbone for risk assessment and the provision of financial products such as lending and insurance amongst traditional institutions. In the absence of traditional data, alternative data is increasingly used. Examples of alternative data include social media activity, utility payments and mobile phone usage patterns. Most initiatives we explore in this chapter use alternative data at the foundation of their offering.

The relationship between alternative data and big data lies in how alternative data can be a subset of big data. Big data is 'the large, diverse sets of information that grow ever-increasingly. It encompasses the volume of information, the velocity or speed at which it is created and collected, and the variety or scope of the data points being covered (known as the "three v's" of big data, or volume, variety, and velocity).'[1] Big data comes from various ever-present sources in individuals' lives, including social media, smartphones and devices, automobiles, transaction processing systems, databases, documents, emails, internet clickstream logs and more. Alternative and big data is readily available amongst almost all segments of populations, regardless of their economic status or location.

Data, in the broadest sense, and AI go hand in. AI is the simulation of human intelligence in machines programmed to think and learn. It encompasses various techniques, including machine learning, where algorithms improve automatically through experience (i.e. exposure to more data). Data is the fuel for AI; it enables AI systems to recognize patterns, make predictions and improve their performance over time. The positive impact AI makes will be discussed in more detail.

While data and AI have numerous applications in mitigating financial exclusion, the standout and most exciting examples within financial services fall in the credit area, and understanding why and how will be the focus of this chapter. We will begin by outlining the nature of data in facilitating credit products, then introduce the concept of alternative data in credit and highlight how it can mitigate existing challenges. We will explain how AI reduces costs and opens up vast opportunities to offer credit and lending to those not captured via traditional data or in credit bureaus. Next, we explore how alternative data impacts micro-lending, a critical aspect of lending to the under- and unbanked. We will then highlight the challenges faced in utilizing alternative data and AI and conclude this chapter by showcasing a selection of noteworthy initiatives and use cases.

Why credit?

When we look at the range of financial services needed by individuals and small businesses that are under- and unbanked, we see notable progress in payments, accounts and savings, many of which are highlighted in previous chapters. With these advancements in mind, credit and lending are the next areas for significant innovation. These financial products are particularly suited for applying data-centric technologies because they rely on detailed data analysis. Credit and lending are ideal candidates for the impactful use of big data, alternative data and AI.

Credit and lending products are highly data-centric due to these services' inherent risks and complexities. In the case of credit products, lenders must assess the risk of default by borrowers. This requires a detailed analysis of various financial indicators such as credit scores, income and employment history. The objective is to predict the likelihood of repayment, minimizing the risk of financial loss for the lender.

Using big data generated from individuals' digital footprints, such as mobile money transactions and phone usage patterns, can reveal behavioural patterns that could help assess creditworthiness. Fintechs and banks can leverage mobile phone data to facilitate credit access for MSMEs. For example, FarmDrive in Kenya uses satellite images and weather forecasts, big data sets, among other data sources to create credit profiles for farmers. This data-driven approach provides access to credit and essential services like insurance and quality farm inputs, crucial for enhancing productivity and income levels.[2]

Alternative data and AI are the secret ingredients to more inclusivity in credit and lending. Apart from spatial, weather and macroeconomic data, several personal data points can and are increasingly being used in offering credit and lending products. These include:

- telco data, which includes call duration, call destinations, call origin location, duration of sim ownership, porting history, handsets used, number of missed calls and other data types
- shopping history at merchants
- rent, utilities or bill payments, which includes the amount, cadence and any late payments
- behaviour on social media

Alternative data applied to credit scoring offers several advantages. It provides a more comprehensive view of an applicant's creditworthiness, beyond traditional credit scores, by analysing data like phone top-ups and bill payment patterns, which are readily available. This enriched data helps lenders make better-informed decisions, balancing risk exposure effectively.

On the other hand, social media data is less ubiquitous because the data is unstructured and governments and businesses are hesitant to take a 'Big Brother' approach to determining credit, similar to what we see in China with the social credit scoring system.[3] There are, however, two use cases for using social media data as an alternative data set. The first is for niche banks servicing creatives and influencers. One example is Karat Financial, which assesses a potential customer's creditworthiness based on their followers.[4] Another use case, although still nascent, is using business sentiment analysis based on customer reviews to understand the creditworthiness of a business.

The potential of alternative data also extends to creating more accurate risk models and mitigating risk defaults. A report by Experian found that 89 per cent of lenders agree that alternative credit data allows them to extend credit to more consumers.[5] Ninety-six per cent of lenders agree that in times of economic stress, alternative credit data allows them to more closely evaluate consumers' creditworthiness and reduce their credit risk exposure, and three out of four consumers believe they are a better borrower than their credit score represents.

The above gains are made possible via utilizing AI. In addition to credit scoring, AI also provides value in automating loan processing. By streamlining the lending process, AI reduces the time and bureaucracy involved in loan approvals. This benefit is particularly valuable for the underbanked, who often require quick access to funds. Additionally, AI enhances risk management and fraud detection capabilities. Through sophisticated pattern recognition, AI systems can identify potential fraud and assess risks more accurately, ensuring a secure lending environment.

AI's impact extends to the personalization of financial products. By analysing vast datasets, AI can identify specific financial needs and preferences within the underbanked population, leading to the development of tailored financial products. This customization is crucial in addressing the unique challenges faced by the underbanked.

Moreover, AI-powered tools like chatbots and virtual assistants revolutionize financial education and assistance. These tools provide valuable guidance and information, helping the underbanked to navigate financial decisions and understand their options better. This aspect of AI empowers individuals and fosters a more financially literate society.

As mentioned previously, the operational efficiencies brought about by AI result in lower costs for lenders, which can translate into more affordable credit for consumers. This aspect is particularly beneficial in the context of the underbanked, who are often more sensitive to borrowing costs. Additionally, AI contributes to developing more inclusive lending policies by identifying and rectifying biases in traditional lending models, paving the way for fairer access to financial services.

Finally, integrating AI with mobile banking platforms is a game-changer in terms of accessibility. For many underbanked individuals, mobile phones are the primary means of accessing financial services. AI enhances the functionality and user experience of mobile banking, making it an even more powerful tool for financial inclusion.

The role of the micro-loan

Micro-lending, or micro-loans, refers to the practice of offering small, short-term loans to individuals, typically those who lack access to traditional banking services and credit. These loans are designed to empower people, especially in developing countries, to start small businesses, fund agricultural activities or support personal needs where formal financial services are unavailable or unaffordable. The evolution of micro-lending is deeply tied to the goal of financial inclusion, aiming to bring the financially underserved into the formal economy.

Traditionally, micro-lending data has come from basic financial information and personal interactions. Lenders often rely on assessments of an individual's character, business plan and community standing, as credit scores and financial histories are frequently unavailable for the target demographic of micro-loans. This reliance on limited and often subjective information has been one of the significant gaps in micro-lending, making it difficult to assess creditworthiness and risk accurately. Traditional data sources do not always provide a complete picture of an individual's financial potential, leading to conservative lending practices and a restricted reach.

Alternative data is transforming the micro-lending landscape by filling these gaps. Alternative data includes non-traditional data sources such as mobile phone usage patterns, utility bill payments, remittance history and even social media activity. This data can provide a more comprehensive view of an individual's financial behaviour and capacity. By leveraging AI and machine learning, lenders can analyse this data to make more informed lending decisions, reduce risks and extend credit to a broader population segment.

A note on challenges and considerations

While in theory alternative data combined with AI holds immense potential with the ability to reach almost all under- and unbanked populations, the reality is different. Critical challenges continue to present themselves and must be worked amongst a number of parties, from financial institution, mobile network operators, governments and businesses. Some key challenges are listed in Table 13.1.

TABLE 13.1 Key challenges of alternative data combined with AI

Data quality and availability	In many underbanked regions, reliable data can be scarce. Alternative data sources like utility payments, mobile phone usage or rental payments may not be consistently recorded or standardized. This lack of quality, structured data makes it difficult to build accurate credit profiles.
Technological infrastructure	The effective use of alternative data requires robust technological infrastructure, including data storage, processing capabilities and advanced analytics tools like AI and machine learning. Such infrastructure may be lacking in many underbanked markets, which hinders the collection, analysis and application of alternative data.
Regulatory and compliance issues	Regulatory frameworks in many countries may not have evolved to encompass the use of alternative data for credit assessment. Issues around data privacy, consumer protection and credit reporting regulations can pose significant challenges.
Literacy and trust	Financial literacy levels in underbanked populations can be low, leading to a lack of understanding and trust in new financial products that utilize alternative data. Educating consumers on how their data is being used and the benefits of credit products is crucial but it can be challenging.
Risk of bias and discrimination	There's a risk that alternative data might unintentionally incorporate biases, leading to discrimination in credit decisions. For example, data like location or social network characteristics could potentially disadvantage certain groups.
Digital divide	In many regions with large underbanked populations, access to digital technology and the internet is still limited. Since alternative data often relies on digital footprints, a significant portion of the population might continue to be excluded.

(continued)

TABLE 13.1 (Continued)

Integration with traditional systems	Integrating alternative data approaches with existing financial systems and practices can be challenging. This includes aligning them with traditional credit scoring methods and ensuring they complement rather than conflict with existing practices.
Market dynamics and consumer behaviour	Understanding these regions' unique market dynamics, cultural nuances and consumer behaviour is crucial for effectively using alternative data. Misinterpreting these factors can lead to inappropriate credit offerings or marketing strategies.
Skills and resources	Many companies in these markets face a shortage of skilled professionals in data science and financial technology, coupled with constraints in resources for necessary technological infrastructure, research and development, and ongoing training.

Case studies and applications

In this section of the chapter, we discuss noteworthy and interesting case studies and applications.

Consumer credit

When exploring live use cases and initiatives, it is encouraging that both fintechs and incumbent banks alike utilize alternative and big data. Table 13.2 highlights a selection of examples.

MSME and SME credit

In India, traditional lending institutions meet only about 5 per cent of the demand for short-term working capital financing.[6] This leaves a significant number of micro, small, and medium enterprises (MSMEs) without access to affordable, short-term working capital, resulting in a large credit gap. Many MSMEs struggle to provide the collateral or documentation required by conventional lenders. Even if they could, these institutions, including non-banking finance companies (NBFCs), mainly offer costly term loan products that don't suit the working capital needs of small businesses.

TABLE 13.2 Examples of alternative and big data

Company	Location	Initiaitve
Commercial International Bank of Egypt (CIB) and Fawry	Egypt	CIB partners with Fawry, an electronic payments provider, to integrate bill payment solutions into its CIB Smart Wallet. This integration is expected to yield valuable data on customer payment habits, which will be useful for tailoring lending and deposit products. CIB's collaboration with Careem, a leading ride-sharing company, is notable. By combining transaction data from CIB Smart Wallet with Careem's driver performance and ratings, CIB can construct detailed driver profiles and assign credit scores, thereby facilitating targeted lending to high-performing drivers.
FinScore	Philippines	Offers a Telco Score, which utilizes mobile network operator data. It uses the most advanced machine learning algorithms and has a high predictive power (42% Gini coefficient). The Telco Score was designed for the underbanked segment, training the score on an underbanked segment.
Grameen	USA	Grameen America stands out in its approach to micro-lending by relying on something other than traditional credit reports or scores. Instead, it gathers data directly from customers using mobile devices, storing it in the cloud. This data is then utilized to evaluate repayment methods, refine service offerings, decide on subsequent loans and guide community outreach efforts.
R5	Colombia	Uses AI to offer fast and low-cost loans. It uses customers' vehicles as collateral, even if traditional banks have denied them. Customers can use these loans to invest in their businesses, consolidate debt, refinance their cars or even remodel their homes.
SCB Abacus (Siam Commercial Bank)	Thailand	Specializes in AI and alternative data to create innovative financial solutions. The company works with various industry partners, focusing on sectors like e-commerce and telecommunications. The company's flagship product, MoneyThunder, is a digital unsecured lending application that serves the underbanked population in Thailand. The platform utilizes SCB Abacus' in-house artificial intelligence and machine learning capabilities to underwrite loans and provide consumers with a completely automated approval experience. SCB Abacus also offers customers a fast time to money of 5–20 minutes from initial registration through loan disbursement. As of August 2021, MoneyThunder has seen close to 5 million application downloads, with loans disbursed surging, increasing by a multiple of 10 in 2021 versus 2020.

Cashinvoice addresses this substantial financing gap by collaborating with large and mid-sized corporations to develop tailored channel financing programmes for MSMEs in their supply chain. Cashinvoice's technology platform integrates validated invoices, historical business interactions with corporate partners and other data points to evaluate the credit risk of these small business vendors and customers associated with anchor partners.[7] For instance, a small business serving as a corporate vendor might opt for immediate payment at a discounted rate against an invoice due in the next 30 to 60 days, the typical credit period. This discount rate is determined dynamically using various data sources and the business's credit profile. Using proprietary data in this process reduces credit risk, lowering the cost of credit for MSMEs.

In a significant move towards financial inclusion, particularly for the agricultural sector, GroVentures is leveraging crowdsourced data from farmers to enhance its analytics platform. This initiative empowers farmers by involving them directly in the data exchange process and ensures that their unique needs are accurately represented in financial models. Farmers contribute their data and receive incentives such as mobile airtime credits or free access to weather and meteorological services.[8] This reciprocal exchange of information and services is poised to improve data collection methods and monitor vital elements of lending profiles, thereby promoting the adoption and implementation of best practices for the benefit of all involved.

Policymakers can further bolster these financial inclusion efforts by providing open access to data and aiding commercial entities like GroVentures. This approach is crucial in overcoming outdated and inefficient infrastructure challenges. By integrating diverse data sources, companies like GroVentures are equipped to offer tailored financial services, addressing the specific requirements of the agricultural community and fostering a more inclusive financial ecosystem.

Conclusion

The exploration of big data, alternative data and AI in this chapter underscores their pivotal role in enhancing financial inclusion, particularly for credit and lending. In markets with limited traditional banking services, the lack of comprehensive financial histories for individuals and SMEs poses a significant challenge. Alternative data emerges as a key ingredient in bridging this gap, offering new ways to assess creditworthiness beyond conventional metrics. This data, ranging from mobile phone usage to social media activity, provides a richer, more nuanced picture of potential borrowers. When paired with AI and machine learning, this data transforms into a powerful tool for crafting more inclusive credit products. The ability of alternative data to create more accurate risk models and lower default rates demonstrates its potential to revolutionize the credit landscape, particularly for underbanked populations.

Micro-lending, a critical facet of financial inclusion, also benefits significantly from integrating alternative data. Traditional micro-lending relies heavily on basic financial information and subjective assessments, often leading to conservative lending practices. The infusion of alternative data fills these gaps, enabling a more comprehensive evaluation of borrowers' financial behaviours and potential. This approach enhances the accuracy of credit assessments and broadens the reach of financial services to those traditionally excluded from the formal economy. The evolution of micro-lending through alternative data is a testament to the transformative power of these new information sources in promoting economic growth and inclusion.

However, deploying alternative data and AI in financial services is not without challenges. Data quality, technological infrastructure, regulatory compliance, financial literacy and the risk of bias are significant hurdles that need addressing. Additionally, the scarcity of skilled professionals in data science and financial technology, and resource constraints, pose further obstacles for companies working in certain markets. Despite these challenges, the potential of alternative data in financial inclusion remains immense. Noteworthy initiatives and use cases across the globe, from leveraging telco data for credit scoring to using satellite imagery for agricultural loans, highlight the innovative ways alternative data is harnessed to bridge the financial inclusion gap. The future of financial services lies in the strategic, ethical and effective use of data and AI, promising a more inclusive and equitable financial landscape for all.

Notes

1 T Segal (2024) What is big data? Definition, how it works, and uses, Investopedia. www.investopedia.com/terms/b/big-data.asp (archived at https://perma.cc/M59A-8J8B)
2 EWB Canada (nd) FarmDrive. www.ewb.ca/en/venture/farmdrive (archived at https://perma.cc/95PP-ZQAY)
3 Velocity Global (2023) The Chinese social credit system: What to know as a business owner. velocityglobal.com/resources/blog/chinese-social-credit-system (archived at https://perma.cc/F3FB-ABNR)
4 Trykarat (nd) Homepage. www.trykarat.com (archived at https://perma.cc/P375-TWDM)
5 L Burrows (2020) 2020 state of alternative credit data: Experian insights, Experian. www.experian.com/blogs/insights/2020-state-alternative-credit-data (archived at https://perma.cc/ZA7Y-WQWU)
6 Yubi (2022) Lending bias and credit gap in India's MSME sector. www.go-yubi.com/blog/credit-gap-msme-sector-causes-effects (archived at https://perma.cc/7H5Z-46U8)
7 Cashinvoice (nd) Homepage. www.cashinvoice.in (archived at https://perma.cc/L9RZ-EQXN)
8 C Byrne (2013) Data-driven lending could help African farmers feed the world, Fast Company. www.fastcompany.com/3019953/data-driven-lending-could-help-african-farmers-feed-the-world (archived at https://perma.cc/R44H-Z9SN)

14

Blockchain and distributed ledger technology

Introduction

In this chapter we will introduce distributed ledger technology (DLT), blockchain and tokenization, the backbones of the Web3 revolution. The relationship between DLT and Web3 is foundational and synergistic, with DLT representing the critical technology underpinning the Web3 vision. This vision represents the next evolution of the internet, where decentralized networks, ownership and control over data are vital themes. This is in contrast to the centralized, platform-dominated experience of Web2. After outlining the technological and conceptual foundation for Web3, in Chapter 15 we will discuss the impact and potential of cryptocurrency and decentralized finance (DeFi), two finance-focused technologies and concepts that emerge from Web3.

DLT, blockchain and tokenization gained traction within financial services in the mid-2010s. Although it has yet to upend the entire financial services space, institutions, governments and fintechs are capitalizing on the technology and Web3 concepts to change parts of the financial services fabric, identity and ownership. From the financial inclusion perspective, DLT is a technology that, although nascent, holds potential and is at a critical point as the foundation for new financial concepts and products such as tokenization, DeFi, cryptocurrency and the issuance of central bank digital currencies (CBDCs).

All of these areas have the capacity to reduce financial exclusion, with the impact and use cases discussed throughout this chapter as well as in Chapter 15 (DeFi, Cryptocurrency and Web3) and Chapter 16 (CBDC).

The potential and excitement for DLT is driven by a number of factors. The first is that DLT inherently provides greater transparency in transactions, thus reducing corruption and encouraging those who distrust traditional financial services to access an alternative financial services ecosystem. Second, DLT and its subsequent financial products such as cryptocurrency, DeFi and CBDCs are all 100 per cent digital in nature and can be stored and transferred digitally, without the need for banking branches, agencies and traditional banking infrastructure. Third, for the most part, DLT and blockchains reduce the cost to service, especially when it comes to international payments. As a result, using DLT for remittance holds a massive potential to give migrant workers significant financial savings. Lastly, new financial products born out of DeFi that mimic traditional financial products such as loans and insurances are issued without intermediaries and credit bureaus, providing financial opportunity for those traditionally excluded due to a lack of trust and low or invisible credit histories.

Despite the potential DLT and Web3 have, there remain some challenges to adoption from consumers, traditional financial institutions, regulators and governments. Several key challenges around DLT and blockchain must be resolved, including interoperability, regulation and harmonization. These have proven to be the most significant challenges to mainstream adoption not only for banks but also for private organizations and governments. Nonetheless, similar to the potential of other technologies and business models addressed throughout this book, the potential of DLT is immense in ushering in inclusive finance through tackling high costs to serve, the removal of unnecessary intermediaries and the ability to provide immutable, instant proof of identity and lendability. The use cases for DLT in mitigating exclusion extend beyond core financial services and have important implications for identity and agriculture, two root causes for financial exclusion.

This chapter will begin with a brief history and overview of DLT. We will then introduce blockchain and tokenization, followed by a deep dive into the primary challenges of DLT and exploring companies and government initiatives aiming to solve these challenges. We will wrap up with an overview of the various use cases that DLT, blockchain and tokenization have in financial inclusion, providing case studies and examples of pioneers where applicable.

DLT: When, who and how?

DLT is a broad technology category encompassing distributed databases managed by multiple participants across multiple nodes. A node is essentially a computer or server that holds a copy of the database and participates in the network. Each node works independently but follows the same rules for processing and recording transactions without central authority or oversight. In a distributed database, each participant (node) has a complete or partial copy of the database. When changes are made, such as a transaction, these changes are made to all copies of the database across all nodes. This ensures all data remains consistent and up to date across the entire network. This method of distribution helps enhance the security and accessibility of the data, because even if one or a few nodes fail or are compromised the rest of the nodes still maintain the integrity of the database. The principles underlying DLT involve decades of research and work in cryptography and computer science. Key concepts such as cryptographic hashing, public key cryptography and consensus mechanisms have been studied and developed since the 1970s and 1980s. Applying these concepts to create a decentralized ledger that could be securely and transparently maintained across multiple nodes was a significant innovation that led to the development of blockchain technology.

DLTs allow the recording, sharing and synchronizing of transactions in their respective electronic databases as each node maintains an identical copy of an immutable, verifiable, transparent ledger of records. This ledger holds a history of every transaction made, with all copies of the ledger maintained via a consensus mechanism rather than via a trusted third party. This distributed nature enhances transparency, security and resilience against fraud or failure, and it is this characteristic that can disrupt and enhance financial services, identity and access to assets.

When a transaction is made on a DLT, it is typically verified through public–private key pairs. The concept of public–private key pairs predates the emergence of Bitcoin and blockchain in 2008. Public-key cryptography is the field of cryptographic systems that use pairs of related keys. Each key pair consists of a public key and a corresponding private key. Key pairs are generated with cryptographic algorithms based on mathematical problems termed one-way functions. The security of public-key cryptography depends on keeping the private key secret; the public key can be openly distributed without compromising security. Public–private key cryptography is also known as asymmetric cryptography because it uses two keys that perform different functions but are mathematically related. The public key is used for encrypting data or verifying a digital signature, whereas the private key is used for decrypting data or creating a digital signature. The critical point is that even though the keys are related, the operations are not reversible without the other key. In cryptocurrencies, DeFi, NFT and other tokenized assets, a popular term, 'not your keys, not your coins', highlights the importance of the private keys in fully owning the asset. On the flip side, there are many anecdotes of individuals losing their private keys and, subsequently, forever losing access to their tokenized or digital assets.

Another notable feature of a DLT is the accessibility and governance of its systems, which are broadly categorized into public and private types. Further distinctions can be made between permissionless and permissioned:

- With permissionless DLTs, participation in the validation process is open to all. This inclusivity allows any individual to host a validator node and partake in the consensus protocol, facilitating the verification of transactions. Examples of permissionless networks are Bitcoin and Ethereum.

- Permissioned DLTs operate under a different paradigm, necessitating explicit approval from a governing body for one to contribute as a validator node. This setup ensures a more regulated approach to the validation of transactions. Banks and governments would use permissioned networks. R3 is an example.
- Public DLTs stand out for their openness, allowing users to execute transactions on the ledger without restrictions. Litecoin and Oceanprotocol are examples of public DLTs in addition to Bitcoin and Ethereum.
- Private DLTs operate more exclusively, limiting the privilege to append new entries to the ledger to a single, centralized authority. While reading the ledger might be open to all or restricted to a selected group, it underscores the exclusive nature of private DLTs. Hyperledger Fabric is a permissioned and private blockchain framework created by the Hyperledger consortium to help develop DLT for a variety of business applications. The consortium is made up of companies such as Airbus, Cisco, American Express, IBM and Intel.

Blockchain and tokenization vs DLT

Blockchain is a type of DLT and one of the most recognized and widely implemented forms. It can be public, private, permissionless or permissioned. It organizes data into blocks, chained together using cryptographic hashes. Each block contains several transactions, and once a block is filled it is added to the chain in a linear, chronological order. Blockchain is the technology that underpins most tokenization platforms due to its security, transparency and ability to operate without a central authority.

The first blockchain was conceptualized and developed by an individual or group using the pseudonym Satoshi Nakamoto. It was implemented as the core component of Bitcoin, which was introduced in a white paper titled 'Bitcoin: A peer-to-peer electronic cash system' in 2008.[1] This implementation marked the first successful deployment of DLT to achieve consensus (the process through which all the participants (nodes) in the decentralized network agree on the validity and order of transactions) in a decentralized network, enabling Bitcoin's launch in January 2009. Key to blockchain is smart contracts, which are self-executing contracts with the terms of the agreement directly written into lines of code within the DLT. These smart contracts run on blockchain, ensuring that the contract is executed automatically when predefined conditions are met, without an intermediary.

As these digital contracts enable parties to transact securely and transparently, the terms are predefined, agreed upon and immutable once deployed on the blockchain. This immutability comes from the decentralized nature of DLT, where transaction records, including the execution of smart contracts, are replicated across multiple nodes in the network, making them virtually tamper-proof. Smart contracts can automate a wide range of processes, from financial agreements, like payments and loans, to operations in supply chains, legal processes and even decentralized applications (dApps) that function without any central authority. dApps are the decentralized version of the apps we use on our smartphones and share a number of characteristics: because they are decentralized, no single party controls the entire application, they are typically open source, they maintain built-in economic incentive systems through cryptocurrencies which encourage participants to maintain the development and use an algorithm to generate tokens and maintain consensus across the blockchain.

Tokenization refers to converting rights to an asset into a digital token on a blockchain or DLT platform. This can include anything from fiat currencies, stocks, real estate or even unique items like artwork. Tokenization leverages the security and efficiency of blockchain technology to create and trade these digital tokens in a secure, transparent and efficient way. The tokens represent ownership or a claim on the underlying asset. They can be traded or transferred on digital platforms and allow for greater access to assets, faster settlement and greater autonomy. Table 14.1 outlines the benefits and challenges associated with tokenization.

TABLE 14.1 The benefits and challenges of tokenization

What?	Pro	Con
Accessibility	Tokenization lowers barriers to entry for investing in various assets. People can purchase fractional tokens of expensive assets, such as real estate or art, which democratizes access and potentially diversifies investment opportunities across different economic segments.	Understanding how tokens, blockchains and digital wallets work can be daunting. Investors need to be educated about these technologies to manage their investments effectively.
Liquidity	By converting physical assets into digital tokens, they can be traded more easily on digital platforms. This increases market liquidity, making it quicker and easier for investors to enter or exit positions.	Tokenization allows for the division of assets into smaller, more affordable units, which theoretically should increase liquidity. However, this can also lead to market fragmentation if different platforms issue tokens for the same type of asset without interoperability.
Settlements and security	Transactions involving tokenized assets can be settled almost instantaneously on the blockchain, unlike traditional systems where settlements might take days. This speed enhances the efficiency of trading and reduces counterparty risks.	While blockchain itself is secure, other parts of the ecosystem, including digital wallets and exchanges, can be vulnerable to hacks. Understanding and mitigating these risks is vital.
Costs	Since blockchain transactions can bypass many traditional intermediaries (like brokers and banks), the associated costs can be significantly lower, making transactions more economically viable even for smaller assets.	Digital assets can be highly volatile. A deep understanding of market dynamics and risk management is crucial. This level of financial literacy is often lacking in the under- and unbanked populations.
Reach	Tokenization on a blockchain allows for cross-border transactions without the need for currency exchange or international banking services, opening up global markets to investors.	The legal frameworks around tokenized assets are still developing in many jurisdictions. Investors need to be aware of the regulatory status of these assets to avoid legal pitfalls.

As Table 14.1 illustrates, while these benefit both the financially included and excluded in managing their financial assets, the benefits can only be realized with substantial financial literacy, something we will assume is present in discussing the potential of tokenization, interoperability and clear regulation.

Key challenges: Harmonization and interoperability

One of the most significant barriers to DLT taking off regionally and globally is the need for harmonization. Aligning DLT systems with the diverse legal and regulatory frameworks, specifically AML, KYC and data privacy, across different regional jurisdictions can be complex. Laws governing data protection, financial transactions and digital signatures vary, requiring DLT implementations to adapt and comply with multiple regulations, posing a challenge to DLT's potential in inter-nation identity and cross-border payments.

Yet, there are promising signs of regional cooperation. LACChain is a collaborative effort among Latin American and Caribbean (LAC) entities, managing a public, permissioned DLT network encompassing the LAC region. This consortium offers a governance and membership structure that honours the autonomy of each participating country, simultaneously delivering a cutting-edge technology platform throughout the region. LACChain's primary mission is to fast-track the creation of a cohesive regional DLT ecosystem, aiming to unlock this technology's vast economic and social inclusivity advantages, such as improved remittance services, streamlined regional supply chains, education verifications and ease of general mobility.[2]

With hundreds of different blockchains globally, interoperability becomes a critical challenge that affects the scalability, efficiency and widespread adoption of blockchain technologies. A lack of interoperability impacts the ability of different blockchain networks to communicate, share information and understand each other without intermediaries. This is crucial for creating a seamless and integrated blockchain ecosystem where various platforms and applications interact effortlessly. To address interoperability issues, several approaches and technologies have been developed:

- **Cross-chain technology:** Solutions like Polkadot, Cosmos and Avalanche are designed to enable different blockchains to interoperate and share information. They use various mechanisms such as bridges, sidechains and layer 0 protocols to facilitate communication between blockchains.
- **Interledger protocols:** These protocols enable payments across different blockchain networks. For example, the Interledger Protocol (ILP) is designed to connect different ledgers and allow for secure transfers.
- **Blockchain agnostic protocols:** Some projects aim to be blockchain-agnostic, meaning they can operate on top of multiple blockchains without favouring any particular network. This approach increases the flexibility and potential reach of applications.

A private global organization, Quant, seeks to mitigate the challenges and solve interoperability issues. The company's mission revolves around making blockchain simple, trusted and future-proof. Quant believes in the power of interconnected networks to build the future of finance, where value, in the form of smart money, tokenized assets and information, flows freely between different blockchain systems.

Quant's flagship offering, Overledger, is a blockchain operating system designed to connect different blockchain networks, facilitate the creation and management of digital assets and enable the development of multi-chain applications (MApps).[3] This platform is built on principles that emphasize simplicity, trust, security and future-proofing, making blockchain technology accessible to entities without requiring them to have in-depth blockchain expertise.

Quant addresses critical areas such as financial inclusion, tokenization, identity and cross-border payments by leveraging its interoperability platform, Overledger, and aims to bridge the gap between traditional banking systems and blockchain technology for financial inclusion, enabling unbanked and underbanked populations access to financial services through DLT. By connecting different blockchain networks, Quant facilitates the creation and transfer of tokenized assets, democratizing access to investment opportunities and enabling seamless asset management. This process includes tokenizing real-world assets and securing digital identities, ensuring users can transact on these platforms with trust and privacy.

Mitigating challenges around interoperability is critical for developing groundbreaking and sustainable use cases for DLT in creating financial inclusion. Similar to the impact of other technologies discussed throughout the book, solving interoperability and ensuring DLT is a future-proof technology will lead to less financial exclusion by lowering barriers to entry, enabling micro-transactions, specifically low-cost cross-border payments and supporting identity verification.

Unpacking the use cases

Identity

Identity is an area in which DLT can have an immense impact on financial exclusion. As discussed in Chapter 12, identity is at the foundation of any financial services relationship. It is also a root cause of many challenges banks and financial institutions face when combatting financial inclusion. Applying DLT to an identification system has the potential to bring in several benefits. It almost instantly overcomes many current challenges in centralized identity systems by promoting a self-sovereign identity (SSI). The beauty of using DLT as a means for identification is that the very nature of the technology makes fraud virtually impossible. Identification becomes portable and is trustworthy.

The most noteworthy initiative of DLT-based identity within financial services is R3, a consortium of over 80 financial institutions and regulators worldwide tasked with designing and delivering DLT within financial services. As early as 2016, several R3 member banks developed a proof-of-concept for a KYC registry that operates on the R3 Corda platform.[4] This registry allows the identity of individuals and entities to be managed by the identity owners. It also allows other participants on the platform to access their digital identity for client onboarding and KYC and AML purposes. From the AML perspective, DLT has the potential to dramatically reduce compliance costs and enhance workflows and processes for onboarding and maintaining customer accounts. According to KPMG, in 2014 the global cost of complying with AML laws and regulations was estimated to be about $10 billion.[5] Implementing DLT can eliminate inefficiencies such as silos, duplication and fraud. The system described above allows for inter-organization sharing with users' consent. It can be critical for the underbanked to access additional products and services more quickly and straightforwardly.

Looking to the future, should a DLT-based identity system expand between financial institutions and mobile network operators (MNOs), unbanked individuals who have a relationship with an MNO could, in theory, quickly and frictionlessly become included in the traditional financial system through the elimination of repetition and the ability to share real-time customer data.

Settlement and remittance

A second high-impact area for DLT in mitigating financial exclusion is the remittance space. DLT can help banks improve their clearance and settlement mechanisms. Sending or receiving money across international borders is expensive and cumbersome as the process involves multiple parties, intermediaries, banks and often different financial systems. All of this means that international payments can take up to three days. By leveraging DLT, a decentralized blockchain can make redundant the need for any intermediary and enable banks to process international transfers almost as soon as they are initiated, a significant benefit for both customers and banks.

A noteworthy initiative regarding interbank clearance and DLT comes from South Africa's central bank, the South African Reserve Bank (SARB). This initiative, known as Project Khokha 2, builds on the success of the original Project Khokha, which demonstrated the potential of DLT in improving interbank payment systems. Project Khokha 2 delves deeper into the transformative possibilities of DLT, particularly in asset tokenization, trading, clearing and settlement processes.

Key to Project Khokha 2 was the issuance of a SARB debenture (a debt instrument) using DLT.[6] This included innovative payment mechanisms such as a wholesale central bank digital currency (wCBDC) and a wholesale digital settlement token (wToken). This project phase was marked by a collaborative effort involving key financial institutions and leading technology firms, tackling challenges such as platform interoperability, token portability and the implementation of complex delivery versus payment (DvP) mechanisms. The project highlighted potential benefits such as cost efficiencies, improved operational effectiveness and increased transactional transparency, indicating a future of financial transactions marked by enhanced security and efficiency.

Another example of using blockchain technology to enhance interbank settlement comes from the Philippines, where UnionBank and ConsenSys partnered to launch Project i2i, which aims to connect rural banks through a blockchain platform.[7] Many rural banks in the Philippines are not connected to the country's main payment networks, isolating them from the broader financial system. When a rural bank is not connected to a country's main payment network, its customers face significant disadvantages that affect their financial activities and broader economic opportunities. Customers often have limited access to comprehensive financial services, such as online banking and electronic payments, making it difficult to engage in the modern financial market. Transactions are often delayed, slow and incur high fees due to the need for manual processing or intermediaries. This lack of direct connectivity can also hinder customers' ability to expand businesses or participate effectively in the global economy, as they are unable to perform quick and reliable financial transactions. The isolation exacerbates economic disparities by acting as a barrier to financial inclusion, particularly affecting those in remote areas. Additionally, rural bank customers might rely more on cash, which can be insecure and cumbersome, making it difficult to build credit histories or access credit products. In emergency situations, the inability to quickly transfer or receive funds can be destabilizing and even debilitating, and for communities that depend on remittances from family members working afar the absence of connection to main payment networks complicates and increases the cost of sending and receiving money, necessitating less efficient and more costly alternatives. Project i2i uses blockchain to facilitate real-time payments and connect these banks, improving financial inclusion for rural communities.

Tokenization

By leveraging DLT, tokenization can democratize access to financial services and assets, making them more inclusive and accessible. Tokenization enhances the liquidity of assets by enabling fractional ownership, significantly lowering the entry barrier for investment. This democratization of asset ownership allows people with limited financial resources to participate in markets from which they were traditionally excluded, such as real estate or art. By facilitating smaller investments, tokenization opens up new opportunities for wealth generation and financial participation for underserved populations.

It also paves the way for lower costs to serve, automating financial processes through smart contracts and reducing intermediary involvement streamline transactions, making them faster and less costly. For individuals in developing regions or those without access to traditional banking, these efficiencies mean that participating in the financial system becomes more viable. Lower transaction costs can make a significant difference in the affordability of financial services, encouraging greater participation and reducing exclusion.

As tokenization takes place with blockchain technology, all transactions are transparent, traceable and immutable, which helps to build trust among participants in the financial system. This level of transparency and security is significant for individuals who have been marginalized or have limited access to financial services due to concerns about fraud or corruption. By providing a more secure and transparent framework for financial transactions, tokenization can bring these individuals into the fold of the formal economy.

Tokenization also has the potential to break down geographical and regulatory barriers, allowing investors and participants from around the world to access financial markets and assets previously out of reach. This global accessibility is crucial for fighting financial exclusion, allowing individuals in remote or underserved regions to engage with global financial markets. The ability to participate in a broader range of financial activities can lead to more diversified investment strategies and economic opportunities, contributing to financial inclusion.

Finally, tokenization can facilitate compliance with regulatory requirements by using smart contracts that can be programmed to enforce KYC and AML regulations automatically. This automation can simplify accessing financial services by reducing the bureaucratic hurdles and paperwork that often deter or exclude individuals from participating in the financial system. By making compliance more streamlined and less burdensome, tokenization can significantly open financial services to a broader population.

The future of tokenization is promising. Asset tokenization can unlock liquidity to support economic growth and democratize access to and broaden investment options. Analysts at Citigroup have forecast that $4 trillion to $5 trillion of tokenized digital securities could be issued by 2030.[8] A report from Boston Consulting Group and ADDX predicts that some $16 trillion worth of illiquid assets will be tokenized by 2030.[9]

Beyond core financial services

Tokenization also holds immense potential in other critical areas for the financially excluded. For example, tokenization of land registry documents can also overcome the challenges of providing proof of address by converting ownership or rights to a piece of land into digital tokens on a blockchain. There are already a handful of pilots and initiatives live in this area.

The Republic of Georgia was one of the pioneering countries to implement blockchain technology in its land registry process. In partnership with the US-based blockchain company Bitfury, Georgia's National Agency of Public Registry launched a project to register land titles using blockchain technology. This initiative began around 2016 and aimed to secure land titles and reduce fraud by making the land registry system transparent and immutable.[10] The blockchain-based registry system allows for secure and rapid updates to land records, enhancing trust among citizens and reducing the opportunities for corruption and tampering with land records.

In the agricultural sector, tokenization can facilitate small-scale farmers' access to capital by allowing them to tokenize their expected harvest, thereby securing upfront investment from a broader range of investors. Tokenization allows them to secure upfront investment by offering tokens representing a share of their expected harvest to a broader range of investors. This method not only provides immediate financial resources needed for cultivation but also opens investment opportunities to individuals who traditionally would not have access to agricultural investments. Similarly, in the art and entertainment industries, artists and creators can tokenize their work, offering a piece of their future earnings in exchange for immediate funding, thus bypassing traditional funding avenues that might be inaccessible or unfavourable.

Developing and accessing the renewable energy sector is also a significant potential area. SaFi is a protocol seeking to bridge the gap in the energy sector by tokenizing qualified real-world clean energy projects. With a $1 billion funding gap in the renewable energy sector in Africa and Southeast Asia, the protocol offers finance for renewable energy assets such as solar power systems by connecting investors with borrowers.

Conclusion

In concluding this chapter, we've delved into DLT, blockchain and tokenization, exploring their capacities to reshape the financial landscape. At their core, these technologies offer a new paradigm for recording, verifying and transferring assets in a decentralized, secure and transparent way. DLT, with blockchain, provides a framework where transactions are recorded across multiple nodes, eliminating the need for central intermediaries and reducing potential points of failure. Tokenization further extends this innovation by converting real-world assets into digital tokens, broadening access to investment opportunities and enhancing liquidity in markets traditionally characterized by high entry barriers.

The potential of these technologies to combat financial exclusion is profound. By enabling fractional ownership, DLT and tokenization, individuals with limited capital can invest in a range of new asset classes. This democratization of investment opportunities is a crucial step towards financial inclusivity. Additionally, blockchain-based transactions' inherent transparency and security can build trust in financial systems among underserved populations, encouraging their participation. Smart contracts automate and streamline processes, reducing costs and making financial services more accessible to those traditionally excluded from the banking system.

Several use cases stand out in illustrating the impact of DLT and tokenization. In real estate, platforms are emerging that allow for property tokenization, enabling investors to buy fractions of real estate assets and thereby lowering the investment threshold. Farmers can tokenize their future harvests in agriculture, gaining access to capital by selling these tokens to investors. Governments and central banks are exploring the issuance of digital currencies and blockchain for land registries, aiming to improve efficiency, reduce fraud, and enhance access to property ownership and financial services.

As we transition from discussing the foundational elements of DLT, blockchain and tokenization, it's clear that these technologies hold the keys to unlocking a more inclusive financial future. They challenge the status quo of financial exclusion by providing tools to bridge the gap between the unbanked and the global financial ecosystem. The next chapters will delve deeper into decentralized finance (DeFi) and cryptocurrencies, exploring how these applications of

DLT can further dismantle barriers to financial inclusion, offering innovative solutions to the longstanding problems of access, trust and equity in finance.

Notes

1. S Nakamoto (2008) Bitcoin: A peer-to-peer electronic cash system, Bitcoin. bitcoin.org/bitcoin.pdf (archived at https://perma.cc/7HT5-KGLM)
2. Hyperledger Foundation (2023) LACChain introduces permissioned public blockchain ecosystem to LATAM, LF Decentralized Trust. www.lfdecentralizedtrust.org/case-studies/lacchain-case-study (archived at https://perma.cc/3GK5-TNF7)
3. A Carrier (2023) Quant launches Overledger platform, Quant. quant.network/news/quant-launches-overledger-platform (archived at https://perma.cc/6LCF-DYZB)
4. I Allison (2016) R3 develops proof-of-concept for shared KYC service with 10 global banks, International Business Times UK. www.ibtimes.co.uk/r3-develops-proof-concept-shared-kyc-service-10-global-banks-1590908 (archived at https://perma.cc/CBT3-24WL)
5. KPMG (2015) *Global Anti-Money Laundering Survey 2014*, KPMG. assets.kpmg.com/content/dam/kpmg/pdf/2015/03/global-anti-money-laundering-survey-latest.pdf (archived at https://perma.cc/4XCS-9YJC)
6. BitKE (2023) Next phase of Project Khokha, South Africa's CBDC, to explore interoperability and 'DAO principles'. bitcoinke.io/2023/03/project-khokha-to-explore-dao-principles (archived at https://perma.cc/7Z5N-EDAA)
7. Consensys (nd) Blockchain payments: Project i2i case study. consensys.io/blockchain-use-cases/finance/project-i2i (archived at https://perma.cc/R2WK-3PTB)
8. Citi Group (2023) Money, tokens, and games. www.citigroup.com/global/insights/money-tokens-and-games (archived at https://perma.cc/AK23-ET8H)
9. S Kumar, R Suresh, D Liu, B Kronfellner and A Kaul (2022) *Relevance of On-Chain Asset Tokenization in 'Crypto Winter'*, BCG and ADDX. documents.addx.co/relevance_of_onchain_asset_tokenization_in_crypto_winter.pdf (archived at https://perma.cc/MD57-5T45)
10. Bitfury (2022) The Bitfury Group and Government of Republic of Georgia expand historic blockchain land-titling project. bitfury.com/content/downloads/the_bitfury_group_republic_of_georgia_expand_blockchain_pilot_2_7_16.pdf (archived at https://perma.cc/8LQT-TVV5)

15

Decentralized finance, cryptocurrency and Web3

In this chapter we delve into the advancements brought about by Web3, explicitly focusing on decentralized finance (DeFi). Web3 signifies a transformative stage in internet applications, marked by a shift towards decentralization. This progression builds on the foundations of Web1, which offered online content consumption, and Web2, which facilitated both consumption and content creation. This chapter delves into the intrinsic financial possibilities that DeFi offers in financial inclusion.

As a concept, DeFi means different things to different people and institutions. These include:

- An emerging financial technology based on secure distributed ledgers similar to those used by cryptocurrencies.[1]
- An umbrella term for peer-to-peer financial services on public blockchains.[2]
- An emerging model for organizing and enabling cryptocurrency-based transactions, exchanges and financial services.[3]
- The offering of financial instruments without relying on intermediaries such as brokerages, exchanges or banks by using smart contracts on a blockchain, mainly Ethereum.

This chapter will explore DeFi based on the third and fourth of these perspectives, focusing on cryptocurrencies, exchanges and financial products run on blockchain technology. We include centralized finance exchanges (CEX), which are cryptocurrency exchanges controlled by a central entity, in our broader concept of decentralized finance as cryptocurrencies are at the heart of such exchanges.

Before outlining how DeFi challenges the traditional financial system and how DeFi can promote financial inclusion, we will define critical terms to understand the DeFi ecosystem.

Definitions

Blockchain: A blockchain is a shared database spread across a network of computers. While they're most recognized for their importance in ensuring a safe and decentralized record for digital currencies, their applications extend beyond that. Blockchains can ensure data remains unchangeable in various sectors.

On- and off-chain: On-chain transactions are validated and recorded directly on the blockchain, ensuring security and immutability. Off-chain transactions occur outside the blockchain, offering speed and efficiency but without the blockchain's inherent security.

Cryptocurrency: A cryptocurrency is a digital or virtual currency that uses cryptography for security and operates independently of a central bank or traditional financial institution.

Self-custody: This is when a holder of an asset, especially cryptocurrencies, holds and manages their assets without relying on third-party institutions or intermediaries for the storage or management.

Keys: In cryptocurrency, 'keys' refer to a pair of cryptographic elements: a private key, a secret string used to authorize transactions, and a public key, which generates addresses to receive funds. The private key must be kept confidential, while the public key can be shared.

Stablecoins: Stablecoins are a type of cryptocurrency designed to have a stable value by being pegged to a reserve or reference, such as a specific amount of a commodity or the value of a fiat currency like the US dollar. Their primary purpose is to reduce volatility typically associated with cryptocurrencies like Bitcoin or Ethereum.

Liquidity mining and yield farming: Around mid-2020, the DeFi space popularized concepts like liquidity mining and yield farming, where users could earn returns by providing liquidity or participating in specific protocol interactions.

Ethereum and smart contracts: In 2015, Ethereum, a decentralized blockchain, allowed developers to create more complex financial applications, called DApps (decentralized applications), on its platform. This paved the way for lending platforms, decentralized exchanges and other financial services without intermediaries.

Cryptocurrency exchanges: These function similarly to online brokers, providing the tools and markets to buy and sell cryptocurrency. Exchanges take several forms, including:

- Centralized exchanges are platforms controlled by a centralized entity. They typically require users to undergo KYC, hold users' funds in custody and have access to users' private keys. Notable exchanges include Binance, Coinbase and Kraken. Brokerages, fiat-to-crypto exchanges and crypto-to-crypto exchanges are also centralized.
- A decentralized exchange (DEX) platform operates autonomously, with no central organization overseeing operations. Not all DEXs require KYC, nor are they regulated by local authorities, providing a trade-off for users. On the one hand, they do not have to undergo KYC, but on the other hand their funds are not protected by deposit schemes or regulators. Types of DEXs include:
  - On-chain order books: These DEXs manage and settle trades directly on a blockchain. Examples include StellarTerm on the Stellar network.
  - Automated market makers (AMMs): These include platforms like Uniswap or PancakeSwap where liquidity pools are used instead of order books. Users trade against these pools, and prices adjust using a predetermined algorithm.

- Off-chain order books with on-chain settlement: These are platforms like 0x, which uses off-chain methods for order matching but settles trades on-chain.
- Cross-chain DEXs: For example, platforms like ThorChain, which allow for trading assets between different blockchains.

TradFi vs DeFi

Table 15.1 outlines the key differences between traditional finance (TradFi) and DeFi.

TABLE 15.1 Key differences between TradFi and DeFi

	TradFi	DeFi
Ability to pay interest	Banks give interest on deposits based on central bank rates, generally lower.	Ranges from CEXs offering interest on crypto deposits to decentralized platforms enabling high-yield strategies, albeit with higher risk.
Access	Often, there are geographical or financial barriers, requiring documentation and credit checks.	More inclusive, though CEXs might require identity verification. Many platforms provide open access, regardless of location or status.
Access to loans	Involves credit checks and documentation, and can have stringent approval criteria.	Platforms, including some CEXs, offer crypto-backed loans with streamlined processes. Other platforms provide loans based on over-collateralization without credit checks.
Consumer protection	Established regulations and government oversight ensure consumer protection.	CEXs often have internal measures and some regulatory compliance, offering user protection, but can be targeted for large hacks. DEXs have less explicit consumer protection. Users need to be more self-reliant.
Costs	Often incur higher fees due to operational overheads and intermediaries.	Typically offers competitive rates; decentralized platforms can have lower fees, but CEXs and network congestion might increase costs.

(continued)

TABLE 15.1 (Continued)

	TradFi	DeFi
Ownership	Operates through centralized entities like banks, brokers and regulators.	Includes a mix of decentralized platforms and centralized exchanges (CEXs). While CEXs function with intermediaries, many DeFi platforms operate without them.
Regulation and oversight	Heavily regulated by governments and institutions. Compliance and oversight are central to operations.	A mixed bag: while CEXs often adhere to regulations, many decentralized platforms operate in a more permissionless environment.
Settlement and speed	Transactions, especially cross-border ones, can take days to settle due to intermediaries.	Depending on the blockchain's congestion and design, transactions can settle in seconds to minutes.
Transparency	Operations are often opaque to the general public, with access to detailed financial data restricted.	Typically offers transparent operations, as transactions and protocols are available on public ledgers.

Potential for financial inclusion

To understand how DeFi can solve many of the pain points in traditional finance regarding financial inclusion, it is worth briefly outlining the rationale behind the creation of Bitcoin, the catalyst for the DeFi movement. In 2008, the Bitcoin white paper was published by a person or organization using the pseudonym Satoshi Nakamoto. The primary objective was to create a peer-to-peer version of electronic cash, sending this electronic cash directly from one party to another without needing a trusted third party, like a bank or financial institution.

Bitcoin aimed to eliminate the need for central control and thus censorship of transactions. In addition, it hoped to minimize the reliance on and trust in third-party institutions for financial transactions and have a predictable monetary policy, as the total supply of Bitcoin is capped at 21 million. This, Nakamoto envisaged, would counter the inflationary practices of traditional fiat currencies. Lastly, central to Bitcoin was ultimate transparency, with all transactions recorded on a public ledger, the blockchain.

Out of this vision, DeFi evolved upon these motivations and ethos to recreate a traditional financial system, incorporating lending, borrowing derivatives, exchanges and payments in a decentralized, transparent, less-costly and permissionless manner using blockchain technology. Therefore, the very nature of DeFi overcomes several inherent challenges of TradFi:

- DeFi products encourage open access and financial inclusion by allowing anyone, regardless of location or socio-economic status, to access financial products and services on DeFi platforms. This overcomes the limitation of physical banking access in remote or underserved areas without agency banking.
- The transparency of transactions aims to build trust and security, ensuring fairness and helping to build trust in the system, overcoming a hurdle by TradFi regarding fairness and inclusion.
- Innovation in DeFi is permissionless, as developers can, in theory, create new financial products and services without requiring approval from a central authority. Rapid innovation to solve niche or ubiquitous pain points is achievable.
- Due to transparency, operational efficiency, standardized protocols, automation from smart contracts and removing intermediaries, transacting in DeFi is typically less costly than in TradFi. This becomes critical for remittances, and several DeFi solutions target the remittance market, offering faster transaction times and minimal fees
- In recent years, DeFi has created alternatives to traditional means for earning interest and receiving loans, as there is no stringent credit-check barrier. There are no minimum deposit barriers and no central institution setting interest rates.
- In some markets with high levels of financial exclusion, local currencies experience significant volatility, for example, Turkey, Venezuela, Nigeria and Lebanon. DeFi has facilitated a solution to this via the creation of Stablecoins.

DeFi presents a Catch-22. From an accessibility perspective, it offers immense potential to support consumers and businesses excluded from traditional finance but at significant risk, including a lack of regulation and consumer protection, price volatility, custody risks, liquidity concerns, technical complexity, a steep learning curve and customer support. When these risks materialize, they are often so paramount that they leave customers worse off and equally, if not further, excluded.

Despite the risks, trailblazers operating in the DeFi space are numerous. Naturally, there is a high skew to start-ups and organizations that are capitalizing on the DeFi movement to mitigate financial exclusion via bringing the under- and unbanked into a financial services ecosystem, albeit in the decentralized finance world. The remainder of this chapter will profile selected trailblazers using cryptocurrency and DeFi to bring about financial inclusion.

Exchanges and investments

Cryptocurrency exchanges differ from traditional finance exchanges by focusing on digital assets like Bitcoin, offering benefits such as enhanced financial inclusion for the unbanked, reduced transaction costs due to lower fees, and improved transparency and security through blockchain technology. These exchanges provide access to financial services in regions lacking traditional banking infrastructure, facilitate cost-effective transactions, and ensure secure and transparent transactions through decentralized networks. Overall, the benefits of cryptocurrency exchanges for the financially excluded include increased accessibility, lower fees and enhanced security compared to traditional finance exchanges.

Buscha

Busha is one of Africa's leading digital assets platforms, facilitating Nigerians to trade over 40 cryptocurrencies. It aims to create a financial system that is open and available globally, focusing on innovation and efficiency.

Busha solves a pain point in several markets with high levels of financial exclusion: a volatile local currency. To mitigate this and ensure individuals can secure savings and investments, it offers Busha Yield, which allows users to earn interest on USD Stablecoins (USDT and USDC). The barrier to entry is low, with a minimum investment of 10 USDT. Busha offers a wallet that allows users to get cashback in Naira by spending their cryptocurrencies.

While the above features are standard for leading crypto exchanges, Busha is trialling a 'commerce' feature allowing merchants to accept Stablecoins. Furthermore, Busha ensures its product is 'localized' for the cash economy as it also operates an agency model called Busha Connect.

Valr

Valr is one of the largest digital exchanges in South Africa, servicing over 100,000 clients. Its objective is to allow users to 'be borderless' through the buying and selling of cryptocurrencies. Although Valr is not regulated, it states it is built on highly renowned security protocols and stores cryptocurrencies in both cold storage and hot wallets. Furthermore, Valr states that fiat money is always held in segregated accounts.

In October 2023 Valr announced a partnership with Visa, allowing the exchange to issue Visa cards and deliver innovative digital payment solutions.[4] Crypto cards are either debit or credit cards typically issued by an exchange where users can spend directly from their crypto or fiat balances, bridging the fiat and crypto spaces. In markets or areas where traditional banking is costly or inaccessible, crypto cards offer a way for individuals to safely spend their money out of the cash-based economy. However, the utility of crypto cards for financial inclusion rests on two criteria: a user must have a formal ID to obtain the card and fund the card exchange via fiat or cryptocurrency in the first place.

In addition to a centralized exchange, Valr offers Valr Pay, a peer-to-peer payment app that allows users to send fiat and cryptocurrencies to anyone instantly and for free. Valr capitalizes on messaging app ubiquity, incorporating WhatsApp and Telegram as channels in which users can send funds to each other, in addition to mobile numbers and email addresses of their VALR Pay ID. Facilitating payments via messaging apps overcomes education and usability barriers for the under- and unbanked who may need to be more accustomed to using traditional banking platforms.

Accrue

A pan-African app providing users with a number of fiat and cryptocurrency financial offerings, including USD virtual card creation, which can be funded with MoMo, M-Pesa, bank transfer or Stablecoins, interest-bearing accounts on Stablecoins, auto-investing in stocks, Stablecoins and cryptocurrencies, and sending money to anyone in Africa within minutes. Currently available to users in a number of African markets, including Ghana, Nigeria, Kenya, South Africa, Cameroon, Uganda, Zambia, Tanzania and Mali, it is truly tailored to the African market as it allows for payouts to M-Pesa and other mobile money operators. It also encourages essential money management via shared savings goals and budgets and goals.

By integrating local payment systems like MoMo, M-Pesa and other mobile money operators, Accrue ensures wider accessibility, even to those without traditional banking. Its presence across multiple African countries further broadens its reach. Additionally, by fostering financial literacy and empowerment through features like shared savings goals, budgets and investment options in stocks and cryptocurrencies, the app provides transactional solutions and encourages sustainable financial growth and independence.

Payments and remittance

Blockchain-based cross-border payments offer several advantages over traditional payment rails, including substantially lower transaction costs by eliminating intermediaries, faster and more secure transactions and improved transparency through immutable records on the blockchain. Cryptocurrencies and Stablecoins can be used as bridge assets to facilitate currency conversion without relying on banks. However, challenges remain around compliance with anti-money laundering regulations, crypto volatility and the need for reliable off-ramps to convert crypto to local currency.

Traditional cross-border payment methods via banks and SWIFT still dominate, but innovative blockchain solutions are emerging to address pain points like high costs, slow settlement times and lack of transparency. Large global banks have less incentive to adopt new blockchain-based payment rails, while smaller banks and fintechs are more eager to leverage the technology to gain market share and provide better customer experiences.

Hurupay

Hurupay is a payments app for consumers and businesses, which likens itself to a 'Stablecoin Bank'.[5] The mission of Hurupay is to mitigate the impact of currency depreciation and slow and costly cross-border transactions. According to Hurupay, cross-border transactions originating from Africa incur an 8 per cent fee on average and take up to three business days.[6]

Hurupay facilitates quick cross-border money transfers, allowing payments directly to Mobile Money wallets using a mobile number, name and operator. Globally, anyone can send payments to Hurupay users in mere seconds without any fees. The platform introduces the concept of saving in Stablecoins like cUSD, USDT and USDC. With a 2 per cent withdrawal fee and free intra-Hurupay transactions, the platform prioritizes affordability. Multiple transaction methods, including Momo, M-Pesa and Bank Account, make it adaptable and tailored to African users.

The focus on businesses here is a first mover in the DeFi space. Hurupay provides SMEs free in-app advertising, in addition to the promotion and enablement of Stablecoin payments, simplified via QR codes.

Hurupay's offerings are pivotal in reducing financial exclusion in Africa. Its use of Stablecoins ensures that savings are protected from volatile local market shifts. The platform's approach to international transfers is cost-effective and swift, promoting broader financial inclusivity. Its simplicity ensures even those without traditional banking can participate, and by offering SMEs tools for financial stability it promotes broader economic growth in the region.

Coins.ph

Founded in 2014, Coins.ph facilitates the exchange of cryptocurrency to fiat money and vice versa in the Philippines. The platform enables Filipinos to buy Bitcoins and ether easily, serving as a conduit for various financial transactions. Users can pay utility bills, purchase mobile loads, and engage in bank transfers and remittance services through Coins.ph. By making cryptocurrency transactions more accessible, Coins.ph contributes towards financial inclusivity.

Bloom Solutions

Serving the Filipino market, Bloom Solutions aims to make remittances more efficient. While initially serving remittance corridors in Australia, Hong Kong and South Korea, the overarching goal is to enhance the efficiency of remittance companies using blockchain technology. The company provides a fast, safe and secure way of executing remittances, working alongside existing remittance companies rather than competing with them.

Sendcash

Sendcash is a digital platform designed for facilitating quick and cost-effective fund transfers to and from Nigeria, addressing the often tedious and expensive traditional methods of cross-border money transfers. Sendcash allows for immediate fund transfers from Nigeria to over 80 countries worldwide and vice versa, with competitive exchange rates.

The primary functionality of Sendcash revolves around using Bitcoin for executing cross-border transfers. Users can send Bitcoin converted and deposited as Nigerian Naira in the recipient's bank account in Nigeria. This streamlined process is typically completed within five minutes, marking a significant speed advantage over traditional money transfer methods.

Furthermore, Sendcash has expanded its payment method offerings to include USDT (Tether), USD accounts and bank card transactions, catering to a broader user base and offering more flexibility in transferring funds. The addition of these payment methods also suggests an adaptability to various financial preferences and global monetary frameworks.

While the platform primarily facilitates personal fund transfers, making it easier for individuals to send money to family and friends in Nigeria or receive payments from clients abroad, the potential business applications could be inferred, especially in the context of freelancers and small businesses engaging in international transactions.

The offerings of Sendcash are instrumental in addressing the challenges of financial inclusion and economic growth, particularly in regions like Nigeria, where traditional banking systems and cross-border transactions can be cumbersome and costly. By leveraging cryptocurrency and other digital payment methods, Sendcash is making cross-border transactions not only more accessible but also more efficient and affordable, which, in turn, could have a ripple effect on economic growth and financial inclusivity in the region.

Infrastructure

While blockchain-based financial infrastructure is discussed in further detail in Chapters 14 and 16, it is worth highlighting a number of decentralized infrastructure supporting fintech and bank innovation particularly for the under- and unbanked. These trailblazers, doubling down on DeFi as a means to solve the financial inclusion problem, tend to target corporates in addition to start-ups, making them an agnostic player amongst their partners.

Stellar

The Stellar Development Foundation (SDF) is a non-profit organization that aims to create equitable access to the global financial system through blockchain technology. The Stellar network is an open-source blockchain for various payment and remittance applications. It highlights four use cases for its blockchain: cross-border payments, asset tokenization, on- and off-ramps, and aid disbursements. Stellar caters to pure-play DeFi projects but is also used by traditional institutions such as MoneyGram, Latamex and the UN United Nations High Commissioner for Refugees (UNHCR).

UNHCR, in partnership with the United Nations International Computing Centre, is pioneering the use of Stellar Aid Assist, a Stellar-based aid disbursement solution, to deliver cash assistance directly to beneficiaries with speed, efficiency and security. This innovative approach ensures full traceability and accountability in transferring aid, laying the foundation for future financial innovations in cash assistance and donation programmes. Leveraging the Stellar Disbursement Platform, Stellar Aid Assist enables instant bulk disbursements of USDC Stablecoin, backed by cash and short-dated US Treasuries, through the low-fee and efficient Stellar network, reaching recipients globally without the need for traditional bank accounts. This initiative not only empowers vulnerable populations by providing access to funds through digital wallets like Vibrant but also enhances transparency, traceability and real-time monitoring for aid organizations, ensuring timely and targeted assistance delivery.

Celo

Celo's mission is 'to build a financial system that creates the conditions for prosperity – for everyone'.[7] To date, Celo has over 1,000 projects building upon its infrastructure. It is a project and platform that allows anyone to access and build DeFi products as long as they have a mobile phone. Two important features that mitigate challenges with the financially excluded include phone number-based identity and an 'ultra-light' client. Phone number-based identity allows users to send and receive payments using phone numbers instead of wallet addresses. At the same time, the ultra-light client is a lightweight version of the Celo blockchain that can run on mobile phones without needing a stable internet connection or processing power.

Humaniq

Humaniq is a company that addresses financial exclusion by providing access to financial services. Utilizing blockchain technology, it offers a secure and transparent platform for financial transactions via the Ethereum blockchain. It aims to mitigate the challenge around formal identification and banking history as a means to access financial platforms by leveraging biometric identification systems. At the heart of Humaniq, users can engage in lending and donation activities. They can lend money to businesses they wish to support, either as grants or with the expectation of a return. The platform's blockchain technology is highlighted for simplifying this process, making it easier for users to engage in lending and donation activities securely and transparently.

AgenteBTC

Established in 2019 in Peru, AgenteBTC aspires to democratize financial access in Latin America. The core mission of AgenteBTC is to provide higher returns, lower remittance rates and enhance financial accessibility. Through its initiative, KasNet, AgenteBTC is setting up 15,000 centres across Peru to serve up to 32 million previously underserved customers. The company emphasizes engagement with local communities to redefine financial accessibility in the region, offering crypto assets through over 14,000 physical cash-in points. AgenteBTC's approach is designed to bridge the financial divide, offering an alternative to traditional banking services in Latin America.

Conclusion

This chapter examined the possibilities that DeFi and cryptocurrencies offer under the broader umbrella of Web3 in tackling financial exclusion. By delving into the primary difference between TradFi and DeFi, we demonstrated how the inherent nature of DeFi aims to create an inclusive financial ecosystem via greater transparency and the removal of intermediaries. Through this system, DeFi and cryptocurrencies help to create cheaper and quicker means to send money, and, through the introduction of Stablecoins, engage in stable savings, investing and lending.

When investing and trading cryptocurrencies, a high degree of speculation and volatility poses a significant risk to those already in a precarious financial situation but provides a platform to grow their wealth. Decentralized platforms that cater to the Agency Model, popular in Africa and Latin America, demonstrate a unique approach to bringing DeFi to physical channels. Platforms such as Busha, Valr, Accrue and Hurupay stand as more than mere innovations – they are active players in combatting the longstanding issues of financial exclusion.

Notes

1 R Sharma (2024) Decentralized finance (DeFi) definition and use cases, Investopedia. www.investopedia.com/decentralized-finance-defi-5113835 (archived at https://perma.cc/2LJH-MFBF)

2 Coinbase (nd) What is DeFi? www.coinbase.com/learn/crypto-basics/what-is-defi (archived at https://perma.cc/9NXG-KV3K)

3 S M Kerner (nd) Decentralized finance (DeFi), TechTarget. www.techtarget.com/whatis/definition/decentralized-finance-DeFi (archived at https://perma.cc/2247-QKSV)

4 VALR (2023) VALR and Visa unveil new crypto card in South Africa and beyond. blog.valr.com/blog/valr-and-visa-a-new-era-of-digital-payments-in-south-africa-and-beyond (archived at https://perma.cc/YJY9-UTJ5)

5 Hurupay (nd) Homepage. www.hurupay.com (archived at https://perma.cc/J24X-3X24)

6 Hurupay (nd) Homepage. www.hurupay.com (archived at https://perma.cc/2YR3-ZADX)

7 Celo (nd) Discover Celo. docs.celo.org/general (archived at https://perma.cc/5L7G-84DV)

16

Central bank digital currency

Central bank digital currency (CBDC) represents a digital currency issued by a central bank, directly linking its value to the broader financial ecosystem. While it is commonly perceived that CBDCs can play a pivotal role in integrating the financially excluded into the formal financial system, this viewpoint has its complexities. It's essential to acknowledge that the concept of CBDC as a tool for financial inclusion is still nascent. Its effectiveness in addressing financial exclusion remains largely speculative. This uncertainty stems from several factors crucial to the success of CBDCs in fostering financial inclusivity and will be discussed in this chapter.

Nevertheless, 93 per cent of central banks are exploring CBDCs, and 58 per cent consider that they are likely to or might issue a retail CBDC in the short or medium term. Almost 60 per cent of emerging and low-income countries see financial inclusion as one of the top three motivations for issuing a CBDC.[1] Live CBDCs, or past pilots, carry different policy objectives; therefore, no CBDC is created equal.

There are many reasons why governments and central banks are exploring and launching CBDCs as part of their financial inclusion strategy. The common denominator is the ability to generate payment data, which is currently impossible with cash. Because cash is anonymous and typically used amongst financially excluded households, a CBDC programme can generate transaction and payment data needed to fuel inclusion in products core to financial inclusion: identity, credit, lending, savings, insurance investments and accounts.

This chapter will explore how CBDC can be used to fight financial exclusion, identifying three key criteria for success: contributing to the shift towards the formal financial sector, creating consented transaction and payment data, and reducing the cost of transacting. We will also cover the challenges and key requirements when launching a CBDC, specifically highlighting privacy and trust concerns, the need for a complementary instant payment system and overcoming the digital divide. Then, we will highlight 10 design specifications of a CBDC to ensure adoption, gain trust and generate the critical payment and transaction data. We will conclude the chapter with a list of noteworthy CBDC pilots and launches.

CBDC as a tool to mitigate financial exclusion: The pros

We consider a CBDC a successful financial tool in bringing about financial inclusion if it fulfils three criteria, which are significantly intertwined:

- **Criteria 1:** Contributing to the shift from the informal to formal financial sector by providing easy digital access through internet-enabled devices, bypassing traditional physical banking barriers to reach unbanked and underbanked populations.
- **Criteria 2:** Creating (consented) transaction and payment data, which can reduce the cost to serve financially excluded individuals, SMEs and MSMEs for banks, fintechs, MNOs and other brands in credit, savings, insurances and investments.
- **Criteria 3:** A reduction in the transaction cost for the financial excluded, whether via peer-to-peer payments, remittances or government disbursements.

Beginning with the first criterion, CBDCs can eliminate the need for traditional physical banking infrastructure, such as branches and ATMs, through their digital reach. Unlike cash, agency banking and ATMs, CBDCs are more closely aligned with the current shift towards digital financial services, including widespread mobile money usage and central bank instant payment systems. This alignment makes CBDCs a more effective tool in mitigating financial exclusion. By leveraging internet-enabled devices, CBDCs can extend their reach to even the most remote and underbanked populations, bypassing geographical barriers that have historically impeded access to financial services. This approach positions CBDCs as a critical instrument in the ongoing movement towards more inclusive financial systems.

The second criterion focuses on the generation of usable transaction data through CBDCs. Unlike anonymous cash transactions, which don't produce digital data, CBDC transactions create valuable digital footprints. Chapter 11 highlights that these footprints are essential in integrating financially excluded individuals into formal finance. This is especially true for credit, lending and insurance products, where such alternative data can be pivotal.

CBDC transactions can provide a rich source of alternative data, helping to evaluate an individual's financial behaviour and creditworthiness, notably when conventional credit histories are lacking. This digital transaction data reduces the information asymmetry typically associated with cash transactions, addressing a significant obstacle in offering credit, insurance and savings services.

The real value of a CBDC lies in its capacity to capture payment data securely and efficiently, facilitating a smooth flow of information from consumers to banks, fintechs or other financial service providers. With the consent use of this data, financial service providers can better assess and serve their clients. While programmable, digital money with a predefined set of rules such as restrictions or limits, or non-programmable digital money, does offer benefits, it only partially captures the potential of a CBDC in combatting financial exclusion with this data capture capability.

Unpacking the third criterion, CBDCs hold an opportunity to lower transaction fees. Traditional banking services often come with various fees, including account maintenance and transaction fees, which can be prohibitively expensive for low-income individuals. CBDCs utilizing a centralized blockchain can drastically reduce or eliminate these costs, making financial transactions more accessible and affordable. Furthermore, because they are blockchain-based, transactions can be processed in real-time or near-real-time, a massive improvement over many outdated payment rails, especially regarding cross-border transactions. This immediacy is particularly beneficial for those in the informal finance sector who rely on quick access to funds.

The clear cost-saving a CBDC can offer is reduced cash handling costs. Handling cash can be costly and complex for individuals and small businesses, with various factors contributing to these expenses. One of the primary concerns is security; safeguarding cash requires secure storage like safes and robust security systems to prevent theft. In some cases, especially in high-risk areas, this might also involve hiring security personnel, further adding to the costs. Additionally, transporting cash to banks often involves transportation costs and theft risk during transit, which can be particularly significant for businesses in remote areas. Banks may also charge fees for cash deposits, especially for more significant amounts.

The labour involved in managing cash represents a considerable cost. Counting, sorting and handling cash consumes valuable time and diverts staff from engaging in other productive activities. The risk of human error in cash transactions, such as miscounting or mishandling funds, can lead to direct financial losses. Additionally, the lack of traceability in cash transactions complicates accounting and financial management tasks, such as tracking income and expenses, tax filing and financial reporting. This complexity is especially burdensome for small, underbanked businesses, which may already face challenges accessing traditional banking services. For these businesses, embracing digital payments can offer significant advantages, including reduced handling costs, improved financial record-keeping, and enhanced access to credit and other financial services. There's often a misconception among business owners with limited financial literacy that cash is cheaper to accept than card payments or digital money, overlooking the broader benefits of digital financial inclusion.

Transactions in cash can also be less efficient than digital transactions, potentially leading to longer wait times for customers and affecting business operations. Additionally, funds held as cash are not earning interest, representing an opportunity cost, as these funds could be earning interest in a bank account or invested elsewhere.

CBDC as a tool to mitigate financial exclusion: The cons

Examining the other side of the coin is crucial. There are drawbacks and challenges to using CBDCs to fight financial exclusion. While CBDCs hold great promise, they are not without their limitations and potential issues, especially when tackling financial exclusion. The uncertainty around CBDC stems from several interconnected factors.

Firstly, without the right infrastructure, namely a digital instant payment system, the positive impact of a CBDC will be minimized. Such a system is fundamental for CBDCs to function efficiently and inclusively because, with ubiquitous access to fast or instant payments, the potential benefits of CBDCs will be maximized. The introduction and subsequent launch of instant payment schemes, such as SWISH in Sweden or Vipps in Norway, catalyse a migration to a cashless society, an end goal of a CBDC.

In Nigeria, the e-Naira, one of the most closely watched CDBCs in a market with a high level of financial exclusion, is integrated into the existing instant payment system. In two markets with highly successful central bank-led digital faster payment systems, India (UPI) and Brazil (PIX), interoperability with a CBDC is currently being developed in the case of India, and cited as a potential feature in the case of the Brazil Central Bank. When a digital payment system, such as PIX, is already ubiquitous and available to users with a prepaid or non-bank payment card, the foundation is laid for migrating to a cashless society.

Secondly, the success of a CBDC in promoting financial inclusion is heavily contingent on ensuring that commercial banks, fintechs and other relevant entities have guaranteed access to the data generated through CBDC transactions. This data access is vital for these institutions to serve as gateways into the formal financial economy.

Another significant challenge is the digital divide. CBDCs, although designed to be accessible on various mobile devices, still rely on some form of digital connectivity and literacy. In many rural or underdeveloped areas, where financial exclusion is most acute, the lack of reliable internet access and general digital literacy can severely limit the effectiveness of CBDCs, thus putting an immense focus on offline functionality. Offline functionality, though a desirable feature of CBDCs, may come with its own set of limitations, including double spending and forging and loss of funds.[2] Double spending means duplication of spend or going beyond the available balance. A World Economic Forum paper warns that 'double spend transactions could be sent to entities that are offline without the high-security validation process that would normally occur online'.[3] Loss of funds refers to the user losing their device used to facilitate a CBDC-based transaction, specifically when offline spend is backed up in device storage The annual risk of device loss has been estimated at between 8–16 per cent.[4] This opens up the door for bad actors to commit forgery and fraud, harming those most economically vulnerable. Therefore, without proper design, launching a CBDC with a strong digital divide can perpetuate, rather than alleviate, financial exclusion for a significant portion of the population. The effectiveness of such functionality in remote or connectivity-poor areas still needs to be tested on a large scale, and it may need to be more reliable and robust.

Finally, a lack of trust is a potential deal-breaker for a CBDC, driven by fear over data security and government surveillance. While CBDCs aim to maintain user privacy, the very nature of digital transactions makes them more susceptible to privacy infringements compared to anonymous cash transactions. Building trust among populations unfamiliar with or sceptical about digital currencies, technology and data is another significant challenge. While incentives and education are part of the strategy to overcome this scepticism, more than these measures might be required in areas with a history of unstable financial systems. Without consent, the critical criterion for success around data generation and utilization by banks, fintechs and brands will remain valid.

Considerations to design a successful CBDC

While CBDCs represent a groundbreaking step towards financial inclusion, these potential drawbacks highlight the need for careful and inclusive design, robust technological infrastructure and comprehensive strategies to ensure their benefits effectively reach underbanked and unbanked populations. The design of CBDC systems will vary based on the objective and market. To provide maximum benefits with widespread adoption, a central bank developing or in the early stages of considering launching a CBDC to combat financial exclusion explicitly should ensure it incorporates the positive attributes of cash while seamlessly capturing consented payments and transaction data.

The following attributes could lead to a successful CBDC programme for underbanked and unbanked populations, especially in rural areas:

- Wallets are available to individuals without a formal bank account.
- Omitting authentication for small-value transactions to remove friction.
- No minimum balance requirements.
- Offline functionality to ensure continuity in connectivity-limited areas.
- Compatibility across devices, from basic feature phones to smartphones.
- Easy conversion between digital and physical cash.
- Universal acceptance
- Building trust through targeted incentives and educational initiatives.
- Privacy and consent are engrained in the DNA.
- A user-friendly interface with a minimal learning curve for easy adoption.

Despite their nascence, several pilots and launches have taken place with an explicit aim of achieving financial inclusion and higher rates of financial literacy. We have highlighted a select few below.

Digital Student Safe (Hungary)

The Hungarian Central Bank's approach to a CBDC involves the Digital Student Safe pilot project, which focuses on digital financial inclusion for a specific demographic: students aged 8–14. This targeted approach aims to enhance financial and digital literacy among young people who are not yet engaged in the banking system. The Digital Student Safe app allows students to set savings goals and collect digital assets through quizzes and tasks. The project emphasizes educating young users about finance and digitalization while testing CBDC functionalities in a real-world setting. The CBDC pilot aligns with the Hungarian Central Bank's broader objectives of promoting financial awareness and supporting digital transformation in the financial sector.[5]

e-Peso (Uruguay)

Uruguay was the first country to launch a large-scale CBDC pilot. The e-Peso was launched in November 2017. The e-Peso pilot was designed to assess the feasibility of a digital currency complementing cash. It focused on legal, security and technological aspects, including testing system components like digital wallets and transactional infrastructures.

To be eligible for the pilot, users had to be active subscribers of Antel, the state-owned telecommunication network. Ten thousand users were approved to create wallets on a first-come, first-served basis. These wallets, managed by the third-party payments firm RedPagos, could hold a maximum of 30,000 Uruguayan pesos (about $1,000) for consumers and 200,000 pesos (around $6,000) for businesses and commercial users. The central bank planned to issue 20 million pesos (approximately $500,000) worth of digital currency during the trial. There were specific incentives for the first 1,000 users who cashed in through RedPagos. Moreover, active users of the e-Peso were eligible for random, monthly monetary incentives throughout the pilot.

Key features of the e-Peso included instant settlement of transactions without the need for an internet connection, offering anonymity and traceability. The platform functioned as a registry for digital banknotes linked to phone numbers, enhancing security and mitigating risks like double-spending and falsification. The e-Peso addressed operational risks by assigning unique ID serial numbers to each digital note, enabling traceability and security. The pilot also established a clear life cycle for the digital currency, testing all system components and ensuring business continuity.

Analysis of the e-Peso usage indicated that transactions were predominantly small payments and transfers, standard throughout the pilot period. This pattern aligns with positioning CBDCs as complements rather than substitutes for cash, addressing financial inclusion without disrupting other payment methods. A critical aspect of the e-Peso pilot was its role as a complement to existing payment systems and bank deposits rather than a competitor. By imposing limits on the amount of e-money in e-wallets, the pilot aimed to mirror the use of cash for small payments while potentially enabling new services and enhancing payment system efficiency.

The project aimed to contribute to financial inclusion in several ways:

- **Accessibility without internet:** One of the most significant features of the e-Peso was its ability to function without internet connectivity. It used Unstructured Supplementary Service Data (USSD), allowing users with basic mobile devices to access digital funds without needing a smartphone or an active cellular connection. This feature was essential in reaching parts of the population that lacked access to sophisticated hardware or internet services.
- **Pilot programme structure:** The pilot, which had a six-month duration, required users to be active subscribers of the state-owned network Antel. The e-Peso wallets issued during the trial had a maximum limit, with different caps for individual consumers and businesses. This controlled approach aimed to integrate digital currency into the financial ecosystem without causing disruptions.
- **Eliminating reliance on physical cash:** The Uruguayan Central Bank's goal with the e-Peso was to reduce the country's reliance on physical cash. This move was expected to lower the costs associated

with cash usage, which accounted for a significant portion of the nation's GDP and was mainly borne by the private sector, especially retailers.

- **Impact on banking and monetary policy:** While the e-Peso was deemed successful in its pilot phase, the IMF noted that further research was needed to understand its impact on monetary policy, financial institutions and the broader economic landscape. There were concerns that widespread adoption of the e-Peso could lead to increased funding costs for banks if it replaced traditional bank deposits, potentially causing a rise in interest rates.

The project was deemed a success by the central bank, as it gained significant traction among users, businesses and even private banks, and it did not experience any security breaches or technical errors. However, following the conclusion of the successful pilot in mid-2018, the Uruguayan Central Bank has remained relatively quiet about the future of the e-Peso. It is unclear whether the country's plans for a CBDC have been postponed or if development of the token continues. Uruguay is possibly waiting to see how other countries implement their own CBDC solutions before making further decisions.[6]

e-Naira (Nigeria)

The e-Naira, launched by the Central Bank of Nigeria (CBN) in October 2021, represents a significant effort in Nigeria's efforts to enhance financial inclusion. With a large portion of Nigeria's unbanked or underbanked population, the e-Naira is a digital form of the Nigerian naira aimed at bridging this inclusivity gap, accessible via a smartphone application or USSD codes.

Despite a rather seamless launch, uptake of the e-Naira has been low. As of the end of November 2021, the total number of retail eNaira wallets was 860,000 or 0.8 per cent of Nigeria's active bank accounts. Merchant wallet download reached roughly 100,000 in June 2022, about one-eleventh of the number of merchants with POS terminals.[7] Furthermore, the majority of wallets remain inactive, with the average number of e-Naira transactions at 14,000 per week since its inception. This amounts to only 1.5 per cent of the number of wallets out there. This means that 98.5 per cent of wallets, for any given week, have not been used even once. It is worth noting that the e-Naira is being launched in a phased approach, with those with a bank account only allowed to use the CBDC. It is therefore difficult to judge the success for combatting financial inclusion, but nevertheless it is still worth highlighting the intentions of the CBDC in tackling financial inclusion.

The e-Naira targets several areas to improve financial inclusion:

- **Ease of access:** Initially available to bank account holders, the e-Naira is expected to expand its reach to anyone with a mobile phone, regardless of banking status. This expansion is crucial, considering that about 38 million adults (36 per cent of the adult population) in Nigeria do not have bank accounts. The move aims to enable up to 90 per cent of the population to use the e-Naira.
- **Reduced transaction costs and facilitation of remittances:** The e-Naira promises to reduce transaction costs significantly. Nigeria, a significant destination for remittances in sub-Saharan Africa, received around $24 billion in 2019. The e-Naira aims to lower remittance transfer costs, making it more feasible for the Nigerian diaspora to send funds home. Wallet-to-wallet transfers of e-Naira would be free, contrasting with the 1–5 per cent fees charged by traditional international money transfer operators.
- **Improved payment systems and government disbursements:** The e-Naira ensures more efficient payment systems and can be used by the government to disburse funds directly, thus enhancing transparency and reducing leakages in social aid distribution.
- **Financial literacy and inclusion:** The e-Naira is accompanied by efforts to improve financial literacy, encouraging more people to engage with the formal financial system.
- **Reduced informality:** The e-Naira, being account-based and fully traceable, contrasts with the anonymity of token-based crypto assets. Its widespread adoption could bring transparency to informal transactions, strengthening the tax base and benefiting informal and formal businesses.

Dinero Electrónico (Ecuador)

From 2014 to 2018, the Dinero Electrónico (DE) was a real-time gross settlement retail mobile payment system developed by the Central Bank of Ecuador. It allowed citizens to transfer money using the USSD protocol, similar to Kenya's M-Pesa. Although it did not run on a blockchain, it is considered a CBDC as it was initiated and maintained by the central bank.

The design emphasized ease of access. Users could open an account by registering their national identity number and answering security questions. At its peak, the DE had 500,000 users. The system was designed to increase financial inclusion, which is especially beneficial for a developing country like Ecuador. The e-Dinero was employed for various services, including public transportation, online purchases, e-government services and nano-credits. However, its adoption faced challenges, and 71 per cent of the accounts were not used at all by December 2017.

The motivation included addressing a shortage of physical cash after the 2008 oil shock and optimizing the use of the dollar. However, the initial launch faced pushback from private banks and underwent several regulatory changes. The system was eventually terminated in March 2018 due to a shift in government policy and criticism from the banking sector. The majority of criticism came from the fact that the DE was believed to be a parallel currency. Ecuador uses US dollars as its official currency, and critics challenged whether the DE was backed by 100 per cent cash, therefore making the DE a new form of sovereign currency.[8] Other criticisms included the DEs inability to be used internationally, its ability to facilitate criminal activity and the low levels in general of digital payment adoption by Ecuadorians. Therefore, there was a strong perception among the population, spurred by critics, that the DE was not real, and therefore it could not purchase real goods.[9]

Sand Dollar (Bahamas)

The Central Bank of the Bahamas introduced the Sand Dollar to increase the efficiency of payments, provide non-discriminatory access to payment systems, achieve greater financial inclusion and strengthen defences against money laundering and counterfeiting. The Sand dollar became legal tender in 2020 after successful pilots on the islands of Exuma and Abaco. It is an 'account-based' CBDC, which means the identity of the payer must be verified by the account, rather than a token-based CBDC where the object used to pay must be verified.[10]

The Sand dollar has a two-tier system. Tier 1 targets unbanked users with a $500 limit and no identification requirement. Tier 2 offers higher limits and the ability to link to a bank account. By February 2023, over one million Sand dollars were in circulation, indicating a growing but still marginal role in the overall money supply of the Bahamas.

Conclusion

CBDCs offer an innovative means to reach unbanked and underbanked populations, bypassing traditional financial barriers through digital technology. The ability of CBDCs to generate transaction data presents new opportunities in credit assessment and financial service provision, especially in markets where traditional financial records are limited. Additionally, CBDCs can potentially lower the cost of financial transactions, making financial services more accessible to lower-income segments.

However, the implementation of CBDCs involves significant challenges, as highlighted. A comprehensive digital payment infrastructure is essential for CBDCs to function effectively and inclusively. Addressing the digital divide and ensuring accessibility for all potential users, including those in less connected regions, is crucial. Privacy and data security are also paramount concerns that require serious attention to maintain public trust and confidence in CBDCs.

The experiences of CBDC pilots, such as Uruguay's e-Peso and Nigeria's e-Naira, provide practical insights into the challenges and opportunities in CBDC implementation. These case studies underscore the need for CBDCs to be user-friendly and inclusive, catering to the specific needs of their intended users. They also highlight the importance of integrating CBDCs within existing financial ecosystems rather than viewing them as standalone replacements for cash.

In conclusion, CBDCs present a significant opportunity to pursue financial inclusion. Their success will depend on a detailed understanding of user needs, financial system intricacies and the socioeconomic environments in which they are deployed. Whether CBDCs will emerge as primary drivers of financial inclusion or serve as complementary components within existing financial frameworks remains to be determined. As digital transformation continues to shape the global financial landscape, the evolving role of CBDCs in promoting financial inclusion will be an area of continued focus and relevance.

While CBDC offers a new digital payment method, a significant question remains: do we need a new digital payment method to fight financial exclusion, or should central banks and stakeholders focus on enhancing or building faster payment methods while simultaneously building on existing approaches to bringing the under- and unbanked into the formal financial services system?

Notes

1 A Kosse and I Mattei (2023) Making headway: Results of the 2022 BIS survey on central bank digital currencies and crypto, *BIS*. www.bis.org/publ/bppdf/bispap136.pdf (archived at https://perma.cc/Y6HT-2JH9)

2 J Stewart (2022) Between a rock and a hard place: Offline use in CBDCs, ProgressSoft. www.progressoft.com/blogs/between-a-rock-and-a-hard-place-offline-use-in-cbdcs (archived at https://perma.cc/4UUU-JAD7)

3 World Economic Forum (2021) *CBDC Technology Considerations*. www3.weforum.org/docs/WEF_CBDC_Technology_Considerations_2021.pdf (archived at https://perma.cc/U7N9-V7VX)

4 C M Kahn, M R C van Oordt and Y Zhu (2021) *Best Before? Expiring Central Bank digital currency and loss recovery*, Bank of Canada. www.bankofcanada.ca/wp-content/uploads/2021/12/swp2021-67.pdf (archived at https://perma.cc/TXE9-XKXC)

5 P Fáykiss, A Nyikes and A Szombati (nd) *CBDC: An opportunity to support digital financial inclusion: Digital student safe in Hungary*, BIS. www.bis.org/publ/bppdf/bispap123_i.pdf (archived at https://perma.cc/X7C9-GP6K)

6 A Sarmiento (2022) Seven lessons from the e-Peso pilot plan: The possibility of a Central Bank Digital Currency, Banco Central del Uruguay. https://www.bcu.gub.uy/Sistema-de-Pagos/Documents/Vigilancia/Libros/CBDC%20march2022.pdf (archived at https://perma.cc/L48S-HJDX)
7 J Ree (2023) Nigeria's eNaira, one year after, IMF Working Papers 2023, 104, A001. www.imf.org/en/Publications/WP/Issues/2023/05/16/Nigerias-eNaira-One-Year-After-533487 (archived at https://perma.cc/2H8K-9GJ6)
8 A Arauz, R Garratt and DF Ramos F (2021) Dinero Electrónico: The rise and fall of Ecuador's central bank digital currency, *Latin American Journal of Central Banking*, 2 (2), 100030. www.sciencedirect.com/science/article/pii/S2666143821000107 (archived at https://perma.cc/EC4J-ZYEZ)
9 A Arauz, R Garratt and DF Ramos F (2021) Dinero Electrónico: The rise and fall of Ecuador's central bank digital currency, *Latin American Journal of Central Banking*, 2 (2), 100030. www.sciencedirect.com/science/article/pii/S2666143821000107 (archived at https://perma.cc/EC4J-ZYEZ)
10 Digital Euro Association (2022) Lessons from the first implemented CBDC: The Sand dollar. blog.digital-euro-association.de/lessons-from-the-sand-dollar (archived at https://perma.cc/BJ5W-W5KP)

PART THREE

What can be done?

17

Call to action

Exploring the next steps

In the previous chapters we have discussed why global financial inclusion is so important and what is being done to improve it across the world. To simplify the upside of inclusion we introduced the concept of the three impacts (social, economic and financial) of financial inclusion. The effects of making sure that every person and organization has access to the banking, financial services and payments services they need are very straightforward, as illustrated in Figure 17.1. In this chapter, let's take a closer look at the three impacts.

FIGURE 17.1 Benefits of greater financial inclusion

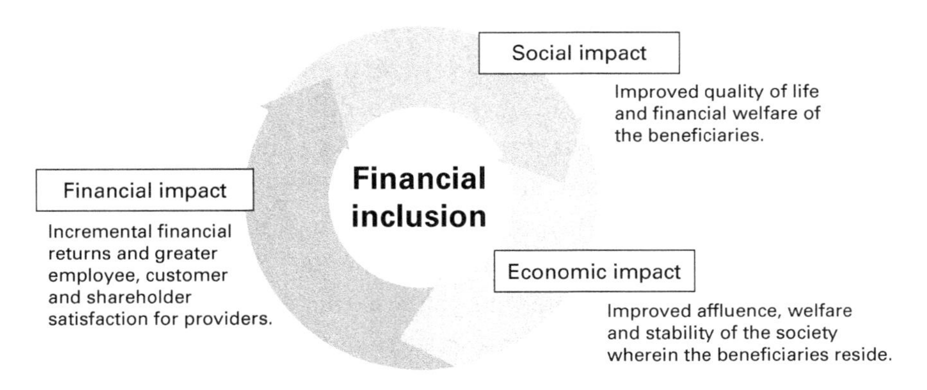

SOURCE The Pacemakers Ltd, 2024

Social impact

The social benefit of financial inclusion may seem obvious, but it has some unexpected outcomes that are worth mentioning. Of course, it is the 'right' thing for society to make sure that certain groups are *not* excluded from the benefits of finance because of their lack of wealth, education or even because they belong to a certain social group. The provision of financial services, especially in the era of digital banking and fintech, should – as we have extensively repeated throughout this book – be seen as a right for everyone.

Financial inclusion can have effects on society that can be described as transformational. A previously underbanked individual, who, thanks to the innovation brought about by fintechs, is now able to access financial services and engage with payers and debtors, is able to save surplus liquidity and is able to get a fairly priced loan to build a business. This individual will slowly become less poor, can achieve higher standards of living and, eventually, this will lead to a more wealthy and, hopefully, equitable society.

Businesses that are able to help the unbanked use fintech innovation to gain access to the financial services can benefit in many ways. We mentioned the financial and economic return above but other benefits should also be considered. Customers are keen to support businesses that have a positive social impact, employees are increasingly keen to work with firms that have positive impact on society and investors are increasingly focused on investing in businesses that are socially minded.

Financial inclusion can have a profound impact on the social cohesion of society. When certain groups of people are denied access to the means to improve their lives, society risks being polarized along the lines of the 'haves' and 'have nots'. Unwittingly the 'haves' often look down on the other group and treat them as if their situation is self-inflicted. The deprived groups sometimes feel that this is because the other group has set up the rules to make sure they remain excluded. Both these outcomes are exacerbated by technology. Almost all members of modern society are socially connected and therefore the awareness of how the 'other half' lives has never been greater.

This awareness of partial views of the other group's lives can increase social tension, discrimination and resentment.

Economic impact

As more people gain access to financial services that are right for them, they will grow the wealth of the market they live within. This will not only mean the growth of the financial service industry, it also means that these newly banked individuals will have the ability to buy goods and services that they could not access previously. This access should not be seen as offering people the means to take on buying things that they cannot afford. Smart regulation will of course be needed to protect new banking customers from abuses but, all in all, being able to pay, be paid, save and borrow will have the effect of growing the size of the economy and impact the welfare of more than just the newly banked.

Newly banked individuals and businesses will slowly become more affluent and generate more economic wealth. Even just access to the global digital payments networks will allow the formerly unbanked to access work opportunities from a wider range of buyers than they previously had access to. Their ability to save and invest will create nest-eggs that can be used to make larger purchases than were possible before. And the ability to affordably borrow will allow these now banked individuals and businesses to buy cars, homes and grow their businesses. The economic impact of this new liquidity will be felt by the whole economy.

Financial impact

This impact is the most straightforward to quantify. Put simply, providers of financial products and services can benefit from delivering these to individuals that do not have them. Reaching new segments that are neglected by existing providers is the dream of every business, especially if these can be served profitably – and of course equitably and reliably. As we said previously, the financial exclusion of many has been driven by issues that can be overcome by simple changes in processes, pricing, rules and technology. This impact can be measured in revenue generated by providing banking, finance and payments to the unbanked.

Bringing financial services to new segments means growing the savings pool leading to increased capital for bank lending. Use of financial services makes more people visible to credit rating agencies, making the pool of eligible credit customers greater. The latter will reduce the grip of informal lenders, making the financial services market fairer and more reasonably priced. All in all, increased inclusion means that the overall banking and finance market will inevitably grow, positively impacting the financial services industry.

The use of technology can be an effective way to address the unacceptable persistence of financial exclusion. But this requires a coordinated effort from disparate parties, including national governments, incumbent players and fintechs. Let us take a closer look at what each one can do to make sure the use of technology and fintech innovation can make financial exclusion a thing of the past.

National governments

The eradication of financial exclusion should be a key goal for all governments. They should make sure that no citizen is unbanked. They also need to aim to reduce the underbanked population. Governments can achieve this by openly making financial inclusion a national priority. This would mean clearly stated goals that the governments ensure will trickle down to all departments and regulators. Some of the key initiatives that government should pursue are detailed here.

Smarter regulation

Access to straightforward digital banking is often cited as a powerful tool in fighting financial exclusion. The fintech wave of the last two decades has seen the emergence of a solid segment of challengers that are transforming the range and accessibility of financial products. Earlier in this book we mentioned several examples of success stories where innovative players enabled previously excluded segments to gain access to finance.

Across many countries, lack of understanding, limited support and sometimes even hostility to innovation in financial services by certain regulators are often cited by fintech entrepreneurs as a real barrier to the growth of digital banking. Governments should be more vocal in demanding that their financial regulators keep the right balance between protecting users and the market while also promoting evolution and change. Many countries have very consolidated banking markets, where a handful of financial institutions dominate the market. By promoting the fintech, regulators can ensure that competition makes the supply of financial services competitive.

Promote financial inclusion

As we said previously, frequently, different forms of discrimination lie at the core financial exclusion. Discrimination has many causes, from racial, religious or sexual bias to simple laziness in updating legacy practices and mindsets that are obsolete and detrimental to the welfare of the industry and the economy. Governments could create legislation that increases scrutiny on situations where bias and discrimination are the causes of exclusion. The OECD Development Centre's Social Institutions and Gender Index (SIGI) measures discrimination against women in social institutions across 179 countries.[1] It uses a score from 0 to 100, where 0 means there's no discrimination, and 100 means full discrimination against women. In doing this, SIGI looks at laws, social norms and practices that might hold women back. It focuses on five main areas:

- how women are treated in families
- women's physical safety and health
- women's access to jobs and money

- women's freedoms in society
- women's legal rights

SIGI collects information on these areas and combines them into one score. This score helps show how much discrimination women face in a country overall.

Their analysis suggests that many countries still uphold laws that unfairly discriminate against women. A reversal of these laws would be a real step forward. Interestingly, religious customs are seen as an issue, but according to this report strict religious countries are actually not as discriminatory as some of the less religious ones.

In parallel to removing barriers to inclusion, governments can also establish penalties for providers that persist in not being inclusive. They could enact and enforce anti-discrimination laws that prohibit financial institutions from discriminating based on protected characteristics like race, gender, disability, etc when providing services.

Furthermore, they could require financial institutions to collect and report data on their diversity and inclusion performance, including demographic data on customers served, allowing for monitoring of potential discriminatory patterns. In late 2023 the UK's two key financial regulators, the Financial Conduct Authority and the Prudential Regulation Authority, both issued consultation papers setting out proposals to boost diversity and inclusion to support healthy work cultures, reduce groupthink and unlock talent in the financial services sector.

Simplify identity

Many countries have national identity programmes that allow every individual to be identified from birth. These enable anyone to prove their identity with potential providers of financial products. According to the World Bank's Identification for Development (ID4D) initiative, across all countries, not having access to a national ID system has a direct impact on financial inclusion. In lower income countries only 19 per cent of those with IDs have bank accounts whilst 45 per cent of those with ID have access to financial services.[2]

But national ID programmes can be controversial and costly. Reasons for the lack of uptake in national IDs can be both because they are not offered and because they are not taken up by potential users. In some affluent countries such as the UK, Denmark, Canada and the USA, concerns about privacy are often stated as a reason for not offering national ID systems to all citizens. These are often supported by global privacy organizations. The concerns about privacy in the age of digital technology and social media are very apt, but the possibly unexpected outcome of these privacy efforts can be that certain individuals are unable to access the financial products they deserve. Another issue with the lack of the uptake of ID programmes can be cost. The inability of states to implement national – and free – ID systems results in the cost of identification being passed down to end-users, with many of them not being able to afford the national IDs and therefore remaining unbanked. According to ID4D 40 per cent of adults attribute not having a formal ID to the costs they would have to bear to get one.

Improve financial education

We said that one of the reasons behind financial exclusion is the unbanked's lack of understanding of what financial services can do for them. OECD research in 2023 reiterated that a substantial segment of the unbanked do not have the right understanding of what financial services can do for them. Research across the globe clearly confirmed that financial exclusion goes hand-in-hand with education.[3] Financial exclusion declines across all segments of society as the level of education rises. Worldwide, national governments are using financial education as a tool in fighting financial exclusion. According to a study on financial education run by the OECD between 2011 and 2015, the number of countries implementing national programmes to address financial literacy grew by 200 per cent.[4]

Governments should not only promote financial education in schools, but they should also drive the financial education of individuals that have already left national education schemes with ad hoc programmes (delivered by governments, non-profit organization or even businesses) aimed at improving the understanding of the real benefits and risks of financial products and services.

Internet access

Digital technology and digital communication have transformed banking and will continue to do so in the coming decades. Across the globe, access to payments, banking and finance have become simpler, faster and less onerous for large segments of society. As society adopts digital banking and payments, governments need to make sure that the lack of access to digital communication does not become a barrier to financial inclusion. Governments should promote programmes that enable the less privileged and more remote members of society to have access to the level of communication that they need to be able to benefit from what finance can do for their livelihood. Governments need to ensure that all citizens have access to digital data networks and digital communications devices that are useful and affordable.

Governments across the world are developing solutions to make sure the underprivileged segments of society have access to digital communications. India's BharatNet and the USA's Connect America Fund are good examples of this approach. Both programmes aim to address the digital divide by providing high-speed internet access to underserved communities, enabling them to access education, healthcare, economic opportunities and government services. While BharatNet focuses on connecting village councils in India, the Connect America Fund targets rural and underserved areas in the USA.

In parallel to internet access, the availability of affordable smartphones needs to be considered. According to the Alliance for Affordable Internet, a global coalition of institutions and businesses, nearly 2.5 billion people live in countries where the cost of the cheapest available smartphone is a quarter or more of the average monthly income. Governments need to establish programmes to procure less expensive smartphones. Governments such as India, China, Vietnam, Egypt, Kenya and Brazil are promoting the local production of smartphones to address this issue.

Governments play a pivotal role in combatting financial exclusion and promoting financial inclusion for all citizens. By implementing smarter regulations, promoting financial inclusion through anti-discrimination measures, simplifying identity systems, improving financial education and ensuring widespread internet access, governments can create an environment where financial services are accessible to everyone. These efforts not only empower individuals and communities but also contribute to overall economic growth and social stability.

As technology continues to reshape the financial landscape, it is crucial for governments to remain proactive and adaptive in their approach, ensuring that no one is left behind in the digital financial revolution. By prioritizing these initiatives, nations can work towards a more inclusive, equitable and financially literate society where every individual has the opportunity to participate fully in the modern economy.

The incumbent players

The incumbent providers of financial services are the primary providers in most countries. They often have greater capability, range, distribution, capital and reputation than any other provider. They are often both the cause of financial exclusion and the best way to eradicate it.

As we said previously, the incumbents' inability to end financial exclusion is largely due to legacy. But these legacy issues are more complex than one would expect. When digital innovation hit financial services, the main concern was technology legacy. We have all heard stories about banks having to upgrade their banking platforms because the increased IT demands were crashing them. Once the platforms were upgraded the banks started realizing that the processes that were executed by these platforms were not optimal. These processes were the result of fixes and patches implemented by the banks' IT teams and what they resulted in were what some called 'Frankenstein' platforms, where outdated and inefficient processes were kept alive and not replaced, usually to address cost and urgency issues.

In the first stage of banking transformation, business leaders tried to unwind the platforms, trying to understand the code, quickly realizing that they no longer had the skills required to be able to read code written in Fortran or Cobol 30 years beforehand. So a large redesign occurred, but instead of reviewing the processes they merely remapped the old processes onto the new platforms. The technology was better, the processing was quicker and more reliable, but all the process inefficiencies and defects were still there. These new platforms were in fact digitizing unsuitable processes created in pre-digital times and not delivering the possible benefits and improvements that the new technology could bring to end-users – especially the less affluent or the rural ones. The often-flawed adoption of digital technology by the incumbent providers has become a key cause of modern financial exclusion.

But what can incumbent banks do to address these issues?

Redesign processes

Banks should review the processes they are moving to digital platforms, adopting multiple perspectives. While they are already focusing on improving efficiency, simplicity and compliance, they should also focus on unnecessary discrimination and exclusion. Understanding the impact of specific requirements they impose on customers for opening accounts, sending or receiving money, borrowing or accessing savings products, especially those that may not be fully literate, live a long way away from a branch or are unaware of which bank product is right for them is crucial.

Additionally, it is important to ensure that risk management and compliance processes are suitable for serving unbanked customers. KYC requirements pose a significant challenge, largely due to processes adopted before the digital revolution. Many traditional banks are still applying processes created for a pre-digital world. For example, they may require new customers to visit a physical branch in-person to open accounts, as my daughters were asked to do when opening their first accounts in the UK with an incumbent bank – their experience with a challenger bank was entirely digital.

Also, as digital technology makes online banking more appealing, banked customers are visiting branches less frequently. Branches in less affluent and rural areas are quickly becoming unprofitable compared to those in wealthier areas, which sell higher margin products or have more foot traffic. Consequently, traditional banks are closing branches in these areas, making it harder for unbanked or underbanked residents to access banking. Lack of branches combines with the continuing prevalence of legacy processes that interpret financial regulations with a pre-digital era mindset, undermining the inclusivity potential of incumbent banks. As a result, fintech, challenger banks and digital wallet issuers have become better solutions for the unbanked. Taking a closer look at how legacy processes are resulting in financial exclusion should be a priority for incumbent banks.

Identify bias

Many established financial institutions rely on management practices that lead to discrimination. We have already mentioned gender and race bias indirectly resulting from the application of such practices. Financial institutions should review the outcome of their policies to see if certain segments of society are being discriminated against. This is often easier than it sounds – simply looking at the makeup of the existing client base compared to the demographics of the markets they operate in is a great starting point.

Once these biases are identified, the leadership of these incumbent players can create a 'carrot and stick' policy whereby greater inclusion is rewarded and exclusion identified and eliminated.

Diversify leadership

Large organizations such as many incumbent banks and financial services providers are often very diverse at the entry level. As people move up in the organization, diversity falls. Almost all large organizations around the world today have diversity policies that are implemented with great PR fanfare. This is great news, but it is simply not enough. The diversity policies of today are correctly focused on fighting discrimination based on gender, race, ability and sexual orientation. A more diverse management is slowly being built in all incumbent financial institutions. This will inevitably lead to a greater scrutiny of financially exclusive policies that result in certain groups being let down. But we are not there yet.

The incumbent institutions should empower their leadership to transform the firm by challenging legacy. The famous expression that many incumbents have been proud of – 'That's how we do things here' – should no longer be seen as a sign of reliability and trust. It should be seen as a red flag signalling the potential risk of discrimination and unfair treatment of select segments of society. The greatest impact of leadership diversity could be that of challenging the status quo.

Motivation

One mistake that many incumbent institutions make is that they believe that financial inclusion is a social initiative where the firm spends money to do good, with no financial upside in mind. Support for financial inclusion is often seen in the same way as charitable giving. In most large organizations, charitable expenses are the first expense line that is cut if business needs to reduce costs. This is a mistake that results in firms not giving financial inclusion the right level of support or attention. The incumbents need to realize that financial inclusion is also a business opportunity (we do realize that this statement is controversial).

The unbanked and underbanked should be seen as a segment with its own specific needs and challenges but one that with a bit of creativity, imagination and smart use of technology can be engaged with as any other customer segment, generating positive outcomes for the incumbent, the unbanked and society at large. This does not mean that the incumbent should feel free to charge unfair prices or offer onerous conditions to serve this group. It merely means that many unbanked are unbanked because the incumbent banks are not providing them with adequate, user friendly, reasonably priced products and services, even though they could.

It is key for the incumbents not to look at serving the unbanked as an act of altruism but to look at the underbanked as an 'underserved' segment that deserves the same amount of focus and attention as any other customer segment they work with.

Fintechs

When aiming to address financial exclusion, fintechs and challengers face the same challenges as the incumbents. That said, the fact that they often have technology, processes, policies and teams that are less impacted by legacy issues of the past can be a real benefit when looking at financial exclusion.

Fintechs have often (though not always) based their proposition on rethinking the way financial products are delivered. This should reduce the risks of built-in bias and discrimination towards certain segments and make them more sensitive to the risks of groupthink and legacy behaviours. So potentially, new players in the market have some built-in advantages in addressing financial exclusion. But challengers and fintechs also have some disadvantages that need to be addressed.

Credibility

We have seen previously that one of the reasons some people decide to go unbanked is they do not trust the financial services providers. One of the big challenges of a fintech company can be that of recognition and therefore trust. It is unlikely that an unbanked individual will seek to get their first account from a new player with little name recognition – and therefore trust – rather than reaching out to an established player which they are familiar with.

To address this issue, the challengers should aim to create awareness and visibility within the un- and underbanked communities. This can be done through traditional PR, press and social channels but also by working with non-profit organizations and governments. Collaborating with non-profit organizations, charities, foundations, national and local governments can be an effective way for a fintech to receive the recognition and therefore trust they need. Another option is to be available in stores that serve communities that have a high incidence of underbanked individuals. In many less developed countries, fintechs have positioned themselves as a safe and quick way to send and receive cash by operating in small local retail stores. Firms like PayTM in India, M-Pesa in Kenya, WeChatPay in China and bKash in Bangladesh have been very successful with this strategy. Credibility and trust are key requirements to attract unbanked users. Partnering can be a great strategy for fintechs to get the necessary recognition.

Access

We mentioned that incumbent banks tend to rely on physical branches to engage with customers. This is largely due to legacy issues and processes often created before the arrival of the digital era.

A challenger or fintech could create new processes that, amongst other things, can allow them to engage with customers in ways that are less challenging for the unbanked or underbanked. Some processes that will improve access could be:

- **Enable digital onboarding:** Enable customers to onboard entirely on mobile devices.
- **Innovate scoring:** Start implementing new processes that allows the scoring of the customers based on data that is not traditional credit agency information, making it possible to onboard individuals with little or no financial history.
- **Use field agents:** Create a team of local individuals employed or rewarded by the fintech to identify, engage and onboard new customers.

- **Improve user experience:** Make it simpler for consumers to open bank accounts through easy-to-use interfaces such as biometric identification or remote agent authentication.
- **Review the offering:** Make sure that the portfolio of products offered are suitable to unbanked or underbanked customers.
- **Review pricing:** Make sure that the pricing of the products is fair and affordable to both the customer and the provider.
- **Partner with non-banks:** Create the means for customers to engage with them through digital devices and through non-bank organizations such as post offices and retailers. This strategy has been adopted by many neobanks in many different countries. A quick, simple and safe digital engagement is a key component of every successful fintech's proposition – these capabilities are also a key requirement in attracting unbanked customers.

Provide education

One of the greatest barriers to financial inclusion comes from lack of understanding of what the product can do for the customer. This knowledge gap has many dimensions. The 2021 FDIC National Survey of Unbanked and Underbanked Households in the USA revealed these perceptions:

> 'Banks do not offer what I need.'
>
> 'I don't have enough money to meet minimum requirements.'
>
> 'Banks fees are too high.'
>
> 'Banks fees are too unpredictable.'
>
> 'Avoiding a bank gives more privacy.'[5]

Banks provide information on their products to their potential customers in their branches, online and in their call centres. But is this enough? To differentiate themselves, fintechs could take this approach to a different level, through digital, interactive training and the use of AI chatbots to create personalized content delivered on mobile devices. Worldwide, good examples of firms doing this are Monzo in the UK, M-PAiSA in Afghanistan and Paga in Nigeria.

Investors

Investors such as angels, VCs and private equity are powerful supporters of fintech innovation but often they can become a barrier to financial inclusion. Investors naturally wish to generate returns from the capital they invest, so they invest into businesses that they believe will generate a real upside that earns them good returns from their investment. This approach often does not see financial inclusion as a sound growth opportunity.

Financial returns

Many investors mistakenly see businesses focused on financial inclusion as non-profit organizations. This perspective is similar to the mindset of 'asset allocators' in incumbent banks, where they see a focus on financial inclusion as a social investment and not business investment. This is not true.

Providing financial services that are socially inclusive can be a profitable endeavour for a business, and as such is worthy of venture investment. To make sure that these funds flow it is important that the different stakeholders remember these factors:

- **Founders:** It is important to keep in mind that socially inclusive businesses can have a financial upside – so make sure these are clearly explained when fundraising.
- **Investors:** Do not automatically think of a financially inclusive business as a non-profit. Financial inclusion expands the size of the addressable market. Keep that in mind when making decisions on investing.
- **The incumbent:** When deciding to back an inclusive proposition internally, do not look at it as a 'charitable' initiative. Keep in mind

that investments in financial inclusion can provide a good return on investment for existing providers, and they can also have a positive impact on employee, market and investor perception of the social responsibility of the goals of the business.

Non-financial return

We are increasingly hearing the emergence of Capitalism 2.0. To oversimplify a very complex topic, this is fundamentally the recognition that a business must have objectives beyond financial return. In the Capitalism 2.0 world, businesses will have to make decisions about (an investment in) activities that not only have a financial return consideration, but they also look at all stakeholders, including employees, customers, suppliers, communities and the environment.

Investing in financial inclusion can be a great way to back initiatives that not only consider shareholders but also all other stakeholders.

Social investors

Lastly, it is worth mentioning that a number of non-profit organizations are also investing in financial inclusion. These include governments, charities, foundations and more. These organizations do not have financial return as an objective. This is a great goal, but many walk away from initiatives that impact financial exclusion but are also profitable. Non-profit organizations should feel comfortable with backing businesses that have an impact on financial exclusion but also make money from doing so.

Big Tech

Big Tech is a very broad term that brings together many different players and industries. These include social platforms, retailers, hardware manufacturers, software firms, service providers and more.

These players are changing society profoundly and they should play an active role in fighting financial exclusion. Firms such as Google, Apple, Meta, Microsoft, Alphabet, Alibaba, Tencent and many more global leaders, simply based on their size, reach and capabilities, could have a huge impact on financial exclusion. The top causes of financial exclusion are identification, access and education, all of which can be very effectively addressed by Big Tech.

Identification

Big Tech firms operate across continents with a presence in practically every country in the world. They could become actors in creating a digital ID for every human being. They could provide a service that, if opted into by the user, could enable a user to be identified and authenticated, making it extremely simple for a person or business to access financial services. An ID service could be incorporated in services such as the social profile of an individual, a service built into their mobile device and more.

In particular, the ability to provide authentication through facial and touch recognition could considerably simplify the access and use of payments and financial services. Most Big Tech firms use ID and authenticate their customers when delivering their services. A scenario where Big Tech – with the blessing of the national governments and regulators – could provide banks and fintechs with a digital ID and authentication services would have a huge impact on financial exclusion.

Access

As we have said across this book, a fundamental cause of financial exclusion is access to providers. Many of the unbanked worldwide live in the poorer parts of cities or away from big urban centres. These locations are increasingly underserved by physical banking options as digital banking is being increasingly adopted by banked customers. Creating the means through which fintechs and challengers can reach customers can be a very effective way for Big Tech to help fight financial exclusion. Big Tech can do this in several ways:

- **Internet access:** Big tech is already creating a number of solutions to enable the delivery of internet access to poor and remote areas. This will have to be affordable for the users so Big Techs are often collaborating with NGOs, charities and governments to provide internet access through initiatives such as providing satellite internet access to rural communities or supporting the rollout of internet access to deprived areas of big cities. Google, Meta, Starlink and many more Big Tech firms are working with local authorities to make affordable internet available to the rural and less affluent.
- **Devices:** Access to a smartphone is a key enabler to internet access. But smartphones are often too expensive for many underbanked individuals. So Big Tech companies are working on addressing this issue. Some manufacturers have established initiatives making it easier for less affluent customers to get access to basic smartphones that are cheaper but still provide most of the services of more expensive models. There are also established processes to provide second-hand refurbished phones and initiatives led by global organizations and supported by Big Tech.

Education

Big Tech companies could use their platforms, resources and partnerships to provide financial education to the unbanked and the underbanked. Offerings such as direct educational programmes and digital literacy initiatives integrating financial education into their products and services could play a significant role in growing financial inclusion. Worldwide, Big Tech firms have engaged in some programmes with local governments, charities and NGOs to support financial education and literacy at the grass-roots level, but these remain small and relatively regional.

All in all, the contribution of Big Tech firms in helping the financial education of the unbanked and underbanked falls short of its potential. Building on the resources that are available to the likes of Google, Amazon, Meta and Apple and their Asian equivalents Baidu, Alibaba and Tencent, we could see global programmes being run at the local level that would deliver sufficient levels of awareness and knowledge to lift many millions of people out of financial exclusion. This could be a valuable, relatively low-cost initiative that could transform the lives of millions worldwide. Let us hope that we will see such initiatives taking place in the near future.

Going forward

The most effective means to achieve economic and social welfare is the ability to earn a living. Today more than ever, earning a fair living is inexorably linked to access to financial services. In order to get paid or to pay someone, to protect a bit of excess earnings, to borrow to buy a home or to fund a business, we all need access to a provider of financial services.

This lack of access is resulting in poverty, social exclusion, poor health and lack of education – robbing many of a fair and fulfilling life. As with most aspects of modern society, digital technology has changed and is changing finance. Incumbent banks, fintechs and other challengers are using digital technology to reshape the financial services, banking and payments landscapes across the globe. But they are doing this primarily to the benefit of certain segments of society, excluding others. This particular sort of financial 'discrimination' is further marginalizing large parts of global society.

As a society, we should aim for every individual (person, business and more) to be able to benefit from the transformation of finance. *Every person* should be able to:

- send money and receive money legally from any other individual or organization anywhere in the world
- store their cash in a safe, quick and inexpensive manner

- access financial products and services that allow them to safely and securely gain financial benefit from any funds that are in excess of their needs
- connect with entities that are willing to provide them with credit with fair conditions
- access trustworthy information and advice on how to manage their money

The achievement of all of these goals can be made possible by a smarter use of the methodologies, resources and technologies available today. We do not suggest that existing providers, regulators, governments and other actors should abandon all constraints and reasons in providing financial services; rather, we believe that every market should be able to provide the right framework to enable:

- a free basic current account for every individual
- a free basic savings account that is safe and earns interest where local customs do not prevent it
- everyone to be identified and authenticated remotely
- access to inexpensive domestic and cross-border payments
- access to affordable credit that adequately reflects the borrower's needs and affordability
- any individual to own the financial data that pertains to them and to grant and deny access to financial institutions that can use the data to offer a needed financial product

The road to full financial inclusion is long and tedious, but the destination is within reach. The benefits it will generate for all involved far outweigh the efforts. So, let's all get on with this.

Notes

1 OECD (2019) *SIGI 2019 Global Report: Transforming challenges into opportunities, social institutions and gender index*. doi.org/10.1787/bc56d212-en (archived at https://perma.cc/PQ7C-8UTL)

2 J M Clark, A Z Metz and C S Casher (2021) ID4D global dataset 2021: Volume 1 – Global ID coverage estimates, World Bank Group. http://documents.worldbank.org/curated/en/099705012232226786/P176341132c1ef0b21adf11abad304425ef (archived at https://perma.cc/2VYS-FNN2)

3 OECD (2023) OECD/INFE 2023 international survey of adult financial literacy, OECD Business and Finance Policy Papers, 39. doi.org/10.1787/56003a32-en (archived at https://perma.cc/N2GC-ZRYU)

4 OECD/INFE (2015) *National Strategies for Financial Education: OECD/INFE policy handbook*. www.gpfi.org/sites/gpfi/files/documents/06-OECD-INFE%20Policy%20Handbook%20on%20the%20Implementation..._0.pdf (archived at https://perma.cc/D9ZZ-7CLP)

5 Federal Deposit Insurance Corporation (2021) *FDIC National Survey of Unbanked and Underbanked Households*. www.fdic.gov/analysis/household-survey/2021report.pdf (archived at https://perma.cc/F5GL-XN8R)

18

Engaging the financial inclusion ecosystem

Resources and references

The drive to eradicate financial exclusion is a multidimensional endeavour. This is driven by a large number of entities, each with their own take and each with the goal of making a difference. In this appendix, we have gathered some of the major organizations that are leading the way. They are global organizations, governments, non-profit organizations and a select number of corporates aiming to eradicating financial exclusion across the world.

Global

Governmental institutions

BANK FOR INTERNATIONAL SETTLEMENTS

Headquarters: Switzerland
Focus: Global

The Bank for International Settlements (BIS) conducts research and provides guidance on issues related to financial inclusion. The BIS actively contributes to promoting financial inclusion through several initiatives that focus on the integration of innovative financial technologies. A key aspect of the BIS's work in this area includes the exploration and research into CBDCs. The BIS has identified

CBDCs as a potential tool to enhance financial inclusion by creating more accessible digital payment systems. This work is spearheaded by the BIS Innovation Hub, which conducts research and develops public goods in the technology space to improve the functioning of the financial system globally.

Furthermore, the BIS, through its Committee on Payments and Market Infrastructures, has engaged in significant efforts to understand and enhance the payment systems which plays a crucial role in achieving broader financial inclusion. These activities aim to ensure that financial services are not only more accessible but also efficient and secure, catering to the needs of underserved populations.

Overall, the BIS's approach to financial inclusion encompasses a blend of innovation in financial technology and enhancement of global payment infrastructures, making a substantial impact on the way financial services reach all segments of the population.

G20 GLOBAL PARTNERSHIP FOR FINANCIAL INCLUSION

Headquarters: Distributed
Focus: Global

The Global Partnership for Financial Inclusion (GPFI) is an inclusive platform for all G20 countries, interested non-G20 countries and relevant stakeholders for advancing financial inclusion globally.

Established during the Korean G20 presidency in 2010, its focus is on advancing financial inclusion by improving access to and the use of formal financial services to help reduce poverty and enhance economic growth.

The GPFI's efforts are structured around the Financial Inclusion Action Plan, which outlines key strategies and goals to promote financial inclusion. This plan emphasizes the importance of digital financial services to increase the financial inclusion of individuals and MSMEs. Through its ongoing work, the GPFI encourages peer learning, knowledge sharing, policy advocacy and coordination among its members, making it a cornerstone in global efforts to foster financial wellbeing and support productivity through more inclusive financial systems.

INTERNATIONAL FINANCE CORPORATION

Headquarters: USA
Focus: Global

International Finance Corporation (IFC) is a member of the World Bank Group and serves as the largest global development institution focused exclusively on the private sector in developing countries. Established in 1956, IFC's mission is to advance economic development by encouraging the growth of private enterprise in developing countries.

IFC's approach to addressing financial exclusion encompasses direct investments, advisory services, partnerships and initiatives that target the underlying causes of financial exclusion. By focusing on SME finance, gender initiatives, digital inclusion, venture capital investments in Fintech and global collaborations, IFC aims to create a more inclusive financial system that supports economic growth and poverty reduction in developing countries.

INTERNATIONAL MONETARY FUND

Headquarters: USA
Focus: Global

The International Monetary Fund (IMF) engages in various initiatives to promote financial inclusion to achieve macroeconomic stability and growth. Financial inclusion plays an important role in this. The IMF promotes inclusion by focusing on both global policy formation and practical implementation to ensure that more people worldwide have access to beneficial financial services. The IMF's efforts include providing technical assistance and policy advice to member countries to improve their financial sectors and increase access to financial services.

One significant area of the IMF's work is its emphasis on the role of digital technologies, which can transform financial services to be more inclusive, especially for underserved populations in remote or rural areas. This includes support for digital payments systems that can help low-income households and businesses engage more fully in the economy. The IMF also explores the potential benefits and risks of CBDCs as a means to promote financial inclusion by offering a digital form of money that is accessible and cost-effective for all segments of the population.

Furthermore, the IMF's seminars and workshops frequently address financial inclusion, bringing together experts and stakeholders to discuss strategies and share best practices.

UNITED NATIONS CAPITAL DEVELOPMENT FUND

Headquarters: USA
Focus: Global

The United Nations Capital Development Fund (UNCDF) focuses on offering financial services to low-income people in less-developed countries. It works to create a financial market that serves the needs of poor populations to improve their livelihoods and economic opportunities.

UNITED NATIONS HIGH COMMISSION FOR REFUGEES

Headquarters: Switzerland
Focus: Global

United Nations High Commission for Refugees (UNHCR) is a United Nations agency mandated to aid and protect refugees, forcibly displaced communities and stateless people, and to assist in their voluntary repatriation, local integration or resettlement to a third country. According to UNHCR, at the end of 2022 there were 108.4 million people who had been forcibly displaced from their homes across the world.

UNHCR actively works to enhance financial inclusion for refugees, aiming to help them become self-reliant and economically independent. A significant part of this effort includes promoting access to financial services such as bank accounts, which is essential for managing money, receiving wages and starting businesses. Recognizing the challenges that refugees face in accessing these services due to regulatory and documentation hurdles, UNHCR collaborates with partners to pilot initiatives that ease these barriers.

UNHCR has been instrumental in implementing digital cash transfer programmes, which not only provide immediate financial assistance but also serve as an entry point for refugees into the financial system. Additionally, the organization advocates for the rights of refugees to access financial services and works with financial service providers to raise awareness about the economic potential of serving this demographic.

WORLD BANK

Headquarters: USA
Focus: Global

The World Bank plays a significant role in promoting financial inclusion globally through its Financial Inclusion Support Framework (FISF). This initiative aims to accelerate and enhance the effectiveness of country-led actions to achieve national financial inclusion goals. The World Bank also provides technical assistance, policy advice and financing to support financial inclusion.

Through initiatives like FISF, launched in 2013, the World Bank assists countries in enhancing their national financial inclusion strategies and infrastructure, such as payments systems and credit reporting. This framework is supported by substantial international funding, including contributions from the Netherlands Ministry of Foreign Affairs and the Bill & Melinda Gates Foundation, which has enabled significant progress in countries like Rwanda, Indonesia and Mozambique.

Additionally, the World Bank supports the digital transformation of financial services. This includes promoting the use of digital transactional platforms which facilitate a wide range of financial activities including savings, payments and credit, making it easier and safer for users, especially in developing countries. This digital push was crucial during the Covid-19 pandemic, helping to deliver government-to-person payments efficiently to those affected by the crisis.

Overall, the World Bank's commitment to financial inclusion not only focuses on expanding access but also emphasizes the quality and usage of financial services to ensure sustainable benefits for underserved populations.

Organizations

ACCION INTERNATIONAL

Headquarters: USA
Focus: Global

Accion is a global non-profit dedicated to creating a fair and inclusive economy by developing and scaling financial solutions for underserved communities. With a focus on responsible digital financial services, Accion works to empower individuals to make informed decisions and improve their lives. The organization collaborates with local partners to innovate and provide access to financial services, supporting initiatives like microfinance and fintech for inclusion. Accion also invests in companies that bring financial services to those who need them most, demonstrating a commitment to reducing poverty and creating opportunities through financial inclusion.

Over the years, Accion has significantly influenced the microfinance sector and continues to support financial service providers globally through its advisory services and investment strategies. It has more than 110 partners in 50 countries.

AGA KHAN DEVELOPMENT NETWORK

Headquarters: Switzerland
Focus: Global

The Aga Khan Development Network (AKDN) is a global organization dedicated to improving living conditions and opportunities for people in some of the world's poorest regions, particularly in Africa and Asia. Operating in over 30 countries, AKDN focuses on a wide range of development issues, including health, education, economic development and cultural preservation. The network employs approximately 96,000 people and takes a holistic approach to development by integrating social, cultural and economic projects. With a commitment to long-term sustainability and partnerships with local communities and governments, AKDN fosters self-reliance to enhance the quality of life for marginalized populations.

The AKDN promotes financial inclusion through various initiatives targeting underserved populations. Key efforts include establishing Community-Based Savings Groups, providing microfinance services through the Aga Khan Agency for Microfinance and embracing digital financial services. AKDN also supports formal banking, offers entrepreneurship support and conducts financial literacy programmes. These initiatives span multiple countries in Asia and Africa, including Afghanistan, Pakistan, Tajikistan, Kenya, Tanzania and Uganda. Through these diverse programmes, AKDN aims to foster economic self-reliance and break cycles of poverty in developing regions.

ALLIANCE FOR FINANCIAL INCLUSION

Headquarters: Malaysia
Focus: Global

Alliance for Financial Inclusion (AFI) is a global network focused on enhancing financial inclusion policies. AFI supports policy development through its membership, which includes central banks and financial regulatory institutions from over 90 countries. Its members are predominantly from developing and emerging economies. These members are primarily focused on advancing financial inclusion both within their respective regions and globally, sharing knowledge and developing policies aimed at enhancing access to financial services for the underserved populations.

It emphasizes peer-to-peer learning and knowledge exchange to foster effective policy formulation and implementation. Notable initiatives by AFI include promoting Digital Financial Services, emphasising Consumer Protection in Digital Finance, and addressing environmental challenges through inclusive green finance. Its efforts are aligned with the UN's Sustainable Development Goals, aiming to ensure equitable access to financial services across diverse populations.

BILL & MELINDA GATES FOUNDATION

Headquarters: USA
Focus: Global

A global foundation created by the founder of the Microsoft Corporation and his partner. Its mission is to create a world where every person has the opportunity to live to their potential. It has a number of initiatives, including the Inclusive Finance System, which aims to expand access to digital financial services so people in the lowest-income communities around the globe can build security and prosperity for themselves, their families and their communities. One of its primary focuses is the development of digital payment systems that are accessible, reliable, affordable, valuable and profitable. These systems are designed to reach even the poorest neighbourhoods and smallest villages, aiming to be easy to acquire and understand, while ensuring the security of users' money and information.

The foundation also emphasizes the importance of women's financial inclusion and economic empowerment. Recognizing that women's full economic participation boosts entire communities and economies, the foundation has committed $500 million over five years to advance women's financial inclusion.

The Gates Foundation's efforts include working with governments, private sector partners and international organizations to create scalable and sustainable financial services that meet the needs of the world's poorest populations.

It was launched in 2000 and is reported to be the second-largest charitable foundation in the world, holding $69 billion in assets.

CENTER FOR FINANCIAL INCLUSION

Headquarters: USA
Focus: Global

Center for Financial Inclusion (CFI) is an independent think tank housed at Accion, dedicated to advancing global financial inclusion. It collaborates with various stakeholders to address challenges in the financial inclusion sector using tools such as research, convening, capacity building and communications.

CFI works through a collaborative business model: it forms or connects with groups of key industry participants who come together to address selected challenges. Working with those groups, it applies the most appropriate tools from a toolbox that includes convening, research, publications, campaigns, piloting and knowledge dissemination. In selecting its programme areas, CFI seeks out areas that have a strong fit with its vision of financial inclusion – particularly its emphasis on quality. It looks for aspects of that vision that have been under-addressed by others and where CFI may have a comparative advantage based on its industry relationships and areas of existing competence.

CONSULTATIVE GROUP TO ASSIST THE POOR

Headquarters: USA
Focus: Global

Consultative Group to Assist the Poor (CGAP) is a global partnership of over 30 leading organizations that seek to advance financial inclusion. CGAP's mission is to improve the lives of the poor by helping them gain access to financial services. This partnership operates under the premise that financial inclusion can serve as a catalyst for poverty reduction and can promote financial stability. CGAP focuses on providing data, developing innovative financial solutions and advocating for policies that enhance the reach and impact of financial services. They work extensively in developing countries, providing research, resources and tools to support the expansion of accessible financial services.

Its members include bilateral and multilateral agencies, foundations and development finance institutions. Key members include the World Bank, the European Commission, the Bill & Melinda Gates Foundation, the Mastercard Foundation and the UK's Foreign, Commonwealth and Development Office.

Its areas of focus include microfinance, the exclusion of women and payments innovation.

CONSUMERS INTERNATIONAL

Headquarters: United Kingdom
Focus: Global

A membership organization for consumer groups around the world, Consumers International is actively engaged in promoting financial inclusion through various initiatives aimed at ensuring digital financial services are inclusive, safe, data-protected, private and sustainable. Through the Fair Digital Finance Accelerator, it supports consumer associations in low- and middle-income countries to advocate for consumer rights in the digital finance sector.

The organization emphasizes the importance of transparent digital finance, calling for greater consumer understanding and trust. It also focuses on consumer protection frameworks, advocating for regulations that prioritize consumer outcomes and engagement with consumer bodies.

Consumers International's efforts are supported by partnerships and funding from entities like the Bill & Melinda Gates Foundation and Mastercard, aiming to advance equitable global consumer protection and empowerment in the digital economy

COUNCIL FOR INCLUSIVE CAPITALISM

Headquarters: USA
Focus: Global

The Council for Inclusive Capitalism is a global organization that collaborates with business leaders and various stakeholders to foster a more inclusive and sustainable economy. It acts as a platform for sharing innovative practices and business actions aimed at creating value for a wide range of stakeholders, including employees, communities, shareholders and the environment.

Members of the Council commit to transforming the way businesses operate to promote broader societal benefits and environmental stewardship. This initiative is guided by the belief that businesses can and should play a crucial role in addressing social and environmental challenges through more responsible capitalism.

Its Guardian members are global leaders representing a diverse array of industries and bring a wealth of experience. They include senior executives of large corporations, and political and religious figures.

WOMEN'S WORLD BANKING

Headquarters: USA
Focus: Global

Women's World Banking (WWB) is a global non-profit organization dedicated to improving women's financial inclusion and economic empowerment. Headquartered in New York City, WWB has been active for over 40 years, focusing on providing support to low-income women entrepreneurs in developing countries to help them gain access to financial services and resources. This effort is aimed at enabling these women to build secure and prosperous futures for themselves and their communities.

WWB's network consists of financial institutions across various regions including Africa, Asia, Latin America and the Caribbean. These member institutions collaborate to share best practices and leverage Women's World Banking's expertise in creating inclusive economic systems. The organization uses market research, policy advocacy and leadership programmes to ensure that financial services are both accessible and impactful for women. This strategic focus not only supports women's individual empowerment but also contributes to broader economic growth and community development.

Investors

BLUE HAVEN INITIATIVE

Headquarters: USA
Focus: Global

Blue Haven Initiative is a family office that focuses on investments generating competitive financial returns alongside positive social and environmental impacts. Managed by Liesel Pritzker Simmons and Ian Simmons, Blue Haven Initiative invests across various asset classes, including direct investments in companies that address social and environmental challenges. The portfolio includes traditional equities, real assets and philanthropic programmes

BLUEORCHARD FINANCE

Headquarters: Switzerland
Focus: Global

Global impact investment pioneers with a 20+ year track record, a global reach of over 300 million people and the largest commercial microfinance fund in the world. It aims to combine social and environmental impact with a positive financial return, and to foster inclusive and climate-smart growth while providing attractive returns for investors.

Part of the Schroders Group, founded in 2001 BlueOrchard was the world's first commercial manager of microfinance debt investments. The firm offers a range of impact investment solutions across asset classes, including credit, private equity and sustainable infrastructure, as well as debt and equity financing to institutions in emerging and frontier markets.

BlueOrchard describes its investment strategy as focused on generating lasting positive impacts for communities and the environment while providing attractive returns to investors. It operates with a sophisticated international investor base and is a trusted partner of leading global development finance institutions.

CATALYST FUND

Headquarters: Kenya
Focus: Global

Catalyst Fund is managed by BFA Global and supports fintech innovations that aim to improve financial inclusion for low-income consumers in emerging markets. BFA Global is an impact innovation firm that combines research, advisory, venture building and investment expertise to build a more inclusive, equitable and resilient future for underserved people and the planet.

The Catalyst Fund provides capital along with bespoke venture-building support, and shares insights with the broader ecosystem to accelerate the progress of financial inclusion.

ELEVAR EQUITY

Headquarters: Kenya
Focus: Global

Elevar Equity is a venture capital firm known for its investments in companies that focus on underserved communities and households. It targets firms that bridge the gap in financial services through innovative solutions, aiming to create social impact by empowering communities with essential financial tools.

FINANCIERINGS-MAATSCHAPPIJ VOOR ONTWIKKELINGSLANDEN NV

Headquarters: Netherlands
Focus: Global

Financierings-Maatschappij voor Ontwikkelingslanden NV (FMO, or the Netherlands Development Finance Company) is a Dutch development bank established in 1970. It is a leading impact investor, dedicated to empowering entrepreneurs and fostering sustainable development in emerging markets. FMO invests in sectors with high development impact, including financial institutions, energy and agri-business.

The bank's mission is to enhance the potential of businesses to create jobs and improve lives, promoting inclusive and sustainable growth. FMO provides long-term capital, technical assistance and advisory services to businesses and financial institutions that align with its goals of reducing inequality and addressing climate change.

Headquartered in The Hague, FMO operates globally, with a strong focus on Africa, Asia and Latin America. It partners with other financial institutions, governments and development organizations to maximize impact. By supporting projects that foster economic development and environmental sustainability, FMO plays a crucial role in advancing global development goals.

FLOURISH VENTURES

Headquarters: Switzerland
Focus: Global

Flourish Ventures is an early-stage global venture capital firm with a $500 million fund solely funded by Pierre Omidyar, the founder of eBay. It focuses on innovations that advance financial health for consumers and small businesses. Flourish Ventures invests in a broad range of financial service products, including mobile banks, personal finance, debt management, insurance and backend infrastructure. It also partners with industry thought leaders to support research and policy initiatives that foster a fair and inclusive financial system.

INCOFIN INVESTMENT MANAGEMENT

Headquarters: Belgium
Focus: Global

Incofin Investment Management is an impact investment firm that focuses on fostering financial inclusion, supporting rural and agricultural finance, and promoting inclusive progress in emerging markets. Established with the goal of increasing financial inclusion and promoting private sector developments, Incofin aims to generate both social and monetary returns for its investors. It emphasizes ethics, business conduct and environmental care.

Incofin is an Alternative Investment Fund Manager licensed fund manager with over $1 billion in assets under management. It provides tailored technical assistance to improve the capacities of its investees, maximizing financial, social and environmental returns. Its headquarters are in Belgium and it has local investment teams in India, Colombia, Kenya and Cambodia. Incofin is committed to being an active investor, going beyond investment to support entrepreneurs in building sustainable businesses.

PARTECH AFRICA

Headquarters: France
Focus: Global

Partech Africa is a venture capital fund that targets start-ups using technology to address large emerging market opportunities in Africa. The fund focuses on industries such as fintech, insuretech and new distribution models. Partech Africa aims to support start-ups that have their main activity in Africa and need initial funding between €0.5 million and €5 million. It has made significant investments in African start-ups like TradeDepot and Yoco.

QUONA CAPITAL

Headquarters: USA
Focus: Global

Quona Capital is a global venture capital firm that focuses on fintech for inclusive finance in emerging markets. It invests in financial technology and services companies that promote financial inclusion for underserved populations globally.

Quona Capital manages the Accion Frontier Inclusion Fund, which is the first global fintech fund for the underserved, supported by non-profit inclusive fintech firm Accion. This fund invests in innovative financial technology solutions that can significantly improve the quality and availability of financial services for the three billion people worldwide who are underserved by the financial sector

RESPONSABILITY INVESTMENTS AG

Headquarters: Switzerland
Focus: Global

responsAbility is a leading asset manager specializing in impact investments that contribute directly to the UN Sustainable Development Goals. Founded in 2003 and based in Zurich, Switzerland, responsAbility manages a portfolio of investments across three main themes: financial inclusion, climate finance and sustainable food. These investments aim to finance the growth of micro and small enterprises, contribute to a net-zero pathway and sustainably feed the growing global population.

The company operates with a strong commitment to creating measurable impact alongside market returns. responsAbility is part of M&G plc. Its vision is to become the world's leading independent asset manager specializing in development-related sectors of emerging economies.

Africa

Governmental institutions

AFRICAN DEVELOPMENT BANK

Headquarters: Ivory Coast
Focus: Africa

The African Development Bank (AfDB) is a multilateral institution whose objective is to contribute to the sustainable economic development and social progress of African countries. It comprises three entities: the African Development Bank, the African Development Fund (ADF) and the Nigeria Trust Fund (NTF). The AfDB Group development agenda has five key strategic priorities: to feed Africa, to light up and power Africa, to industrialize Africa, to integrate Africa and to improve the quality of life for the people of Africa. Some of its initiatives include:

- The Africa Digital Financial Inclusion Facility, launched in 2019, aims to accelerate digital financial inclusion across Africa, in partnership with Alliance for Financial Inclusion.
- The AfDB's Gender Equality Trust Fund contributes over $4 million in grant funding.
- Making Finance Work for Africa Partnership promotes inclusive finance.

AfDB's inclusive finance work encompasses a range of initiatives aimed at improving access to financial services for underserved populations, particularly women and SMEs. Through strategic investments, partnerships and capacity-building efforts, the AfDB seeks to foster inclusive economic growth and development across Africa.

Organizations

FIRST CIRCLE CAPITAL

Headquarters: Morocco
Focus: Africa

First Circle Capital targets fintech companies across Africa, prioritizing founding teams that showcase a grand vision, a distinct proposition and the requisite skills for execution. The overarching impact of First Circle Capital's endeavours is significant, where they aim to enhance societal wellbeing by digitizing financial services to improve access and financial inclusion. Its investment strategy not only fosters economic stimulation and job creation through supporting scalable and sustainable business models but also champions a more inclusive technology ecosystem, especially advocating for the increased involvement of women as investors and founders, in alignment with the 2x Challenge and reflecting its identity as a female-founded fund.

AFRICAN RAINBOW CAPITAL

Headquarters: South Africa
Focus: Africa

African Rainbow Capital (ARC), which was formed in 2015, is a fully Black-owned and -controlled company of significant scale focusing on opportunities in the South African and African financial services and diversified investments (non-financial) industries. It focuses on acquiring a shareholding in businesses that deliver exceptional returns on equity. From the outset ARC's vision has been to make a difference in the lives of ordinary South Africans by being the premier Black-owned and -controlled financial services entity.

NORRSKEN

Headquarters: Rwanda, Spain, Sweden
Focus: Africa

Norrsken is an impact ecosystem designed to equip entrepreneurs with everything they need to make world-saving their business. Its mission is rooted in the belief that entrepreneurship and new technology can be powerful forces for positive change.

It provides growth capital and deep strategic value to founders in Africa, while positioning them for international expansion and impact. It says that every investment is a partnership and value-creation goes well beyond just capital.

Norrsken's five funds have raised over $500 million to support exceptional entrepreneurs who blend profit with positive global impact: Norrsken VC, Norrsken22, Norrsken Accelerator, Norrsken Launcher and Norrsken Africa Seed Fund.

As a non-profit, non-partisan and non-religious foundation, Norrsken was founded by Niklas Adalberth, co-founder of the payment services unicorn Klarna.

The Americas

Governmental institutions

NATIONAL CREDIT UNION ADMINISTRATION ACCESS

Headquarters: USA
Focus: USA

The ACCESS initiative was launched by the USA's National Credit Union Administration (NCUA). It seeks to foster financial inclusion and address the financial disparities experienced by minority, underserved and unbanked populations. The initiative helps to develop policies and programmes in support of financial inclusion within the NCUA and the credit union system by addressing the financial services, financial literacy and employment needs of diverse, underserved and unbanked communities.

Through ACCESS, the NCUA provides resources to assist credit unions with their outreach strategies. These resources include educational webinars and the identification of grants and other financial sources to support the development and implementation of financial products and services, to assist members experiencing financial hardship.

INTER-AMERICAN DEVELOPMENT BANK

Headquarters: USA
Focus: The Americas

The Inter-American Development Bank (IDB) plays a pivotal role in advancing financial inclusion across Latin America and the Caribbean through a variety of initiatives and programmes. The IDB supports the design of public policies, fosters public–private partnerships, and provides financial and technical assistance to enhance access to financial services for underserved communities. Notably, the IDB has launched initiatives like FINLAC, which promotes financial inclusion through knowledge sharing, investment and collaboration between public and private sectors.

FINLAC is a joint effort by the IDB, IDB Invest and IDB Lab. It serves as a one-stop shop for advancing financial inclusion, supporting governments, accompanying firms and igniting innovation in developing and implementing effective policies, reforms and business practices to create inclusive financial markets in the region.

INTER-AMERICAN FOUNDATION

Headquarters: USA
Focus: The Americas

The Inter-American Foundation (IAF) is an independent agency of the United States government established by Congress in 1969 to support social and economic development in Latin America and the Caribbean. The IAF funds community-led grassroots development projects across the region, focusing on initiatives that promote inclusive economic prosperity, reduce food insecurity, combat corruption, prevent violence and crime, protect the environment and build resilience to natural disasters.

IAF supports initiatives that promote profitable agriculture, microbusinesses and community enterprises, alongside providing skills training and access to essential services. It emphasizes the inclusion of indigenous peoples, African descendants and other disadvantaged groups, ensuring their participation in economic and social processes. IAF also fosters partnerships among community organizations, businesses and local governments to improve the quality of life and strengthen democratic practices

Organizations

BBVA MICROFINANCE FOUNDATION

Headquarters: Spain
Focus: The Americas

The BBVA Microfinance Foundation (BBVAMF) is a non-profit organization established by BBVA Bank in 2007 as part of its corporate social responsibility initiatives. The foundation is dedicated to promoting sustainable and inclusive economic and social development for people living in vulnerable conditions in Latin America through its Productive Finance mode.

The BBVAMF's mission is to support the sustainable development of vulnerable entrepreneurs by providing financial services, training and advice. The foundation operates independently from BBVA Group, focusing on creating and consolidating a network of microfinance institutions across Latin America. Since its inception, the BBVAMF has disbursed over $19 billion to more than six million low-income entrepreneurs.

The BBVAMF has been recognized by the OECD as the largest philanthropist in Latin America and the second largest globally, following the Bill & Melinda Gates Foundation. It has also been acknowledged for its contributions to gender equality, having invested significant resources in supporting vulnerable women in the region.

JUMP$TART COALITION FOR PERSONAL FINANCIAL LITERACY

Headquarters: USA
Focus: USA

The Jump$tart Coalition for Personal Financial Literacy is a non-profit organization dedicated to improving financial literacy among pre-kindergarten through to university-age youth in the United States. Established in 1995, it collaborates with over 100 national partner organizations from various sectors including business, finance, education and government to advance financial literacy. The coalition operates through a network of state affiliates that implement educational and advocacy programmes at local levels.

The coalition's efforts are focused on ensuring that students are financially literate by the time they graduate, helping them to make informed financial decisions and manage their personal finances effectively. Jump$tart's work includes advocating for financial education standards and supporting the development of financial literacy curricula that reflect the needs of today's digital and diverse world.

Overall, Jump$tart plays a crucial role in shaping the financial literacy landscape in the US, having a significant impact on the educational and financial wellbeing of young Americans.

CREDIAMIGO

Headquarters: Brazil
Focus: Brazil

CrediAmigo is Banco do Nordeste's microfinance programme. It has significantly contributed to addressing financial exclusion in Brazil's north-east. Since its inception in 1997, CrediAmigo has focused on providing microcredit to urban micro-entrepreneurs, many of whom lack access to traditional banking services. This initiative has empowered individuals to start or expand their businesses, fostering economic growth and job creation in underserved communities.

A pivotal moment for CrediAmigo was the introduction of the Crescer programme, which adjusted interest rates and financial transaction taxes, challenging CrediAmigo to adapt by segmenting its customer base to maintain sustainability. Despite these challenges, CrediAmigo has continued to innovate, notably through CrediAmigo Delas, a programme specifically designed to support female entrepreneurs. This focus on women has not only facilitated financial inclusion but also promoted gender equality and community development.

CrediAmigo's success is a testament to the transformative power of microfinance in reducing financial exclusion and enhancing economic opportunities for the marginalized.

Asia and the Pacific

Governmental institutions

ASIAN DEVELOPMENT BANK

Headquarters: Philippines
Focus: Asia and the Pacific

Operating in over 65 countries, the Asian Development Bank (ADB) envisions a prosperous, inclusive, resilient and sustainable Asia and the Pacific while sustaining its efforts to eradicate extreme poverty in the region. The ADB assists its members and partners by providing loans, technical assistance, grants and equity investments to promote social and economic development. The ADB has been actively involved in promoting financial inclusion across the region through various initiatives and programmes.

Key activities include strengthening financial inclusion frameworks, supporting digital financial services and improving financial literacy. The ADB also conducts research and publishes reports on financial inclusion, such as developing new indices to measure its impact on poverty and income inequality. Additionally, the ADB organizes conferences and learning events to share best practices and innovative solutions for expanding financial access across Asia and the Pacific.

ASSOCIATION OF SOUTHEAST ASIAN NATIONS

Headquarters: Indonesia
Focus: Asia

The Association of Southeast Asian Nations (ASEAN) is a regional grouping that aims to promote economic and security cooperation among its. The ASEAN countries have a total population of 662 million people and a combined GDP of $3.2 trillion.

Two initiatives of this association stand out. The ASEAN Working Committee on Financial Inclusion is a dedicated body within the ASEAN that coordinates initiatives to advance financial inclusion. The committee has been instrumental in developing policies and regulatory frameworks to support digital financial inclusion across the region. Another relevant initiative is the ASEAN Financial Innovation Network, a collaboration between the Monetary Authority of Singapore, the ASEAN Bankers Association and the International Finance Corporation, which provides a platform for the development and experimentation of innovative digital financial products and services, often focused on the unbanked and underbanked populations in the ASEAN.

Organizations

ABC IMPACT

Headquarters: Singapore
Focus: Asia

ABC Impact, headquartered in Singapore, is a private equity firm dedicated to impact investing, with a strong focus on financial and digital inclusion among its investment themes. Since its inception in 2019, ABC Impact has been actively investing in companies that aim to provide essential financial services to underserved communities across Asia.

By supporting businesses that offer innovative financial products and digital solutions, ABC Impact seeks to reduce inequalities and drive economic growth in the region. Its investments aim to empower individuals and micro-enterprises with access to financial services, thereby contributing to a more inclusive financial ecosystem. Through its rigorous and evidence-based impact assessment approach, ABC Impact ensures that its investments not only generate financial returns but also deliver measurable social benefits, aligning with the UN Sustainable Development Goals.

CENTRE FOR IMPACT INVESTING AND PRACTICES

Headquarters: Singapore
Focus: Asia

The Centre for Impact Investing and Practices (CIIP) fosters impact investing and practices in Asia and beyond. Based in Singapore, the CIIP was established in 2022 as a non-profit entity by Temasek Trust, a steward of philanthropic endowments and gifts.

To establish impact investing as an effective lever for sustainability, Temasek Trust launched ABC Impact, a private equity fund dedicated to impact investing in Asia, in 2019. Temasek established an impact investing team in 2021 with a mandate to generate a positive impact for underserved communities while achieving market rate returns.

MICROFINANCE INSTITUTIONS NETWORK

Headquarters: India
Focus: Asia

Microfinance Institutions Network (MFIN) is an industry association for the microfinance sector in India. It works to promote responsible lending practices and financial inclusion by supporting microfinance institutions that provide financial services to underserved populations. MFIN also engages in policy advocacy, capacity building and research to enhance the microfinance ecosystem.

SA-DHAN

Headquarters: India
Focus: Asia

Sa-Dhan is a prominent association of community development finance institutions in India. It focuses on promoting financial inclusion through microfinance, self-help groups and other community-based financial services. Sa-Dhan provides a platform for its members to collaborate, share best practices and advocate for policies that support financial inclusion

GRAMEEN BANK

Headquarters: Bangladesh
Focus: Asia

Grameen Bank is a microfinance organization and community development bank founded in Bangladesh. It makes small loans (known as microcredit or 'grameencredit') to the impoverished without requiring collateral. Grameen Bank is founded on the principle that loans are better than charity at reducing poverty: it offers people the opportunity to take initiatives in business or agriculture, which provide earnings and enable them to pay off debt. Grameen Bank is best known for its system of solidarity lending.

PRADHAN MANTRI JAN DHAN YOJANA

Headquarters: India
Focus: Asia

The Pradhan Mantri Jan Dhan Yojana (PMJDY) financial inclusion programme is one of the most notable financial inclusion programmes in Asia in recent years. At inception, the PMJDY programme opened over 18 million bank accounts in one week in 2014. The Indian government introduced the PMJDY programme to provide financial services such as savings and deposit accounts, remittance, credit, insurance and pensions. PMJDY aims to ensure greater access to financial products and services. This is achieved by using technology to lower costs and widen the reach of financial services to rural communities. The number of PMJDY accounts rose from 179 million in August 2015 to over 400 million in August 2020.

Europe

Governmental institutions

EUROPEAN INVESTMENT BANK

Headquarters: Luxembourg
Focus: Europe, Africa

The European Investment Bank (EIB) is the lending arm of the European Union. It provides financing and expertise for sustainable investment projects that contribute to furthering EU policy objectives across Europe and beyond. EIB is actively involved in promoting financial inclusion through various initiatives and funds aimed at improving access to finance for underserved populations, particularly in developing countries.

It focuses on supporting small businesses, innovation, infrastructure, climate action and economic and social cohesion. It supports several initiatives fighting financial exclusion including the Financial Inclusion Fund, focused on micro SMEs, the EU Initiative for Financial Inclusion and Social Inclusive Finance Technical Assistance, supporting microfinance and social enterprise finance providers in the EU.

EUROPEAN BANK FOR RECONSTRUCTION AND DEVELOPMENT

Headquarters: London
Focus: Europe, Africa

The European Bank for Reconstruction and Development (EBRD) is an international financial institution founded in 1991. As a multilateral developmental investment bank, the EBRD leverages investment to foster the growth of market economies.

Initially, the EBRD concentrated on the countries of the former Eastern Bloc. Over time, its mandate expanded to support development in more than 30 countries spanning from Central Europe to Central Asia. Unlike other multilateral development banks, the EBRD has global membership, including countries from North America, Africa, Asia and Australia. The United States is the largest single shareholder. However, the EBRD lends exclusively to its countries of operations.

Headquartersed in London, the EBRD is owned by 71 countries and two European Union institutions. Algeria became the newest shareholder in October 2021. Although it has public sector shareholders, the EBRD primarily invests in private enterprises in partnership with commercial entities.

EUROPEAN FINANCIAL SERVICES ROUND TABLE

Headquarters: Luxembourg
Focus: Europe

The European Financial Services Round Table (EFR) is composed of Europe's largest banks and insurers, advocating for a fully integrated EU financial market. The EFR promotes financial and digital education, public–private partnerships and best practice sharing to enhance financial inclusion across Europe. It was formed in 2001 to contribute to the public policy debate on financial services and financial stability in Europe, and its members include top executives from firms such as HSBC, BNP Paribas, Deutsche Bank, Allianz, AXA, Santander and many other leading European financial institutions.

It is registered as a non-profit organization under Belgian law and promotes the creation of a fully integrated EU financial market with consistent rules and requirements in order to strengthen the competitiveness of the European financial sector globally. Its current priorities include sustainable finance and digital transformation. The EFR serves as a key representative body and policy voice for major European banks, insurers and financial firms at the highest levels of EU decision-making on financial regulation and policies impacting the sector.

EUROPEAN UNION INITIATIVE FOR FINANCIAL INCLUSION

Headquarters: Belgium
Focus: Europe, Africa, Middle East

The European Union Initiative for Financial Inclusion (EUIFI) is a comprehensive programme launched by the European Commission in partnership with four leading European finance institutions: the European Investment Bank, the European Bank for Reconstruction and Development, Kreditanstalt für Wiederaufbau and Agence Française de Développement. The initiative aims to extend financing to MSMEs in the Neighbourhood South, which includes regions such as the Middle East and North Africa.

Through facilitating access to finance and providing MSMEs with the right tools, the EUIFI aims to increase their competitiveness, which in turn creates much-needed jobs and powers economic growth. The EUIFI provides funding to MSMEs through the Neighbourhood Investment Facility whereby the European Commission blends its grants with loans from the four leading EFIs. The EUIFI budget in 2024 amounted to €1.5 billion. The EUIFI is structured into five complementary regional facilities, with different lead financiers, representing a comprehensive package that addresses different aspects and tools for MSMEs in the region.

Organizations

FINANCIAL INCLUSION EUROPE

Headquarters: Luxembourg
Focus: Europe, Africa

Financial Inclusion Europe (FiInE) is a network of experts and academics dedicated to addressing financial exclusion and promoting financial inclusion across Europe. FiInE aims to engage in dialogue with stakeholders and EU institutions to increase awareness and understanding of financial inclusion issues.

The network's primary goal is to develop strategies that can remove the main obstacles to financial inclusion and advocate for policy options that ensure equal participation of financially excluded groups in society.

FiInE activities are designed to provide workable policy recommendations and to advocate for the inclusion of financially excluded groups in society by leveraging its network of experts, engaging in policy advocacy and conducting research to address the barriers to financial inclusion in Europe.

FINANCIAL INCLUSION CENTRE

Headquarters: United Kingdom
Focus: United Kingdom

The Financial Inclusion Centre is an independent, not-for-profit think tank. It aims to promote greater financial inclusion and provision so that consumers' core financial needs are met, and promote fair and inclusive, efficient and competitive, well-governed and accountable, properly regulated financial markets. It focuses on two groups: consumers who could be, but are not, providing for themselves, and consumers who are not commercially viable for mainstream financial services and need alternative solutions to meet their core financial needs.

The Centre collaborates with government bodies, third-sector organizations and the financial services industry to create fair and affordable financial products and services. Key activities include major research projects on financial inclusion, helping authorities develop targeted strategies and setting up organizations like credit unions. The FIC also campaigns against poor market practices and works with firms to design consumer-focused products. Additionally, the FIC addresses the impact of financial markets on climate change and social utility, advocating for sustainable and responsible finance.

Middle East

Governmental institutions

ISLAMIC DEVELOPMENT BANK

Headquarters: Saudi Arabia
Focus: Middle East, Asia

The Islamic Development Bank (IsDB) is committed to promoting social and economic development in its member countries and supporting Muslim communities in non-member countries. The IsDB's initiatives in financial inclusion are part of its broader strategy to support economic empowerment and development in member countries. The bank has established various programmes and funds aimed at increasing access to financial services. These include the Islamic Corporation for the Development of the Private Sector, which focuses on developing the private sector and enhancing the role of the market economy in IsDB member countries

The IsDB is also involved in projects like the Sustainable Finance Framework aimed at mobilizing resources for sustainable development and financial inclusion. This framework aims to finance projects that support economic development while ensuring that financial services are accessible to underserved populations. Also, the IsDB's operational strategies include specific initiatives aimed at poverty alleviation and improving the quality of life through better education, health services and economic opportunities, which are closely linked to financial inclusion

FINANCIAL INCLUSION FOR THE ARAB REGION INITIATIVE

Headquarters: Saudi Arabia
Focus: Middle East

The Financial Inclusion for the Arab Region Initiative (FIARI) is a multi-partnership regional platform created amid growing demand from member institutions in the Arab Region for tailored solutions to regional financial inclusion issues. It was launched by the Arab Monetary Fund and the German International Cooperation at the Alliance for Financial Inclusion (AFI) 2017 flagship event, the AFI Global Policy Forum. The World Bank later joined as a technical partner.

The group aims to support the AFI member institutions in the Arab region and all the Arab countries members of the Arab Monetary Fund to accelerate policies and actions that enhance access to financial services in the Arab region through effective coordination mechanisms and supporting the implementation of national financial inclusion policies. The FIARI uses financial inclusion as a driving force for sustainable economic and social development, aligned with the range of the UN Sustainable Development Goals. It acts as a coordination platform that enables financial inclusion advocacy, capacity building, peer learning, knowledge development and in-country technical implementation support among central banks and financial authorities in the region.

Organizations

FINANCIAL INCLUSION TASK FORCE

Headquarters: Saudi Arabia
Focus: Middle East

The Financial Inclusion Task Force aims to enhance financial services in Arab countries by helping national authorities strengthen regulations and instruments to broaden financial services coverage. It also promotes financial awareness and supports collaboration among supervisory authorities and international organizations. The Task Force serves as a platform for sharing experiences among Arab central banks, fostering cooperation in financial inclusion and harmonizing the region's approach to global financial inclusion issues.

The Task Force collaborates with several global entities, including the World Bank, the German Agency for International Cooperation, the Consultative Group to Assist the Poor, the Alliance for Financial Inclusion and the Islamic Development Bank. It also involves representatives from various international and regional organizations, such as the Union of Arab Banks, Union of Arab Securities Authorities, the Secretariat General of the Gulf Cooperation Council, the Middle East and North Africa Financial Action Task Force, the Bill & Melinda Gates Foundation, the International Finance Corporation and the International Monetary Fund, who participate in its meetings.

INDEX

EU Representative (GPSR)

Authorised Rep Compliance Ltd, Ground Floor, 71 Lower Baggot Street, Dublin, D02 P593, Ireland

www.arccompliance.com

www.ingramcontent.com/pod-product-compliance
Lightning Source LLC
Jackson TN
JSHW051426280325
81618JS00004B/18

* 9 7 8 1 3 9 8 6 1 0 4 5 3 *